CW00545180

Bob Dylan: How the Songs Work

Bob Dylan

How the Songs Work

Timothy Hampton

ZONE BOOKS · NEW YORK

2019

© 2019 Timothy Hampton

ZONE BOOKS

633 Vanderbilt Street

Brooklyn, NY 11218

First paperback edition 2020

ISBN 978-1-942130-36-9

Printed in the United States of America.

Distributed by Princeton University Press,
Princeton, New Jersey, and Woodstock, United Kingdom

Library of Congress Cataloging-in-Publication Data
Names: Hampton, Timothy, author.
Title: Bob Dylan : how the songs work / Timothy Hampton.
Description: New York : Zone Books, 2019. | Includes bibliographical
    references and index.
Identifiers: LCCN 2018045504 | ISBN 9781942130154 (acid-free)
Subjects: LCSH: Dylan, Bob, 1941—Criticism and interpretation. |
    Popular music—United States—History and criticism.
Classification: LCC ML420.D98 H32 2019 | DDC 782.42164092—dc23
LC record available at https://lccn.loc.gov/2018045504

there is no right wing
or left wing . . .
there is only up wing
an down wing

— Bob Dylan, "11 Outlined Epitaphs"

Contents

INTRODUCTION
A Maker   9

I   *Containing Multitudes:*
Modern Folk Song and the Search for Style   25

II   *Ramblin' Boy:*
"Protest" and the Art of Adaptation   45

III   *Absolutely Modern:*
Electric Music and Visionary Song   83

IV   *Tangled Generation:*
Memory, Desire, and the Poetics of Escape   119

V   *Turn, Turn Again:*
A Poetry of Conversion   157

VI   *"A Wisp of Startled Air":*
Late Style and the Politics of Citation   193

CONCLUSION
Frankness: Voice and History   225

Acknowledgments   235

Notes   237

Bibliography/Discography   265

List of Songs Cited   273

Index   279

A Maker

A drumbeat from your finger releases all sound,
and a new harmony begins.
—Arthur Rimbaud, "To a Reason"

This is a book about songs and how they are made. It is about the intersection of lyric, music, and performance. It studies how the forging of these elements produces art that is more than the sum of its parts. My topic of study is the songs of Bob Dylan, the most influential popular songwriter of the last half century. Although Dylan's acceptance of the 2016 Nobel Prize in Literature has elevated his status, pushing him — controversially, of course — out of the world of popular music and into some larger sphere of creative achievement, much of the critical writing about Dylan has tended to skirt or neglect the artistic nuances that give life to the work of this most dynamic and skillful writer and composer. This book offers a close investigation of how the songs work as compositions, as structures, as systems of signs that create meaning and elicit emotion. Neither a technical musicological study nor an exercise in traditional literary criticism, it seeks out places where language and music shape and support each other. It studies in detail Dylan's writing technique, his intertwining of lyric and music, and his engagements with broader cultural and political topics. It is intended as an investigation of the work of a major artist, an exercise in the close analysis of song, and, on a more practical level, a set of guideposts to Dylan's compositions.

The massive body of writing about Dylan's career and the size and variety of his recorded output have generated an entire collection of different Dylans and of different ways of framing his work. Three approaches come to mind as particularly influential and insightful. The first is what we might call Dylan as disruptor. Dylan is an entertainer, "a song and dance man," as he once described himself. His initial success was linked to the way he introduced serious and complex lyrics into the mainstream of popular music — a development that transformed the field. Because many of his songs touch on political or moral concerns, he was quickly labeled a philosopher or spokesman, an existentialist prophet, "the voice of a generation," able to offer up gnomic pronouncements at will.[1] His innovative art, when coupled with his personal evasiveness and concern for his privacy (in contrast, say, to a figure like John Lennon, for whom self-exposure came to be a virtue), has generated a body of writing that seeks to figure out what he "believes" about this or that topic. Moreover, Dylan's personal and professional courage in following his own interests, regardless of popular taste or the preferences of his fans, has lent his trajectory a dramatic shape that is obviously appealing to biographical criticism or mythography. This leads to a critical approach that combs through his many interviews and occasional writings, looking for statements that might illuminate the songs and tell us what he "really thinks." It builds the edifice of criticism around the fragile core of the biography. And since no artist can be consistently disruptive or transformative in the ways that Dylan was at the beginning of his career, we are left with a somewhat predictable narrative of triumph and decline, as much of Dylan's later work is taken to be somehow "less" than his earlier, "disruptive" work.[2]

As Dylan's stature has grown, it has become clear that certain themes are consistent across his work. From his earliest days he has not shied away from passing judgment or casting light on racism, greed, corruption, and the miscarriage of justice. This tendency has taken on new importance with the Nobel Prize in Literature, which has often gone to artists known for their moral visions or political stances (Boris Pasternak, Pablo Neruda, Nelly Sachs, and Toni Morrison, among others). Indeed, some of the best work on Dylan of the past two decades sees him as a kind of moral philosopher, setting him in dialogue with other writers, from Virgil to Eliot, yielding insights into the ethics, as well as the mechanics, of his writing.[3] This work has drawn its strength and wisdom from a close consideration of Dylan's lyrics, to the relative exclusion of his music. And if the narrative of Dylan as disruptor often casts his artistic trajectory as a story of decline, here we run the risk of a version of Dylan that fails to account fully for the changes in his work, setting him up as always doing more or less the same thing. My book will track how his approach changes, how his moral concerns can both remain constant, yet be articulated — both lyrically and musically — in vastly different ways across time.

Dylan's deep sense of history and his curiosity about different musical traditions — from Mexican border ballads to western swing — have led some commentators to see his work as a kind of parable about American identity and inclusiveness. Here he is taken less as an existentialist hero or a great ethicist than as a quintessentially American bard, the heir to Walt Whitman and William Carlos Williams, speaking of and to the promise of America. This is a critical approach that has occasionally considered both music and lyrics and has opened important perspectives on the work, not least by showing how Dylan moves between what used to be called "high" culture and "popular" culture. That I put scare quotes around those two terms is itself testimony to the success with which Dylan, along with a few of his contemporaries, has succeeded in blurring once distinct categories. Yet, a strict focus on Dylan's "Americanness" (more scare quotes) runs the risk of limiting our sense of the songs' aesthetic impact and formal complexity. Much of the power of Dylan's art emanates from how he breaks conventions, or merely gestures toward them as he passes by. For example, he does not sing the blues: he uses the blues.[4] To be sure, Dylan's work is deeply indebted to American song traditions; he is not a global musical tourist in the ways that, say, Paul Simon, David Byrne, and Caetano Veloso are. But that doesn't mean that the impact of the work is limited to the national imaginary. Art means beyond the space and time of its production. Music doesn't like borders; it moves easily. Poetry moves less easily, yet it still moves, and the drag or resistance produced out of its movement is itself part of its energy. The aesthetic range of Dylan's achievement is especially important to acknowledge going forward, as his work now circulates in a global musical culture. And the next generation of listeners, working in a new digital soundscape, will doubtless hear (and sample) this music in ways that we can scarcely imagine today.[5]

My own discussion will focus on how Dylan gets his job done. I want to look at features of the work that can help us grasp questions of politics, history, and ethics beyond the level of theme or argument. My interest will be in style and form — features that should ground any broader consideration of the author's cultural importance. For it is in the intersection of lyric and music — in the details of structure — that Dylan's art generates new types of knowledge. Lyric poetry, like much song, often seems to live outside of history and the flow of social conversations. Yet, precisely for this reason, we can turn to lyric forms for insights into social experience. As the poet Robert Pinsky has noted, in lyric, "Communal life, whether explicitly included or not, is present implicitly in the cadences and syntax of language: a somatic ghost."[6] Whereas many of Dylan's first fans lamented that he early on abandoned "political" music (by which they meant topical songs about current events), it is clear that his most original insights into social and political reality often come through his depictions of power, love, memory, desire, and art itself. Through the ways in which they shape language and rhythm, poetry and song grasp how politics works. As Pinsky points out, poetry is a form of art that brings the body into the social world. "Poetry penetrates to where the body recognizes the stirring of meaning," he writes, in lines that are doubly true for song, which seizes the body and moves it. "That power," Pinsky continues, "is social as well as psychological. If all art is imitation, what does the art of verse imitate? It imitates the social actions of meaning."[7] Put differently, songs are most political when they are not talking about politics, but when they are giving voice to the social relations and the play of power and resistance that shape our collective experience. For it is then that song — like any art — can generate new types of knowledge, grasping what cannot yet be conceptualized in thought.

Yet, one might wonder, why focus on one author who will be singled out for attention? Does this not in some sense privilege an idea of the songwriter as "genius" (as outmoded as that idea may be today) — and a "white male genius" at that? Would it not be better to set Dylan up as one of a pack, in the history of a mode of representation (in this case, rock and roll), or in the history of a moment (American popular culture's rise to global dominance)? The answers to this are several. First, as will be clear, Dylan's work is obsessively about dialogue and about the multiple voices through which art takes shape. In this regard, we might understand "Bob Dylan" less as some type of discrete "genius" than as a site, a wavering node of influences that coalesce to speak in new ways, through which we can reflect on the kinds of knowledge that art makes happen. But more compelling, perhaps, is that Dylan's own art, from its very first manifestations, has consistently questioned, taken apart, and criticized every feature of the very culture that has made it possible, from the arrogance of stardom to the vacuity of the press and the capitalist machine underpinning middle-class consumerism. And he has developed modes and tools for understanding and grasping collective experience, our relationship to language, memory, and form — our "somatic ghosts." This is why even when Dylan's art is irritating or confrontational, it elicits attention from listeners. For it is clear that something is happening in it that speaks to both our moment and beyond our moment, something that points to the space where ideas end and where, as Pinsky puts it, "the body recognizes the stirring of meaning." To do this, as we will see, Dylan's art steadfastly refuses to limit itself, to offer convenient "positions" on topics of "importance." These are the "positions" (on race, identity, sexuality, state power, commercialism, and so on) that are often set forth in the art of Dylan's colleagues. They are, in themselves, useful. What sets Dylan apart is that his work registers the impact of social and political change, not only on selves and communities but also on art itself, as the medium of communication.

Throughout the book I will be using the somewhat grand-sounding term "poetics" to refer to Dylan's different ways of working. What I have in mind is an approach that touches on the content or themes of Dylan's songs, on their formal structures, and on the interplay of theme and structure, both musically and lyrically. As we will see demonstrated in a number of instances, Dylan can best be understood as a combiner. He is a maker, which is the original meaning of "poet" (*poiein*, in Greek, means "to make"). So, a *poetics*, in this context, is quite simply a way of making things. Our task then becomes to explore how, at certain moments, songs are made and how specific literary and musical techniques work to generate particular manifestations of style in song.

When we speak of style we can touch on several interlocking senses of the word. For much literary, visual, and musical criticism, style involves the way in which artists manipulate different levels or historically defined registers of representation — the "high" style of tragedy, the ornamented style of the "Baroque," for example. The concept of style works as a point of intersection where the individual pulse of artistic creation interacts with the collective dimension of artistic reception. The individual artwork inevitably unfolds within and against convention, tradition, commonplace, cliché. Style means not only individual expression but also the conformity of the individual voice to broadly accepted notions of what is appropriate or even fashionable. Thus, the Petrarchan poet of the Renaissance or the country music balladeer, for example, channels her or his personal experiences through conventions of a style recognizable to a readership or listenership. Style shapes and, we might say, cushions the violence of individual expression, making it palatable for a reading or listening public. This means that no matter how dramatically an artist may change direction, he or she must remain within a certain set of parameters that are recognizable to the listener, viewer, or reader. And it follows that older styles will continue to leave their traces, ghostlike, in the very works that seem to be departing in new directions.[8]

We can link artistic technique to the more general social world by recalling for a moment the work of the Russian critic Mikhail M. Bakhtin. For Bakhtin, the language of art is inherently dialogic, not in terms of some type of hierarchy of artistic movements or canons (Attic style, Art Deco style) but in the ways it brings different social worlds into contact with each other. In a poem or a novel, words from different contexts are woven together; speakers speak in their own voices, but they also report the language of other speakers or speak in clichés. The text is multivoiced, what Bakhtin's jargon termed "heteroglossic" (bits of language from different communities set in proximity) or "polyglossic" (multiple languages in the same text). Every text is caught up in a web of conversations with other texts, with other speakers, with other linguistic communities.[9] This means that the style of a given text, as it melds together different textual elements, also gestures toward the diverse communities from which these elements come. As we shall see, this question of the multiplicity of languages at work in a specific text, be it linguistic or musical, is important for grasping Dylan's work.

Lyric — in both poetry and song — is about fragmentation, momentary flashes of insight, condensed expression. We could think of Dylan's work in this regard as a kind of "galaxy" or "constellation" of moments in which the combination of lyric, melody, and rhythm generates a force field. If literary art is, in Bakhtin's words, "many voiced," it should be obvious that this concept — taken, as it is, from the world of sound itself — illuminates the construction of musical compositions. It does so nowhere more dramatically than in the realm of popular music, which constantly cites itself, draws on earlier genres and idioms, plays with pitch and rhythm, samples other recordings. In recorded productions, such citation and multivoicedness may be obvious and explicit, as in The Beatles' many sonic experiments of mixing musical idioms and quoting diverse traditions — from Indian ragas to British music hall ditties — in their recordings. But they may also be implicit and "felt," such as the ghostly presence of the Zydeco rhythm that underpins Hank Williams's 1952 song "Jambalaya," which both is "about" Zydeco culture in its lyric and ineluctably performs Zydeco in its meter, no matter how perverse ("countrified," "sweetened," "rock and roll," etc.) an arrangement of the song may be. Our task will be to listen for these many pulses in Dylan's work. For example, how do rhythm and lyric work together? How do alliteration and rhyme enhance (or undercut) moral message or erotic invitation? Why do some chord changes have a dramatic effect, while others bring the lyric to a happy resolution?[10]

One of the keys to Dylan's achievement, I will suggest, lies not in an avant-garde attempt to refuse accepted styles, but in a much more strategic mixing of stylistic registers. This occurs at the level of sound and melody as well as lyric. Poetry is, among other things, language organized to generate rhythm and sound. It is, in its origins, closely linked to music. Much writing on Dylan ignores or skirts the question of his musical prowess, of his manipulation of melody and harmony. Too often he is dismissed as a musical "primitive" or simply ignored as a musician. But his "poetic making" also involves melodies and rhythms, and the forging of sense and sound together into something bigger than the sum of its parts. Thus, a study of the "multivoiced" character of the songs must, when possible, take into account the manipulation of sound, via melody and harmony, as well as the way sound and sense shape each other.

It is fair to say that Dylan's work reveals a complexity and compaction not seen in the work of most other popular artists. That is, Dylan's work feels "denser" or "deeper" (in an almost tactile sense, not necessarily in any philosophical sense) than that of most of his contemporaries. The American writer Ezra Pound emphasized that the poet is someone who makes language thick, who condenses it—as the German word for poet, *Dichter*, comes from the word for "thicken." As a master of citation, a combiner, a collagist, a paster, a thickener, Dylan is able to lend a new density to song.[11] His singing persona functions as a kind of medium or vehicle through which the listener can glimpse or hear the sonic landscape of some other moment or territory where "Bob Dylan," the composer, seems to roam. This sense of density—what we might call the "Dylanesque" feature of his work—is achieved through a mastery of the art of combination or collage.

The multilayered density of Dylan's songs and the metamorphic energy of the lyrics brings us to yet another sense of style, which links up to the modern idea of "fashion" or "mode"—the conventions that dominate a particular moment but are soon set aside as "old-fashioned" and rejected. This dynamic is, of course, the dynamic of mass production and of the modern culture industry.[12] Dylan's work consistently exploits the way fashion is transformed by the passage of time. He turns again and again to the relationship between the "now" and the "future," on the one hand, and, on the other hand, the archaic, the premodern, the quaint. To a degree unrivaled by any modern popular artist Dylan is a miner of old forms, an expedition-ary heading back into the hoary world of predigital models of expres-sion—old songs, old sentences, old images, old chords.[13]

Dylan's constant reflection on the "old" and the "new," on what the poet Rimbaud called the "absolutely modern," will help us to locate the songs in a history of forms. Dylan's work takes shape in the post–World War II moment, the moment of television and the automobile. Thus, the most pertinent historical context for under-standing his work may be less that of rock music, or of "the Sixties," than of artistic modernism more generally. By "modernism," I have in mind that current of artistic experimentation that expands from the French Impressionists in the nineteenth century through the "geniuses" of the early twentieth (Woolf, Stravinsky, Eliot, Eisen-stein, Ellington, Picasso) and on to the emergence of a late "modern-ist" style after World War II (Pollock, Nabokov, Henry Moore, Char-lie Parker, Orson Welles). Dylan comes of age at the moment at which "modernism" first becomes recognized as a kind of international style in art and at which it begins to reach a mass audience, spreading beyond the world of the avant-gardes. Yet, more pertinent than the history, for our purposes, are the technical discoveries of modernist art: the focus on formal integrity as the response to historical chaos, the importation of "low" culture into "high" culture (and vice versa), the fragmentation of time and space, the continual vexed worrying about the past, about tradition and originality, the idea of culture as a ruin, the emphasis on artificial or invented objects and moments as bearers of peak or authentic experience within an increasingly unreal "real world."[14] Modernist art privileges the moment, an absolute contemporaneity that simultaneously seeks to break with history and take stock of its own relationship to what has been lost. It struggles to come to terms with a world that has been stripped of its religious magic by the logic of capitalism, what Max Weber called "the disenchantment of the world." Dylan's reformulation, "It's easy to see without looking too far that not much is really sacred," from 1964's "It's Alright, Ma (I'm Only Bleeding)" offers a later articulation of the same idea, written from within the swirl of postwar industrial expansion and 1960s media culture.[15]

Dylan differs from several of his contemporaries who went on to develop influential bodies of work as particularly "dense" or "poetic" songwriters. For example, Leonard Cohen's voice and songs seem to come from a bounded place of unusual concentration — at the intersection of the erotic and the spiritual — out of which he generates powerful insights about desire and regret. It is no accident that this type of intensity requires a deep focus on the frailty of the self (which we might see paralleled, biographically, in Cohen's interest in Buddhism and Jewish mysticism). It results in a closely circumscribed, though forceful, poetic vision. Or, to take another example, we could recall the work of Joni Mitchell, which generates much of its energy out of Mitchell's self-dramatizing and romantic re-creations of her own adventures in love and art. This might be linked to her pioneering status, along with Laura Nyro, as one of the first great female singer-songwriters. Lacking the ready-made paradigms of desire and amorous conquest available to her male colleagues, she generated her own counterstories by showcasing her escapades, triumphs, and foibles. This is reflected in Mitchell's insistence on herself as "original" and an "artist."[16] Dylan, by contrast, offered an album called *Self Portrait* that consisted of songs by other people. Quite unlike both Cohen and Mitchell, Dylan radiates outward in his work, and his interest lies in absorbing into his singing persona all of the material of the culture around him.

17

To study Dylan's art and its combinatory power, we need to take into account the different ways in which he uses the "I" who appears in his compositions. This "I" is, of course, a fiction, just as the "I" of Shakespeare's sonnets is a fiction and the "I" of Marty Robbins's 1959 border ballad "El Paso" is a fiction. It is a character that Dylan invents anew for each song. Sometimes that character knows many things. Sometimes it knows little. Sometimes it thinks it knows more than it does. Sometimes it says more than it knows. Moreover, like many self-invented artists, Dylan seems to locate his persona in relationship to various exemplary figures, both real and fictional (Woody Guthrie, Arthur Rimbaud, Jack Kerouac, Jay Gatsby, Billy the Kid, Rhett Butler, Jack London). Yet, what is important about these figures is not their role in the development of personal identity — they will change — but rather the literary and musical resources they free up. In what follows I will be speaking interchangeably of the "hero" or "protagonist" or "narrator" of Dylan's songs. Sometimes, for convenience, I will speak of the "singer," without, however, assuming that the singer caught up in the story is the biographical "Bob Dylan," whoever he may be.

This question of the "I" poses interesting problems when we consider Dylan's own location in his songs. Just as he is often most "political" when least political, so may his hand be felt most clearly in songs that cannot be linked in any narrative way to "Bob Dylan." We can think, in this context, of a song like 1995's "Dignity." The song recounts the adventures of an "I" who appears to be a private detective, much in the mold of Raymond Chandler's Philip Marlowe, who crisscrosses a nocturnal cityscape that feels like Los Angeles, in search of someone, or something, called "Dignity." We watch as the hero goes from scene to scene: a tattoo parlor, a fancy party, a cheap bar, an abandoned apartment, "Asking the cops wherever I go, 'Have you seen Dignity?'" (p. 766). The literary trick of leaving the identity or nature of "Dignity" vague makes the song particularly powerful, as it yokes a seedy crime story to a grand philosophical quest. (Indeed, where can one find something like dignity at the end of the 1980s, the decade of arbitrageurs, Teflon presidents, and Spandex?)[17]

The main character of "Dignity" is a persistent but not particularly competent private eye who has his own problems ("So many dead ends / I'm at the edge of the lake"). Yet he does more than act in a series of misadventures. He cites. "Fat man lookin' in a blade of steel," begins the lyric. "Thin man lookin' at his last meal / Hollow man lookin' in a cotton field, for Dignity." This particular narrator speaks in the language of T. S. Eliot's "The Hollow Men." He also channels Walt Whitman, as he reveals a moment later with, "Wise man lookin' at a blade of grass," not to mention Saint Paul ("I heard the tongues of angels and the tongues of men / Wasn't any difference to me"), Stendhal, the *Financial Times*, and the Book of Ezekiel ("I went into the red, went into the black / Into the valley of dry bone dreams"). This technique of citation is one aspect of the "density" of Dylan's lyrics that I mentioned a moment ago.

But what is the status of these citations with regard to the fiction of the story? We might contrast this approach with the famous citations of Dante, Marvell, and the Greeks in T. S. Eliot's "Love Song of J. Alfred Prufrock," where the main character — a shy intellectual — is so neurotic that he can speak of love only by citing classical poetry. Eliot's world and Prufrock's world are the same world, a refined world where people would drop bits of Dante in casual conversation. Or, we could set "Dignity" against Raymond Chandler's uneasy references to "high literature," such as the moment in 1953's *The Long Goodbye* when Marlowe is asked by an African American chauffeur what he thinks of Eliot's phrase, "In the room the women come and go, talking of Michelangelo." "It suggests to me that the guy didn't know very much about women," quips tough guy Marlowe.[18]

Dylan's citations fit into neither of these patterns, the first of which makes "high" literature a seamless part of the fictional world, the second of which makes "high" (modernist) literature something to be commented on sarcastically to show that Eliot's London is irrelevant to life in the mean streets of Los Angeles. Rather, Dylan's citations are embedded in the fabric of the song, but not linked to its "plot." They tell us nothing about the characters. It doesn't matter, in other words, whether the hero has read Eliot. But the citations do tell us something about the *song* and its purpose. They suggest that the quest for Dignity is not just a mystery tale, as the narrator seems to think. It is a quest for meaning in a meaningless world, for goodness in a den of thieves. *Someone* connected to the song knows that Whitman and Saint Paul are hovering in the area, that they, too, are looking for Dignity. Yet given the fact that some of these allusions are less than obvious, it may not be the listener, either. Indeed, what is most important is that the literary allusions are only of limited relevance to the listener's grasp of the song. They are about tone as much as they are about meaning. They provide the very flavor of the lyric, giving it its strangeness and stimulating our curiosity. "I heard the tongues of angels and the tongues of men / Wasn't any difference to me." What a striking idea! It conveys the alienation of the narrator, who says, in effect, "I have heard it all." Neither the narrator nor the casual listener needs to know that what is at play is Saint Paul's claim in 1 Corinthians 13 that, without charity, the voices of men and of angels are nothing but clanging gongs. Yet the images — the men, the angels — have the effect of marking the surface of the lyric. We sense that they come from somewhere, even if we know not where. And in this regard, in their capacity to make normal phrasing strange, they are the signature or footprint of the author's presence. They are how we know that this is a Bob Dylan song. They are the mark of the Dylanesque style, of a particular layering of intensity that structures an imaginary world at once "high" culture and "low" culture, recognizable (through the style of the film noir) yet unfamiliar, distorted, other.

The implications for authorship of this technique are worth considering. Dylan has always been interested in having it both ways. That is, he has wanted to be taken seriously by his listeners and by the press, but not too seriously. He has wanted to be famous, but to keep his privacy. He has wanted to be popular, but not mainstream. He has wanted to express himself through song, but not to be on display in ways that will lead listeners to pin his compositions to his biography. The poetic technique of "Dignity" shows how Dylan can be "in" his songs *both* as an actor, as the performing "I" who speaks, *and* as the clever commentator who sews the lyric with citations that suggest some larger meaning. He is in his songs, but not of them.

The evasive boundedness of Dylan's lyrics and lyric/sound combinations is strengthened by his musical accompaniments, which are mostly steady and monochromatic compared with the lyrics. In contrast, say, to The Beatles, who in their most experimental period manipulated the sound of every track to follow the lyric (here comes the clarinet . . . oops, there it goes again, and here comes the sitar), Dylan sets his multivalent lyrics against solid, often unvarying, sonic tracks. He rarely slows down or speeds up. Dynamics rarely modulate. This lends him authority over what is happening, as he dips in and out of the worlds in which his characters move. The accompaniment functions as a drone, or a control against which variations can be explored. It keeps the focus on the voice, which is also one of the reasons why listeners who find that voice unappealing often struggle to understand the attraction of Dylan's work. Thus, it is important, as we work through this material, not to focus on the fact that "Bob Dylan" is singing. What is important is the persona he creates at any given moment. Some of these songs could be sung by anybody — and have been. Others are simply unimaginable apart from the raspy voice that puts them over on record.

Song is a particularly powerful art form because it envelops the listener. There is no period of "settling into" it as one settles into a novel, or of sitting quietly in front of it as one does with a painting. Song is simply there — around you and in your head. In some contexts, where songs are performed for communities as part of their shared history, the moment of performance is a moment of transformation, as the singer, shaman, or griot is inspired and listeners are transported to another time and space. When song is recorded electronically and played back, the power of transformation is multiplied exponentially and imposed violently. From the very moment of some of Dylan's most recognizable beginnings — the snare drum beat that opens "Like a Rolling Stone," the steel guitar that begins "Lay, Lady, Lay," the humming chorus of "Knocking on Heaven's Door," the booming piano chords of "Ballad of a Thin Man" — we are outside quotidian reality. This violence visited on our nervous systems hobbles the critical faculty. The overload of sonic and intellectual information makes it difficult to listen and think about listening at the same time. To slow down this process, my own discussion will begin with the lyrics, which are the feature of song to which one can return and that one can analyze spatially, as it were, on the page. Dylan begins his own apprenticeship by writing lyrics to melodies by other composers, not by writing new melodies to lyrics by other poets. Thus, it seems safest to begin with the lyric and move from there to questions of harmony, melody, performance, and sound.

To a degree unparalleled in American popular culture, Bob Dylan has been a shape-shifter. I don't mean that in any type of existential or philosophical sense — that would be, yet again, to make him into myth — but simply in a technical sense. At one point in his career he writes one type of song. At another point, he writes songs that are quite different. How are they different? And can we discern how he

gets from one point to the other? To attribute these shifts and devel-
opments to something as vague as "inspiration," or to the vagaries
of biography, or to politics — or simply to neglect them — inevitably
fails to account fully for how the songs work, and for how some songs
work differently from other songs.

To engage with the variety of Dylan's output, we must focus on
a set of problems faced by any artist who changes direction: How
do old forms continue to weigh on new forms? How can we see new
forms as offering a set of "solutions" to problems or limitations in
older forms? What is the relationship between the "I" who sings and
the listener? Who is that listener? How is her community or situation
implied in the song? What is the role of different forms of language
(repetitions, questions, exclamations, proverbs, curses), of differ-
ent rhetorical tropes (metaphor, simile, allegory)? Are there points
where Dylan seems to be working with models from other writ-
ers, or to be in dialogue with them? If so, how does their presence
shape what we are listening to? What work does the stanza do, or
the chorus? How are different generic conventions in both music and
poetry (the blues, the sonnet, the ballad) deployed? How do shifts in
harmony and cadence, no less than in lyric, work within or against
those conventions?

In what follows, I will argue that Dylan's work unfolds through
a shifting set of innovations and discoveries — different "poetics," if
you will — that often involve engagement with other types of writ-
ing or singing. In Chapters 1 and 2, I show that Dylan learns to write
by practicing a "poetics of adaptation" that both transforms earlier
models — in the spirit of his hero Woody Guthrie — and remains in
dialogue with them. I will show how he draws on different invented
versions of American English and American space as a way of creating
an identity and claiming authority for his singing persona. Later, he
will be interested in exploring the nature of meaning and the limits
of the senses. Here, my account of his rise to eminence will be atten-
tive to his encounters with the works of the great modernist writers
Bertolt Brecht and Arthur Rimbaud (Chapter 3). This is not to say that
Rimbaud was more important for Dylan than, say, Muddy Waters, but
it is to say that by being attentive to Dylan as Rimbaldian modernist
we can learn something about his work that we wouldn't if we only lis-
tened to Muddy Waters. Somewhat later, when Dylan shifts directions
again, changing his sound and persona in the mid-1970s, his approach

to structure, language, and harmony will change as well. He will push past the impasses of some of his expansive 1960s work to focus on tightly constructed stories of escape and evasion, travel and memory. This I discuss in Chapter 4. Chapter 5 will look at Dylan's engagement with evangelical Christianity at the end of the 1970s, stressing the changing positions of singer and listener within a dynamic of conversion. From there, my argument will touch only at moments on Dylan's work during the long 1980s, since his obvious groping for direction and his many collaborations during that period make it difficult to offer even a moderately coherent account. However, in Chapter 6, "A Wisp of Startled Air," I will turn to Dylan's reinvention of his approach in the mid-1990s and point to some of the features of his more recent work. Each of these moments in Dylan's poetic trajectory, I will suggest, is defined and shaped by particular poetic and musical strategies — ways of using figural language, ways of depicting the self, harmonic tics, ways of evoking the audience, and so forth.

New sounds and new approaches require new poetics. The project of the book is to describe these poetics. I will be looking as closely as I can at the versions of Dylan's songs presented on his officially released recordings. The corpus is vast, with multiple versions of some songs, live outtakes, and pirated versions in wide circulation. Dylan himself seems to have only limited patience with the recording process and has often stated that the best versions of his songs may well be in live performance. Fair enough. However, I am not interested in playing the sleuth or archivist, or in tracking down hidden versions or obscure outtakes. The hope is that my discussion can illuminate those versions of the songs that average listeners can access without too much difficulty — for it is those versions that have had such a powerful impact on popular music and world musical culture over the past half century. As will become clear, for the most part I do not pad my close analysis of songs with references to Dylan's interviews or other writings. This is partly because I am not particularly interested in "Bob Dylan," whoever he may be, or in what he thinks about cabbages or kings. Our attention should be on the songs. But it is also because the constant glossing of Dylan's songs with his comments in interviews runs the risk of leveling out the work, reducing it to biography or to a set of documents of cultural history. When appropriate, I will turn to his 2004 memoir, *Chronicles: Volume One*, to help locate the discussion.

The arc of the book will be built on a loose chronology, but it makes no pretense to offer a comprehensive account of Dylan's corpus. There would never be world enough and time to talk about each song. I have attempted to engage seriously with a broad swath of Dylan's most influential work, touching, often in some detail, on most of his signal compositions. Some areas, albums, and periods necessarily receive less attention than others. For example, the songs on the famous *Basement Tapes*, made with The Band in the late 1960s, get only a glance here, simply because, though they seem to mark a renewed dialogue with tradition on Dylan's part, they don't result in major shifts in his songwriting that would break with his officially released material during these years.[19] In other words, I am not interested in the biographical conditions shaping these songs, but in the songs. My focus is on analyzing tendencies in Dylan's compositional strategies, in tracing how these tendencies shift across time. Certain preoccupations will emerge and then disappear. Some songs will be seen in dialogue with each other. Certain rhetorical tropes will be deployed and discarded. Certain forms of character, or techniques of citation, will modulate. Many great songs will not be discussed in any detail, simply for lack of space. My project, in what follows, then, will be to describe some of the nuanced effects of Dylan's art, to see how, in part, it is made, and what that making can teach us.[20]

CHAPTER ONE

Containing Multitudes:

Modern Folk Song

and the Search for Style

In January, 1961 Robert Zimmerman, of Hibbing, Minnesota, drops out of the state university in Minneapolis and hitchhikes to New York. He quickly establishes himself as a folksinger in Greenwich Village under the name of Bob Dylan. He presents himself as a person of great experience, many travels, and mysterious adventures. His eccentric sound and performance style attract the attention of the press, and he begins to write songs that garner a following in the close-knit folk community of the Village. He signs a five-year contract with Columbia Records and records his first album, Bob Dylan. *It does not sell. However, his second album,* The Freewheelin' Bob Dylan, *featuring both love songs and protest songs mostly penned by Dylan, is more successful.*

Near the beginning of *Chronicles: Volume One*, his memoir of his early days in New York, Bob Dylan attends a party where he crosses paths with Mike Seeger. Dylan has recently come east from Minnesota and is presenting himself as an interpreter of the songs of the Oklahoma-born Dust Bowl singer Woody Guthrie, whose mannerisms and intonations he has taken on. Yet he is brought up short by the sight of Seeger, who was the half-brother of the famous folksinger (and Guthrie collaborator) Pete Seeger and a member of the folk revival group The New Lost City Ramblers. Seeger was a formidable character, a virtuoso on a handful of instruments, and a powerful presence: "He was tense, pokerfaced and radiated telepathy," writes Dylan. Even more impressive was the way he seemed to embody the songs he was singing — the very songs that Dylan was trying to put over as his own repertoire. "It's not as if he just played everything well, he played these songs as good as it was possible to play them," writes Dylan. "What I had to work at, Mike already had in his genes, in his genetic makeup. Before he was even born, this music had to be in his blood."[1]

Dylan's description of Mike Seeger might be seen as an ironic meditation on what T. S. Eliot famously called the relationship between "tradition and the individual talent."[2] Seeger's parents were distinguished musicologists and composers; his father was a Harvard professor. Dylan paints him as an aristocrat. Like a member of the nobility in some ancient kingdom, Seeger embodies his greatness and identity. The music is essential to his very being, "in his blood." A member of the WASP elite, he has been raised in the culture of left-wing folk music. He *is* tradition, in several senses of the word. For Dylan, a provincial and a Jew, such ease and familiarity seem beyond reach, no less than nobility is beyond the reach of the peasant. At that moment, says Dylan, he realized that he could only find success if he broke with the tradition that he saw incarnate before him: "The thought occurred to me that maybe I'd have to write my own folk songs, ones that Mike didn't know. That was a startling thought" (p. 71).

Fields

Dylan's response to Mike Seeger's presence raises a set of topics that illuminate his earliest songwriting experiments. For one thing, the folk song tradition itself, incarnated here in one of its princelings, is seen as stifling, limiting, and even exclusive. Given the aristocratic vocabulary that Dylan uses to describe Seeger, his own claim on a place in the music world is also a gesture of democratization, the revolt of the outsider. And it has literary historical implications. Dylan's zeal to carve out his own place also involves a kind of artistic modernism. It gestures toward a new type of folk song, a song with its origins not in shared tradition or collective struggle, but in the individual talent. Yet when Dylan nevertheless calls these songs "folk songs," he gives the phrase "folk song" itself a new meaning. It is no longer simply "a song sung by folks," as Woody Guthrie is said to have described the form. The "folk song" henceforth defines a *style*, a particular authority and attitude in writing, expressed through a certain accent and instrumentation. Guthrie composed his own songs, but he did so in the context of labor struggles and migration. When he writes about himself, he does so as the embodiment of an entire community, as a typical character. Dylan, by contrast, stresses his own individuality. He writes in quest of fame and success, *against* the essentialist poetics of tradition embodied in Mike Seeger. For him, the character of the folk song will henceforth be manufactured, invented, patched together as an artistic and commercial strategy. The "authenticity" of folk music will become, for the young Dylan, as for no singer before him, a kind of brand.

Of course, Dylan is not the first person to compose folk songs or to affect authenticity. But he will be among the most self-conscious about his relationship to traditional forms. The craft involved in creating his voice — in all of the senses of that term — will in turn guarantee its authority to speak on the "folk" themes of proletarian experience and social injustice. Dylan is not primarily interested in writing songs that will be sung by factory workers on strike. He is interested in writing songs that will guarantee his success as a performer. He is, in a stroke, transforming an understanding of the music as temporal — as part of a "tradition" that is handed down through time — into an approach that is, we might say, spatial, with Dylan functioning as one term in a set of oppositions that make up a given space, a field, a market. Dylan's songs will be set against those of the competition, Mike Seeger included — a competition that he will quickly outstrip.[3]

The folk music culture of the late 1950s and early 1960s into which Dylan made his entrance upon his arrival in New York constituted a relatively closed world that saw itself in opposition to mainstream or "square" society. This involved not only musical taste, but politics, lifestyle, and sensibility. Folk music was, paradoxically, both retro-grade and cutting-edge. The folk world was relatively small; from the epicenter of Greenwich Village, folksingers fanned out across the country to perform in coffeehouses, on university campuses, and in clubs. As performers in a left-wing tradition of protest music and union activism, steeped as well in spirituals and Dust Bowl ballads, Dylan's contemporaries saw themselves on the edge of the main-stream, as the proprietors and protectors of a landscape of hipness that nourished resistance to the social conformity of the Eisenhower years. Loosely allied with the jazz world of the beatniks and the underground art culture of the 1950s, the folk music movement at the beginning of the 1960s took on the social mantle of a "modern" urban, sophisticated resistance to convention. The folksingers evoked traditions of protest against political and social injustice dating back to the labor strife of the 1920s and '30s — if not to the Paris Commune of the 1870s. Yet paradoxically, this modernist revolt against social convention took as its vehicle songs that were deeply rooted in premodern America and England. The older the song, the better, the more potentially disruptive and transformative it might be. By singing and circulating songs long forgotten, these singers aimed to carve out a subcultural space beyond the world of plastics, instant soup, and TV westerns. With ancient musical weapons they waged a rearguard action of "authenticity" or sincerity against the phoniness and standardization of emerging consumer culture.[4]

Folk music was popular in the proletarian sense of the word without generally being popular in the commercial sense. It articulated its values within a self-contained world that nevertheless presented a kind of performance of "coolness" for the "straight" world that watched it. This performative dimension of the folk enclave was crucial, as Greenwich Village became a destination for weekend tourists curious to see how "real" bohemians lived. Through the gaze of the tourist, and with the authority provided by the relatively few figures and institutions who actually succeeded at turning folk culture into cash, the folk music world asserted the value of its valuelessness.[5]

Dylan's seizure of folk material was itself made possible by the fact that the "folksingers" in the Greenwich Village scene were themselves, to use a term from the philosophers Gilles Deleuze and Félix Guattari, "deterritorialized."[6] The Village singers were, in a soft sense, refugees, often in flight from small towns or from the suburbs. Their identity was marked by their use of a set of artifacts — songs — that were themselves taken from ethnic immigrant communities or from a rural experience that was not theirs. Like the practitioners of what Deleuze and Guattari call a "minor literature," a body of art existing inside a broader cultural world that does not share its language or traditions, they circulated utterances and texts that stood in opposition to the mainstream culture. Yet the idiom of these utterances was not, strictly speaking, their own idiom. It belonged to the long dead, to the rural poor, to the black underclass, to the immigrant. The folksinger's flight from suburbia was given meaning through his or her ability to take up and assume, like a mask, the language of others. Previously marginalized or forgotten singers (Josh White, Leadbelly) were promoted, and the crucial concept of solidarity was mobilized to build bridges to various movements for justice. The resulting community of singers built a new canon of "American" songs to project a new type of postwar community that could overcome inequality and injustice. Geographical or regional difference (still a factor in American life at that time) was minimized or turned into a marketing technique; racial difference was mostly glossed over, as black, white, and brown performers intermingled. Class difference was carefully sidestepped, since virtually all of the younger players were middle class and most had some college experience. Indeed, class identity made it possible to project the image of a new community destined to change history with the advent of the years of the Kennedy presidency.

At one level, this rootlessness connects with a great theme of the lyric tradition in the West, the sense that the poet is always somehow an exile, estranged from love and home. As María Rosa Menocal showed in an important book on the emergence of Western lyric poetry at the end of the Middle Ages, the theme of exile is essential to modern poetry itself.[7] The earliest "modern" poets saw themselves as displaced, forced from home, in constant motion. In the case of Dylan, the sense of wandering, of homelessness, is one of the themes that binds him to his audience and to the "generation" that, for better or worse, he became associated with when he came to prominence in the 1960s. As we know, some of his most famous songs ("Like a Rolling Stone," for example) touch on this theme. The theme of exile, of symbolic homelessness, is central to the youth culture of the postwar American generation, freed from agricultural work and small-town claustrophobia, provided with the resources to wander and explore.

Dylan's ability to intervene in the world of traditional music was, to a degree, enabled by the technology of "folk culture" itself, as it was being created for and by the postwar generation. From the time of the first collecting expeditions, early in the twentieth century, by folklorists John and (later) Alan Lomax, through the emergence of Moses Asch's Folkways Records as the preeminent recording label for folk music, the folk music boom had exploited the new technology of recorded sound. The kings of folk music circulation and marketing were mostly Jewish males — themselves, like Dylan, in marginal ethnic and cultural positions — eager to create a sound portrait of

American music produced by other marginal figures—black people, poor people, migrants. An important tool was the 1952 *Anthology of American Folk Music*, edited by Harry Smith, which made available a strange collection of work songs, courting songs, and traveling songs from the previous seventy-five years. The *Anthology* helped shape the canon of the Greenwich Village singers, bringing them into contact with social worlds they might not otherwise have been aware of. Most of the songs on the *Anthology* were not, strictly speaking, "folk" or "traditional" songs, much less field recordings. Many had been released as commercial "race" records to black audiences earlier in the century. Yet the *Anthology*, by virtue of its very form and technology, *made* these songs "authentic." It converted them into American folk music. The *Anthology* made possible the circulation of songs that could be reworked by Village singers and reissued on Folkways, thereby generating a kind of low-profit capitalist enterprise inside a field that saw itself as distinct from the capitalist order, as a world of art. Just as the new technology of the microphone makes possible the intimate music of Frank Sinatra or the suffering voice of Billie Holiday, so a technological-literary form—the recorded anthology—shapes the American folk "tradition" in the early 1960s. And it is the technology that makes possible the emergence of "Bob Dylan."

Yet Dylan neither mimics nor offers pastiche. His approach—in contrast to that of most of his contemporaries—was to break up accepted songs, not "embodying" them in the "blood," as Mike Seeger had done, but combining them into a completely new style. Just as James Joyce could rewrite English literature from the marginal position of Ireland, and in Parisian exile, Dylan defines a new way of writing folk music as only someone from outside "the tradition" can do. Moreover, he took a step outside his own community when he secured a contract with Columbia Records, the largest recording organization in the country. He sold out, in order to sell more. His task would then become to write across the apparatus of recording and distribution, speaking to the folk world and for it at the same time.

No less important for an understanding of the ambiguous status of the folk music boom was the phenomenal commercial success of a few folk music acts who both bridged and marked the difference between folk culture and the larger record-buying public. The most famous of these was The Kingston Trio, who topped the Billboard charts in 1958 with a tongue-in-cheek reworking of the Civil War-era

murder ballad "Tom Dooley." The paradoxical situation of acts like
The Kingston Trio was that their repertoire drew from traditional
sources tapped as well by less famous and less commercial singers,
singers who no doubt saw them as a "sellout" to consumer culture.
Yet through their very success they illustrated the potential value
of folk music for a broader public accustomed to crooners and soft
jazz. Though West Coast-based, they offered a window into bohemia
for the uninitiated. Conversely, the folk world could both envy and
scorn their success, thereby affirming its own purity of intent and
transgressive status.

The Kingston Trio's position differed from that of Mike Seeger's
half-brother Pete, who had struck gold with the Weavers in the 1940s
through a hit version of Huddie Ledbetter's "Irene Goodnight,"
before being blacklisted by McCarthyism and relegated to perform-
ing in churches and union halls. Seeger's left-wing politics had been
incidental to the success of "Irene Goodnight." But his having been
blacklisted proved the political rightness and marginality of folk
music. The distance between Seeger's fate and the popularity of The
Kingston Trio indicates the shifting borders between traditional
American songs, on the one hand, and the increasingly commercial
and monitored world of "pop" music that emerged from the 1950s,
on the other. Seeger had been popular and authentic, but, because
of politics, his commercial triumph was past. The Kingston Trio
was popular and present, but they were inauthentic. This situation
left a structural hole in the music business, a space for a figure who
could redefine "authenticity" while gaining popularity. Yet that fig-
ure could only do so through a kind of second-order "folkiness," a
folkiness made-to-order for a changing consumer society that could
tolerate liberalism, but not, say, communism.

Dylan was able to seize this empty space in the structure of the folk
music world, presenting himself as "authentic" yet not "traditional."
He was shrewd enough not to try to reinsert traditional songs back
into their now distant contexts, as would, say, any number of "old-
timey" groups (including Mike Seeger's). Rather, he would invent the
fiction of a new cultural space beyond the mainstream, a space out
of which his songs seemed to emerge, and within whose imagined
atmosphere they could be understood. In this regard the achievement
of his earliest songs has a political dimension. For these songs invent
techniques and approaches by which stories of suffering, injustice,

and longing can touch a new, educated record-buying public — a public looking for songs that were not quaint curiosities and that hadn't been written for the picket line. This is not to say that Dylan was only interested in presenting himself as a kind of brand. Rather, he would continually reinvent "authenticity" as something that could be sold, even as he opened perspectives for reflecting on and questioning the very processes of commodification that made his own success possible.

Thus, Dylan's disruptive relationship to the folk music subculture involved his fictional reinvention, through his persona, of the "authentic" world from which his songs seemed to come. He is quite clear about the job before him. In *Chronicles*, he follows the description of Mike Seeger cited earlier by turning to his own self-presentation: "One thing for sure, if I wanted to compose folk songs I would need some kind of new template, some philosophical identity that wouldn't burn out. It would have to come on its own from the outside. Without knowing it in so many words, it was beginning to happen" (p. 73). Dylan's description of his identity coming "from the outside" suggests the enclosed territory of the folk world. But he also confronts here the question of his own persona, or self-definition in song. What kind of new identity could put the new songs across? The Kingston Trio had tried a "new template" for old songs. Dylan had been trying an "old template" in his imitations of Guthrie. Now new songs needed a new template of the self. What might he find or invent as a "philosophical identity that wouldn't burn out"? How could Dylan be *both* modern (that is, unique, distinct from the competition) and a folksinger (that is, "traditional") at the same time?

Voices

In the paragraph from *Chronicles* that immediately follows his description of the encounter with Seeger, Dylan expands on his insight that he will need to develop his own "template" for music. He describes the repeated experience of sitting up through the night in a cafe with two companions, the singer Paul Clayton and a friend named Ray: "I'd lean back against the wall and shut my eyes. Their voices drifting into my head like voices talking from another world" (p. 74). The key term here is "voice," the vehicle of both language and of music. But which voice, and from which "other world"? Dylan says of Paul Clayton, "He sang a lot of sea shanties, had a Puritan ancestry, but some of his old relatives had been from the early Virginia families." As for Ray, he "was from Virginia, had ancestors who had fought on both sides of the Civil War" (p. 74). If Mike Seeger embodies American WASP musical aristocracy, Clayton and Ray offer something different. Their voices express identities as complex as American history itself. Both of them are linked simultaneously with the North and the South, that is, with both sides of the American Civil War. They quite literally give voice to an American experience that is multiple, split against itself, in conflict, even when inside a single body. And in their voices we can begin to hear the rudiments of a poetics that would counter the essential aristocracy of a figure like Mike Seeger, who carries folk music in his blood.

This hypnotic display of the power of voice is then broken, an instant later, by a disturbing anecdote that adds yet another dimension to Dylan's self-definition. He mentions walking with his friend Mark Spoelstra to a club on Carmine Street run by a man named the Dutchman ("[who] resembled Rasputin" [p. 74]). Arriving at the club, they learn that the Dutchman has just been stabbed. His body is still lying on the sidewalk in front of the club. "Seeing the Dutchman lying there . . . he looked like a mercenary who could have fallen at Gettysburg," writes Dylan. This is a striking expansion on what Dylan has just been saying about Mike Seeger, Paul Clayton, and Ray. The body of the Dutchman (whose name reminds us of the Dutch origins of New York) evokes both the American Civil War and, as a Rasputin figure, the Russian Revolution. His murder is the death of New Amsterdam, the Battle of Gettysburg, and the murder of Rasputin all rolled into one. In this moment of vision, the violence of the present and the violence of the past seem to merge. Gettysburg is replayed every day in the streets of New York. The shock encounter with the dead Dutchman (following the earlier encounter with Seeger) yields yet another insight. Dylan realizes that what he loves about the songs he has been singing is their *language*, an antiquated language, a language marked by history: "I was beginning to feel that maybe the language had something to do with the causes and ideals of the circumstances and blood of what happened over a hundred years ago over secession from the Union. All of a sudden, it didn't seem that far back" (p. 76), he concludes.

Identity, voice, history: these themes hover around Dylan's first songwriting efforts. Dylan sets a task for himself that would involve a swerve away from — or a transcendence of — an aristocratic version of "embodied" identity. Dylan would have to outmaneuver or skirt the world of people like Mike Seeger to mark out a new — and newly democratic — approach to song. He presents his own philosophical identity as the vehicle through which that swerve will be enacted. No less striking is that the quest for a "new template" is a quest for a new *language*. Dylan's poetics will have to emerge out of a practice of listening, of response to the pulses, sonorities, and accents of the American vernacular. And finally, it is hard not to be struck here by the close relationship that Dylan sets up between language and history. The voices of the past are violently available to the imagination at any time. They ring through the present. A body on the street in Manhattan could be from Gettysburg. If Dylan is anything, he is a historical poet.

Virtually all of Dylan's compositions on his first three albums are themselves echoic adaptations — reworkings of other tunes, appropriations of scenarios and structures, citations. At one level, there is nothing particularly unusual about this in the annals of folk music. Woody Guthrie had taken dozens of traditional melodies and dressed them up in new, topical lyrics: the Appalachian tune "Wildwood Flower" becomes the patriotic song "The Sinking of the Reuben James"; the hymn "This World Is Not My Home" becomes the workers' lament "I Ain't Got No Home"; and so on. Conversely, Pete Seeger had taken ready-made lyrics from poems and books and set them to music: "Turn, Turn, Turn" from the Bible, "Guantanamera" from José Martí. By contrast, Dylan will recast traditional forms as the creation of a particular literary persona or "philosophical identity." Dylan is not singing the experience of some community — say, the Okies in California or striking miners. He is singing himself.[8]

Dylan's invention of a new "template" of post-Seeger authenticity is linked to two things. One is his mobility, his image of himself as a traveler or rambler. The defining characteristic of this self-construction is the idea of "experience," the sense that the character has done things no one else has done. The other key element is the notion of *voice*. Language, as Balzac says somewhere, is the capital of the poor man, and Dylan's ability to mix linguistic registers and play with diction constitutes the tool through which he puts the stamp of "authenticity" on his singing and writing. Indeed, one of the features that distinguishes Bob Dylan's art from that of his contemporaries is the variety of voices with which he communicates. At the level of performance, this involves the simple biographical fact that through his career he has changed many times the way he sings. Whereas, for example, Mick Jagger and Paul McCartney continue to sing more or less in the same timbre and register that they have always used, Dylan's voice has bounced around from a nasal keen to a trumpetlike croon to a preacherly shout to a growl to a sob. These verbal variations are tools. They sometimes occur in the same song, as a way of eliciting different emotional effects, as is especially clear in his earliest recordings, where he whoops and groans by turns.

But we can also think about another aspect of "voice" in Dylan. The lyrics are themselves multivoiced. They are produced out of a technique in which bits of language taken from different contexts and registers of American English are patched together in a kind of amalgam. This is characteristic of any text, of course, but in Dylan's case it is central to his approach. The critic Mikhail Bakhtin, whom I mentioned in my introduction, has described the social nature of all texts as follows: "The living utterance, having taken meaning and shape at a particular historical moment in a socially specific environment, cannot fail to brush up against thousands of living dialogic threads, woven by socio-ideological consciousness around the given object of an utterance."[9] At one level, we might think of Dylan's lyrics as a kind of stylistic collage, or, perhaps even more strongly, of a "constellation"—a kind of combinatory force field that radiates in all directions. It is Dylan's combinatory approach—hinted at in the scene of him listening to Ray and Paul Clayton—that generates the complex persona through which he puts his songs across.[10]

Initially, as a thought experiment, we might point to three fairly obvious Dylan "voices" within the world of his early albums. One is Dylan's "hobo voice." This is the feature of his writing that affects a countrified accent and, more important, a deliberately nonnormative use of grammar. The hoboesque or country boy phraseology appears in expressions such as "a-changin'" (with its dropped g), the use of "ain't" ("It ain't no use to sit and wonder why, babe" [p. 78]), the misplacement of verb tenses ("I give her my heart but she wanted my soul" [p. 78]), the mismatching of plural nouns with singular verbs ("By the old wooden stove our hats was hung" [p. 80]), or idiomatic distortions of normal usage ("ifn" [p. 78], instead of "if").[11]

Though these are obvious and familiar features of Dylan's early work, one should not simply skirt over them. There is no consistency to these grammatical affectations. Rather, they are used strategically, when needed. Dylan's hobo voice places him in the heritage of Woody Guthrie, who, unlike the Minnesota-raised Dylan, was an actual Okie and from a deeply rural background. Dylan's statement from the 1964 song "With God on Our Side," speaking of the Midwest, that "I's taught and brought up there" (p. 108) recalls such phrases as Guthrie's "I's a-goin' pretty fast" (from "Talking Dust Bowl Blues").[12] This linguistic pose — quite different, for example, from Pete Seeger's impeccable, clipped, WASP mastery of English grammar — would become, by the mid-1960s, one of a number of tools that Dylan could drop or pick up as needed. In his earliest compositions it has the effect of creating a mask. It is central to the development of his "philosophical personality." It projects an identity or persona that seems to come from a space beyond that of the average educated consumer of popular song.

In *Chronicles*, Dylan recounts his habit, in his early days, of visiting the New York Public Library to study nineteenth-century newspapers for useful words and phrases. "I wasn't so much interested in the issues as intrigued by the language and the rhetoric of the times" (p. 84), he says. Thus, just as important as the hobo voice — though less obvious — is what we might call the "archaic voice," marked by a set of verbal tics and word choices that seem to speak from some earlier moment in the history of the language — perhaps from the moment of Gettysburg itself. These are often bits of antiquated or even mispronounced speech, such phrases as "Come writers and critics who *prophesize* with your pen"; "I'd *forsake* them all"; "I fell asleep *for to take* my rest" (pp. 104, 114, 80). At times these bits of language take on the intonation of the preacher and/or the bluesman, sometimes at the same time ("If you can't quit your sinnin' / Please, quit your lowdown ways" [p. 46]). This is the voice responsible for the biblically inflected language of one of Dylan's first major songs, "A Hard Rain's a-Gonna Fall," which describes present-day life, yet seems to come from some fairytale setting outside of it ("I met a young girl with wild wolves all around her" [p. 76]). If we remember that much of Guthrie's production consisted in taking received melodies and updating them under the pressure of current events, Dylan's approach involves not only applying new lyrics to old melodies, but also filling those new lyrics with bits of language that seem to come from a pre-1950s world. In effect, he is going for his language back before the epoch of his putative models.

I give these "voices" labels not to indicate them as absolutely distinct from each other, but simply to point out how Dylan's writing generates its enormous vitality through the interplay of different stylistic registers. Thus, "With God on Our Side" begins with Dylan sounding like a hobo or rural workingman, as he asserts his lack of status: "Oh, my name it ain't nothin'" (p. 108), he says, in a distant echo of Odysseus's comment to the Cyclops, "I am Noman." This is followed by the grammatically correct but awkward answering phrase, "My age it means less." It is not clear what could be less than "nothing," but the phrase is deceptive, since the age of the narrator matters very much as the song unfolds. He is today's youth, one of the young people — you or me — who have been miseducated. We then get a geographical identification of the singer as from the Midwest, before being led into a complex articulation of the thematic center of the song:

I's taught and brought up there
The laws to abide
And that the land that I live in
Has God on its side (p. 108)

The "hobo" language of "I's taught and brought up there" immediately gives way to the old-fashioned sounding phrase "the laws to abide," which is semantically vague: Does it mean to "tolerate" ("I can't abide him") or to "obey" (in which case it should be "abide by")? Whatever the precise meaning, the phrase generates an alienating effect, as if the singer knew something about grammar that we don't, as if this phrase actually "worked" grammatically in some sociolect somewhere, in some local tongue that we would recognize if we knew what the singer knows. This awkward grammar then gives way to the phrase that sums up the verse: "And that the land that I live in / Has God on its side." However, this summing up is not presented in the nonnormative grammar of the hobo. It is an attack on traditional patriotism and old-time religion — both probably revered by any number of real hobos — and it is in standard English. It is yet a third voice, the voice of a college kid and Greenwich Village lefty who is well read. And yet the final lines take their authority from both the geographical reach and the social experience evoked in the phrasing of the rest of the verse. Without them the final lines would fall flat, as self-righteous liberalism divorced from experience. These diverse voices are necessary as a way of linking personal experience and moral commentary. Dylan has to take on the voice of the rural citizen in order to make his learned claim against official American history.[13]

Writing of the struggles of the dramatist Bertolt Brecht to create, late in his career, a theater that would speak to the German proletariat, Theodor Adorno notes that Brecht's plays are marred by the awkward imposition of "popular" sayings and words that ring false. "Brecht's language affects the speech of the oppressed," he writes. "But the doctrine it champions requires the language of the intellectual. Its unpretentiousness and simplicity are a fiction. . . . Ears that have preserved their sensitivity cannot help hearing that someone is trying to talk them into something."[14] For Adorno, Brecht's archaisms are simply insulting to the proletariat from whose ranks popular language comes. By contrast, Dylan never pauses to assume any particular "voice" for more than a few seconds. The distinct registers of his diction are constantly intertwined, combined and recombined. They take the form of affective instants, bits of phrasing or distortions of common speech that go by with dizzying speed. This is key. Whereas, for example, Paul McCartney takes on the voice and persona of a middle-class Englishman singing to his wife in "When I'm Sixty-Four," Dylan's work largely avoids this type of ventriloquism or playacting. Because his style is combinatory, rather than dramatic, dialogic, rather than pastiche, it leaves space for his singing persona to dip in and out of different identities, while never allowing itself to be enclosed in any one. Dylan is virtually always "in" his songs, but he is never completely absorbed by them. This is yet another aspect of his marginality — a marginality toward his own creations. In this way, to recall a famous phrase from Walt Whitman, Dylan's voice can "contain multitudes." He achieves this in the very fabric of his lyrics, at the level of the poetic line.[15]

Spaces

Dylan's songs differ from Brecht's plays because he can present himself as a figure of wandering, as a rambler who is always on the move. The interplay between erudite language and archaic or popular language is linked to the singer's very claim to speak. It locates him in a world of shared national history in song. In this regard, his account of his movements does important mediating work, knotting different subcultural worlds together. His intent is manifestly not to speak to the rural world from which he has taken his language, but rather to use that language to entertain an urban audience. If anything, his speech may echo distantly listeners' own family histories, now brought back to consciousness and transformed. Dylan thus both grapples with the problem that Adorno points to in Brecht and transcends it through his own self-creation.

"With God on Our Side" addresses the problem of how a single individual, drawing on his limited experience and his linguistic gifts, can make an authoritative claim about a much larger theme — in this case, about American history itself, which he goes on to judge harshly. Dylan's authority, his new "style," if you will, involves not only a blending of linguistic registers, but the use of those registers to create a new sense of space, a collective world in which the singer's struggles and ours are the same. Because Dylan moves, he sings with authority. As a contrast, we could think of Woody Guthrie's outlaw ballad "Pretty Boy Floyd." It sets the scene as follows: "'Twas in the town of Shawnee / On a Saturday afternoon."[6] Guthrie's lines are specific, the work of a chronicler whose listeners have never heard of the town of Shawnee, Oklahoma. By contrast, Dylan opens his "Talkin' New York," with, "Ramblin' out o' the Wild West / Leavin' the towns I love the best" (p. 6). Dylan uses *both* the language of where he has been and the language of his listeners, who all know about the "Wild West" from television and movies. Guthrie located his songs in very specific contexts, linked to particular historical events, often far behind us. Dylan recasts that space so that it includes both performer and listener.

One of Dylan's earliest and most enduring love songs, "Girl from the North Country," begins with these words:

> If you're travelin' in the north country fair
> Where the winds hit heavy on the borderline
> Remember me to one who lives there
> She once was a true love of mine (p. 71)

The language of this verse seems to come from several different worlds. The phrase "north country" is slightly exotic and unfamiliar.

39

It is not obvious where one would locate it on the map of the United States, with its carefully delineated state borders. It could remind us of England, where they have a "west country," or the long-past world of Mark Twain's Huckleberry Finn, who vows to light out for "the territories" as the novel ends. This exoticism is underscored by the adjective "fair," which is not a word applied in everyday postwar American speech to geographical regions. It adds an archaic touch; it makes the phrase sound old.[17] This detail is especially striking when we set the song against the model on which Dylan is building the verse. This is the centuries-old English folk song that begins, "Are you going to Scarborough Fair?"—a song that Dylan presumably learned from the singing of Martin Carthy and that later became a radio hit for Simon and Garfunkel. In that song (which Dylan takes from a minor key to a major key) we begin with a precise place and event: the fair held in the town of Scarborough. It is an event that has no particular age. It could be held again tomorrow, and it would be described with the same phrase. Dylan takes that phrase and rewrites it to invent a vague country described in aesthetic terms as "fair." The *noun* in the original becomes an *adjective* in Dylan's reworking. In the process a place of ritualized commerce becomes a site of affective loss.

Yet no sooner have we entered this slightly mythical imaginative space than we get details: "Where the winds hit heavy on the borderline." The word "borderline" is interesting, since a border is precisely the one thing that doesn't matter to the winds, any more than it could serve to delineate "the north country fair." Moreover, in conversational speech winds don't "hit heavy." Storms hit; winds blow. When a storm hits, it is an event. Heavy winds may "kick up" or "strengthen," but because air currents are virtually always present, we do not think of wind as hitting. The relationship of border and wind suggests the tension between the limits or contingencies that keep the lovers apart, on the one hand, and the flow of emotion that still links them, on the other. The power of the "heavy" hitting here stems from the fact that heavy is an adjective, yet it functions as an adverb. Dylan's point is not that there are "heavy winds," a temporary situation, but that the winds hit "heavily," a habitual state of affairs made possible by his own grammatical malapropism. This unfamiliarity turns the phrase into a kind of instant idiomatic expression—one of the first of many self-contained proverbs that Dylan

generates in his early songs. In this case — and this is the impor-
tant thing — the awkwardness of the grammar locates the singer in
a world of people who see the winds as "heavy" because they have
to live with them. "I have been there," it suggests in a way that the
original reference to the famous fair in Scarborough does not. "I have
been hit by these winds and lived to tell about it." Its colloquial reach
embraces the lexicon of Dylan's idol Guthrie, who characteristically
uses verbs like "hit" to mean "do." "I been hittin' some hard travelin',"
sings Guthrie in the song of the same name. This is the language of
one version of the American rural poor, of Dust Bowl migrants and
hobos. Yet here it is juxtaposed with a romanticized image of a "north
country fair" that contains within it an echo of an old English folk
song. And this makes the phrase "the winds hit heavy" the descriptor
of a world that seems both to exist in real time and space — some-
where on the American continent — and nowhere at all. The singer
is placing us and himself at the edge of two worlds, one a world of
violence and heavy weather, the other a lovely land of mystery. One
exists in an old song, the other in the lives of working people. Dylan
makes them both part of a new song. Indeed, the verse swerves back
from the grit of the heavy-hitting winds to the exoticism of the Eng-
lish ballad when Dylan urges the listener to "remember me" to his
lost love. This is yet another slightly archaic phrase. We can gauge its
quaintness by remembering that when Dylan rerecorded the song a
decade later in a duet with Johnny Cash, Cash muffed the vocal by
replacing "Remember me" with the more colloquial and "modern"
expression, "Please say hello."

My point here is that the striking combination of two linguis-
tic worlds, merry old(e) England and the hardscrabble world of the
American worker, creates a peculiar imaginary landscape within
which Dylan can express the amalgam of tenderness and toughness
that will be characteristic of much of his self-presentation. Simon and
Garfunkel made "Scarborough Fair" "relevant" for modern listeners
by appending a countermelody about war. Dylan simply rewrote the
entire scenario, opening a space in which actor, poet, and listener can
coexist. Indeed, the listener is implicated in Dylan's appropriation of
the original form. "Scarborough Fair" is a song about the failure of
love. With each verse, the song sets up a series of impossible tests that
the lost love must fulfill: "Tell her to find me an acre of land," sings
the canny narrator, "between the salt water and the sea strand." The

41

renewal of love is based on a kind of exchange. The singer can only love again if the love partner will do something impossible to prove her or his worth. It is a challenge song. It evokes the world of work, of women's domestic work and men's agricultural work. It articulates an unbridgeable gulf between daily work and the magic of true love. Dylan elides these references to work and opts for a description of the weather, for the generation of atmosphere and context. He turns a song about fate into a song of sentiment. A song about the immobile laborer's limited power becomes a song about the mobile young lover's limitless memory. Moreover, and most important, he shifts that obligation from the lover to the listener. The hero is a wanderer, not an agricultural worker or a craftsman. This makes it possible for him to both love and move. And he creates a song that places a burden on the listener who is enjoined to be a messenger and a caregiver. Do not challenge my love to accomplish an impossible task; watch out for her. Is she wearing a warm coat? For his part, the singer worries that she has forgotten him: "I wonder if she remembers me at all" (p. 71). This sense of a lost connection, of a slip into oblivion, is linked to the initial replacement of Scarborough Fair by "the north country fair." For it underscores the distance — perhaps, we might say, the American distance — between singer and lost love. You can find Scarborough on the map; as for the north country . . . well, maybe not. The mission of the listener is articulated in the third line of each stanza, where the singer's voice hits the lowest note of the melody: "Remember me," he says; "Make sure she wears a coat"; "Please see for me if her hair's hanging long."

Thus, the problem described by the song isn't a recalcitrant lover and farmer who can prove worthiness only by working miracles, as it is in "Scarborough Fair." It is distance itself — time and space — that weaken the singer and, in the process, underscore the power of the song to communicate. The song repairs the impossible love depicted in the English original. For the solution to the problem of distance is the listener — you, or I — who will travel up north and carry a message to the girl. The song shifts emphasis away from the moral testing of the lovers and onto a community of friends. This imagination of a partner, a listener, a friend, is one of the characteristics of Dylan's early work. "Girl from the North Country" makes an implicit statement about the spatial immensity of America, and about the power of song to overcome that immensity. In the process, in the very inventedness of its language, it projects an imaginary community that binds listener and song. As I will suggest in the next chapter, it is the definition and redefinition of that community that will be central to Dylan's writing during his ascendency to eminence in the early years of the 1960s.[18]

Ramblin' Boy:

"Protest" and the Art of Adaptation

Beginning in 1963, other artists begin recording Dylan's original composi-
tions. Most notably, Peter, Paul and Mary ride "Blowin' in the Wind" to the
top of the pop charts. Dylan is recognized as an important new voice in song-
writing. Over the next five years, "Blowin' in the Wind" goes on to become
one of the anthems of the emerging movements in support of racial justice
and against the war in Vietnam. Dylan's third album, The Times They Are
a-Changin', cements his reputation, as does a triumphant performance at
the 1963 Newport Folk Festival. 1964 brings a shift in focus. Another Side
of Bob Dylan — recorded, like its predecessors, in a stripped-down "folk"
style, with acoustic guitar or piano, harmonica, and minimal accompani-
ment — nevertheless features increasingly ambitious and extended compo-
sitions written in a less topical and more subjective register. These new
songs are marked by clusters of striking images that often challenge easy
comprehension and break with the more journalistic language of Dylan's
earliest work.

Dylan's songs on his first four albums, through their form and dic-
tion, respond to the situation of folk music at the onset of the 1960s.
The collective experience of migration and union organizing in
which Dylan's idol Woody Guthrie had worked has been replaced, for
a record-buying middle class, by the experience of the nuclear family
and emerging automobile culture. That new audience would come to
have its own political projects, as the subsequent history of the 1960s
would demonstrate, but its concerns would not be those in which the
songs of Woody Guthrie had taken shape. Rhetorically, this means
that folk songs, the kind that "Mike wouldn't know," to recall Dylan's

remark about Mike Seeger, must establish new relationships to audiences and a new singing persona.

One way to approach Dylan's self-creation in these early songs is to think for a moment about the choices before him. The young Dylan made exorbitant claims about his past and experiences to fans and journalists: that he had been kicked out of his home, that he had traveled with a carnival, that he was raised in New Mexico, that he had worked at many different kinds of hard labor, and so on. How to cull this kind of information and graft it together into some type of "template" that wouldn't wear out, as he put in *Chronicles?* Dylan was surrounded by singers trying on different styles: the queen of folk music, Joan Baez, sang ancient ballads in an angelic voice; Dave Van Ronk, an early mentor, specialized in blues and early ragtime tunes; Mike Seeger and The New Lost City Ramblers sang in the accents of Appalachia; John Hammond Jr. became a blues specialist. Dylan thus needed to choose a set of characteristics for his songwriting persona. He did so by focusing on the theme of mobility and by exploring the implications of that theme for language, space, and identity. At one level, of course, this mobility simply reflected the life of the touring musician or couch-surfing apprentice. My point is that Dylan gives it symbolic and even political meaning.

Rough Weather

The cultural cliché of the "rambler," of course, has a very long history. In the popular imagination, it goes back to the idea of the medieval troubadour who supposedly travels from court to court and sings for his supper. In the history of modern popular music, the image is first associated with Jimmie Rodgers, "the Singing Brakeman." Dylan's immediate model is Guthrie, who was driven from his home in Oklahoma by the Dust Bowl, traveled to California, and sang for migrant workers before ending up in New York, where he eventually started a family. This figure of the singer as wanderer, who brings some kind of "wisdom" from his time on the road, is central to a certain current of modern American folk music. Another Guthrie heir, Ramblin' Jack Elliot, had written the idea into his very stage name. The wandering folksinger, in Dylan's guise, is not driven by economic desperation or political upheaval. Whereas Guthrie sings about the rambling forced on him by the Dust Bowl, Dylan's persona rambles to get songs that he can then sing ... about his rambling to get songs.[1]

The iconic moment in the depiction of the wandering American bard must certainly be the opening passage of Guthrie's 1943 memoir *Bound for Glory*. There we see the young Guthrie hop a freight train: "I could see men of all colors bouncing along in the boxcar," he begins. The episode proceeds to paint a picture of a restless, unemployed underclass headed somewhere, riding in a stifling boxcar that had recently held bags of cement. The cement becomes a metaphor for the fragile bonds that link the men, as their sweat mixes with the powder and coats them all in gray mud. Jostled and bumped, they shout at each other above the rattle of the wheels, boasting and complaining mostly about work, which all claim to be masters at, but which none of them has. Guthrie's own work is revealed to be music. He defends his labor on patriotic grounds, asserting that the war against fascism will not be won by Tin Pan Alley songs, "a dam bunch of silly wisecracks." "Gonna take work!" he exclaims, on the curious assumption that folk songs somehow require more "work!" than, say, Cole Porter's 108-measure-long masterpiece "Begin the Beguine." When the scene begins to turn violent, Guthrie and an African American friend seek the safety and fresh air of the door and finally climb up on the boxcar roof. As Guthrie lies down and puts his ear to the metal rooftop, he can hear the men singing and fighting down below, like Dylan listening to Ray and Paul long into the night. "Are these men?" asks Guthrie. "Who am I?"[2]

Guthrie's scene is rewritten twice by Jack Kerouac, one of Dylan's literary idols and early influences. Chapter 4 of Kerouac's 1957 novel *On the Road* offers an account of "the greatest ride of my life," on the back of a flatbed truck driven by two smiling, exuberant farm boys ("they liked everything") across the Nebraska plains. Guthrie's restive collection of unemployed men is now welded together into a fraternity of good humor and enthusiasm by the excited voice of the narrator, Sal Paradise, on his first trip west. The singer is replaced by the novelist. As they roll across the plains, Sal strikes up a conversation with a man called Mississippi Gene, only to learn that he and Gene have a mutual acquaintance, the college dropout and professional hobo known as Louisiana Slim (who sounds a bit like the college dropout Jack Kerouac). "Well, damn me, I'm amazed you know him. This is a big country," notes Sal. Guthrie's claustrophobic version of American community, on a train to nowhere, is now rewritten as a romance tale of wandering in which friends lose and find each other via word of mouth, across the vast space of the continent. It is the postwar labor boom, and work is now everywhere, as passengers hop on and off the truck bed, heading out for the harvests. Each rambler gets named after a state, and, as they come and go, the American continent is stitched together.[3]

Three years later, the scene is replayed yet again in the set piece that opens Kerouac's next novel, *The Dharma Bums*. There we see the protagonist Ray headed north: "Hopping a freight out of Los Angeles at high noon one day in late September 1955 I got on a gondola and lay down," is the first sentence. As Ray watches the clouds, he enters into silent communion, across the boxcar, with a solitary hobo whose only action is to pray to Saint Teresa as he shivers in the chill. At Santa Barbara, Ray leaves the miserable man and his prayer and makes a camp on the beach, "one of the most pleasant nights of my life." There, he exults in his solitude and in the space of the heavens above him: "I sat cross-legged in the sand and contemplated my life. Well, there, and what difference did it make?"[4]

"Am I a man?" asks Guthrie. "What difference did it make?" counters Kerouac. These three scenes depict the changing relationship between mobility and community in the postwar years. Guthrie's Depression-era company, which he calls a "carload of sheep," is on the way to nowhere, stuck in an indifferent universe: "Bound for glory? This train? Ha!" Guthrie shouts sarcastically as the rain begins and the chapter ends; "Strike, lightning strike! The sky ain't never as crazy as the world."[5] By contrast, Kerouac's beatnik has no direction, and turns that aimlessness into a goal: "There was nowhere to go but everywhere," exults Sal Paradise. Kerouac knits the country into a unified space through the coincidences of romance narrative. Like knights meeting in an enchanted forest, his beatniks prowl the land, picking up at will the "work" that Guthrie's characters seek with such desperation (Louisiana Slim used to be a student, then he became a lumberjack, now he's a cowboy). Even race is effaced, as white-skinned Gene has "something of the wise old Negro in him."[6] Kerouac displaces the social tension depicted in Guthrie by emptying the crowded boxcar of bodies and turning the "other" (the hobo) into a mystic who shivers like a ghostly apparition.

This shift from worker solidarity to beat solitude registers the changing position of the marginal figure in the new booming manufacturing economy of the post–World War II era. It also gives spiritual voice to the technology that informs that economy — the new culture of the automobile. It is the automobile that, for Dylan's generation, has emerged to replace the earlier, now romanticized, freight train. Kerouac can only glorify the hopping of freights because he has other means of transport — either hitchhiking on a farm truck in *On the Road* or, later in that book, taking up the magical automobile, which can get him from coast to coast in a matter of days. The faster the trip, the better and more "beatlike" it becomes. Yet the increasing solitude of the rambler also attests to the difficulty of representing, in art, the numbing emptiness of the road. Kerouac's travelers speak endlessly of whom they will meet at the next stop, and rarely of what the experience of movement through which they are passing actually feels like or means. Like the contemporaneous figure of the rancher/ cowboy in a TV western (the dominant filmic genre of the late 1950s) who can, in a complete abandonment of plausibility, "ride into town" for lunch and be back by teatime, Kerouac's heroes promote an ethos of mobility that doubles that of the new car-enabled citizen in the late Eisenhower years.

Guthrie listens bitterly as his fellows sing the spiritual "Bound for Glory" through the boxcar roof, unable either to participate or offer an appropriate song that could knit the community together and help fight fascism. His artist is an outsider even in his own community, and the communities that his songs represent — unions, small towns, labor camps — are endangered or gone by the time Dylan comes along. Dylan, by contrast, creates a new community, a community of listeners. It is generated out of his pose as a wanderer. Whereas Kerouac's heroes are intellectuals who must return east to write about their experiences, Dylan's persona writes songs instead of novels and composes as he goes. In contrast to the jazz musicians idolized by Kerouac and his friends, the folkie needs no bandstand or club in which to ply his trade. His contingency is not biographical ("my name it ain't nothing" [p. 108]) but spatial. He is here now; but he might not be here later. Yet that very fiction of mobility is what accounts for his capital as a singer. He converts physical mobility into professional success. It gives him the aura of wisdom beyond his years.[7]

The spatial or geographical mediation offered by Dylan's voice is presented in nearly programmatic terms in "Down the Highway," from 1963's *Freewheelin'* album. There he presents himself in his best rural disguise, singing a simple tune modeled on the acoustic blues tradition, punctuated by the kind of guitar figure one might associate with a singer like Lightnin' Hopkins. What is he doing? "Well, I'm walkin' down the highway" (p. 74). He repeats the phrase, in conformity with the blues convention. Then he expands on it. We learn that he's lonely because his "baby" is in "some foreign land." The problem with this answering line is that the world of the blues that seems to be evoked by the idiom and form of this song is generally not a world in which one's baby goes off to a "foreign land." African American blues singers in the tradition that Dylan is building on here may sing about their baby going off to Chicago, or New Orleans, or Natchez. But not on a trip abroad: that's an experience that, at this particular moment, is still mostly the province of a modern, educated, Caucasian upper middle class. The incongruity between the protagonist's rural "walkin'" and the beloved's journey by ocean liner underscores the awkwardness of the setup. And, indeed, the song seems to have been occasioned by the fact that Dylan's girlfriend of the moment, Suze Rotolo, had left for art school in Italy. Dylan goes on to claim in good rural language that he'll "get lucky" or "die tryin'" as he rambles to reach his beloved. Either way, he laments that she's packed his heart in a suitcase and "took it away to Italy, Italy." The repetition of "Italy" reinforces the rural blues register of the song, as if the singer can't believe where's she's gone; as if he has to say the word twice, to get it right, so unfamiliar is the word to him: Where did you say she's gone? Memphis? Jackson? Italy. I can't believe it myself. Yet the function of the singer is precisely to mediate the experience of two largely incompatible worlds, to bring the moral earnestness of the blues form to the attention of listeners in touch with the most unblueslike phenomenon of study abroad.

Dylan's fictionalized mobility binds the nation together, geographically, at the moment of the postwar emergence of California and the West as plausible spaces to visit and return from. This geographical work is palpable in the way he brings a version of rural art to the ears of urban or suburban listeners. Moreover, the invention of a new type of hobo, just in off the road, is linked to the collage style of lyric writing that I spelled out in the previous chapter. Indeed, the two phenomena — the performing identity and the style of the lyric — are two sides of the same coin. The rambling boy is the thematic embodiment of the poetic technique shaping Dylan's lyric style. Dylan's composite lyricism, drawing on both working-class

American idioms and "exotic" imported song forms, is the manifes-
tation, at the level of form, of his mercurial persona, and vice versa.
It is impossible to say which one generates the other.

The intertwined relationship of identity and musical style
is made clear from Dylan's very first released recording. His first
album, titled simply *Bob Dylan* (1962), featured a number of tradi-
tional folk songs and blues tunes, interspersed with two "original"
compositions: "Song to Woody" and "Talkin' New York." "Talkin'
New York" is the very first officially released recording of a Bob
Dylan song on vinyl. It builds explicitly on a number of Guthrie's
compositions, most obviously "Talking Dust Bowl Blues," in which
Guthrie recounts his misadventures upon leaving his farm in Okla-
homa. The form matters. It is a "talking blues." The talking blues is
one of two relatively open forms that Dylan deploys repeatedly in
his early songs, as a way of defining his persona. Like the blues, it is
built around a set of major chords, over which the singer recounts his
adventures, occasionally expanding the lines in order to intercalate
commentary or to stretch words. The tone is usually ironic; it offers a
perplexed, comic alternative to the drama of much traditional music.
It is the genre of the antihero, whom we see spin out the story of what
has happened to him, as if both astonished at the direction his life
has taken and stoically resigned to the hand that fate has dealt him.
In literary terms we might relate it to the picaresque novel. The job
of the listener is to follow in amusement as the narrator spins story
after story, ending up with a sense of the craziness of the world and
the corrupt nature of those in power.

Dylan carefully manipulates this form to invent a model of the
singing narrator who is both the heir to Guthrie and a much more
modern — indeed, we might say, modernist — version of the same
type. "Talkin' New York" recreates Dylan's arrival in the city in the
winter of 1961. Each verse consists of two rhyming couplets, followed
by some type of formal expansion, often a phrase that comments on
or opens up what has preceded. So, the opening couplets:

Ramblin' outa the wild West
Leavin' the towns I love the best
Thought I'd seen some ups and downs
'Til I come into New York town
People goin' down to the ground
Buildings goin' up to the sky (p. 6)

51

The rhyme scheme of this verse perfectly illustrates one part of the dynamic that powers the talking blues. The rhymes of "down," "town," and "ground" set up an expectation of another rhyme that will complete them. Instead we get "sky," which opens up the sonic pattern of the song, refusing convenient closure. In this disruption of symmetry lies much of the humor of the form.

This break in the rhyming pattern underscores the theme of the verse — and, indeed, of the song more generally. Guthrie's "Talking Dust Bowl Blues" recounted his trip to California. Dylan rambles east, by contrast, answering the westward movement of empire with a personal odyssey. The obvious exaggeration in the phrase "Wild West" (neither particularly wild, in 1961, nor, so far as we know, particularly familiar to Minnesota's Robert Zimmerman, despite one brief trip to Colorado) sets the generic tone. Moreover, and more important, no sooner has he arrived in New York than the directional matrix of east/west gives way to a contrast between "down" (people) and "up to the sky" (buildings). The opening verticalizes the movement of the singer's experience and sets the way for the overarching achievement of the song, which is to present the confusion of the provincial in a major city.

The second stanza (with my emphases) reasserts the disorientation of the singer with its insistence on the cold and on aimlessness:

Wind blowin' the snow *around*
Walking *around* with nowhere to go
Somebody could freeze right to the bone.
I froze right to the bone

The repetition links Dylan to the cityscape. He now becomes "somebody," the everyman, the unnamed common citizen no longer anonymous because he, of all people, has frozen to the bone. And then, as if to celebrate this moment, we get Dylan's first extended talking blues commentary: "*New York Times* said it was the coldest winter in seventeen years / I didn't feel so cold then." As he will so frequently in the years to come, Dylan turns to another text, this time the newspaper, to provide a context for his experience.

The key motif here is the feeling of disorientation. It is continued as stanza three opens. "I swung onto my old guitar," sings Dylan, mobilizing his archaic register. This is of course inaccurate. You can't "swing onto" your guitar. You can swing your guitar onto yourself.

Yet the phrase, with its reversal of subject and object, underscores the sensory and cardinal disorientation that continues as the singer takes a subway car to Greenwich Village, where we learn that "I landed *up* on the *down*town side" (my emphases).

These images of disorientation, of directions and actions that run counter to logic, both establish the experience of the "naive" subject in the city and set up the moral contrast between the foolish, corrupt world of singers and managers that he encounters and his own status as an "outsider" who is, nevertheless, more "real" than they are. He gets a singing job, only to be told that he sounds like a "hillbilly" (which he is not), whereas what is needed are "folksingers." New York turns out to be the space of both disorientation and misnaming. Yet music saves the day, almost. Soon the singer gets a job, "blowin' my lungs out for a dollar a day." The freezing wind "blowin' the snow around" gives way to the breath of music. But even here there is disorientation, as the subject is turned all about: "I blowed inside out and upside down," for a dollar a day.

The exposure of New York as the place of inauthenticity and sensory disorientation is finally brought into focus when, after "weeks and weeks of hangin' around" (there's the notion of "aroundness" again), he gets a real job. Bigger place, "bigger money," and he joins the union. Here we get a turn back to the figure of the labor union as a site of solidarity and help that Guthrie had painted so impressively in songs like "Union Maid." Dylan's account of his union experience constitutes the first four lines of the sixth stanza. And we think that everything has fallen into place. However, the moment of rest is temporary. For it gives way to the longest bit of "commentary" in the song. Dylan evokes Guthrie explicitly:

> Now, a very great man once said
> That some people rob you with a fountain pen
> It didn't take too long to find out
> Just what he was talkin' about

This is an echo of Guthrie's ballad "Pretty Boy Floyd," in which Dust Bowl farmers are robbed by unscrupulous bankers. Dylan applies the lessons of Guthrie's song (bankers are corrupt) to himself.

So, it turns out that the union doesn't work, that the old communities have failed, that protection from unscrupulous bosses is not forthcoming. The music business in the 1960s is as bad as farming in the 1930s. This self-dramatization of Dylan as the victim of the men in suits then gives way to the strangest moment in the song. He goes on: "A lot of people don't have much food on their table / But they got a lot of forks 'n' knives / And they gotta cut somethin'." This ends the long "commentary" or tag on the penultimate stanza. But what are these lines doing in the song? They seem to be a reference to professional rivalries in the Village scene. But they also expand the earlier reference to Guthrie's bandit ballad with a moralizing tag. We seem to have drifted into the world of menace, toward a potential uprising of the poor and dispossessed. At least that is the tenor of the moment. The contrast between this dark moment of social commentary and the lighthearted story of the rambling musician is stark. Dylan seems to have sung himself into a corner in which his form leads him to a social commentary of some type, yet the comments he offers don't quite cohere with the rest of the composition. The drama is humorously and completely personal, and his evocation of the hungry worker rings false next to the portrait of the singer as ironic wanderer. Especially since, in the final stanza, the weather changes, and the singer rambles out of New York, "headed out for the western skies." The West is now New Jersey — to be precise, East Orange. But Dylan is not headed for labor in the orchards of California; he is going to a gig.[8]

The essayist and short story writer Jorge Luis Borges once wrote a meditation called "Kafka and his Precursors," in which (citing the Eliot essay on "Tradition and the Individual Talent" that I mentioned in Chapter 1) he argues that after the writing of Kafka certain earlier writers can never be read in the same way again, since they are now necessarily read, not for themselves, but as the origins of certain features that are more fully developed in Kafka. Certainly, one can make the same claim about what Dylan has done to Woody Guthrie, whom we can never listen to the same way again. This becomes clear if we turn to the other original composition on Dylan's first album, "Song to Woody." The song is built on Guthrie's "1913 Massacre," a song about an episode from labor history in upper Michigan. It tells the story of how the "copper boss thugs" lock the door to a community center where the miners are celebrating Christmas and then cry "fire." The ensuing stampede results in the deaths of women and children. It is not surprising that Dylan builds "Song to Woody" on "1913 Massacre." His own roots in the iron country of Minnesota place him geographically and socially close to the scene of Guthrie's story. If anything, this was a rare instance in which Dylan knew the world of which Guthrie sang better than Guthrie did. Guthrie writes as a chronicler, long after the events recounted, whereas the mining world was the world that Dylan had just fled for New York. The fable of a closed community that literally suffocates its own children could not have been lost on him. Guthrie begins with a collective experience inviting the listener, "Take a trip with me to 1913."[9] We are led into the union hall and watch the festivities with the singer. As the song closes, the singer's voice is taken over by the community itself, as the miners accuse the bosses: "Just see what your greed for money has done." The moral core of Guthrie's story involves a community whose members unwittingly kill their own.

Dylan turns Guthrie's song inside out. He recasts Guthrie's narrative of collective enclosure as a story of personal freedom:

I'm out here a thousand miles from my home
Walking a road other men have gone down
I'm seein' a world of places and things
Your paupers and peasants and princes and kings (p. 8)

The image of following, both literal (on the road) and metaphorical (in time), suggests that though the narrator may be geographically alone, that solitude also puts him in a community of singers. Like the song, he is, by definition, an echo, a repetition. Whereas Guthrie is interested in events, Dylan is interested in the recounting of events. "Hey, hey, Woody Guthrie, I wrote you a song," he goes on. "About a funny old world that's a-comin' along." However, writing about "the world" is precisely what Dylan is not doing. He's writing about a singer who writes about "the world." (We recall Guthrie's exclamation, cited earlier, that "the sky ain't never as crazy as the world.") And it turns out that the "men" who precede Dylan on "the road" are not miners but other singers. The song imagines a new community. But it is a community of musicians, with Dylan among them. The shift is clearest when he quotes Guthrie's paean to migrant workers, "Pastures of Plenty." "Every state in this Union us migrants have been," sings Guthrie; "We come with the dust and are gone with the wind." Dylan cites these lines to evoke not the life of the migrant worker, but the wandering (and well-known) folk-singers who were Guthrie's friends: Cisco Houston, Sonny Terry, and Huddie Ledbetter: "Here's to the hearts and the hands of the men / Who come with the dust and are gone with the wind." In other words, at the very moment that Dylan cites Guthrie's account of migratory labor experience, he turns that citation against itself. Those who wander nowadays are folksingers, not laboring men.

This is modernist canon construction at its best. Dylan is both a latecomer in history and the reinventor of form. "Song to Woody" converts the structure and melody of "1913 Massacre" into a parable of personal liberation and professional belonging. Enclosure and suffocation give way to movement. The world of the miner becomes a community of singers, among whom Dylan now claims membership while pretending humbly to exclude himself ("there's not many men who've done the things that you've done"). These two aspects of the song — self-deprecation and self-promotion — come together in the final lines. "The very last thing that I'd like to do," he sings, "Is to say I've been hittin' some hard travelin' too." Here again, Guthrie is both cited and overcome; his song "Hard Travelin'" offers a catalogue of the backbreaking jobs taken on by the laboring classes ("hard rock minin'," "leanin' on a pressure drill," "dumping that red-hot slag," and so forth), interspersed with evocations of the instability of the laboring life ("ninety days for vagrancy").[10] In Dylan's case, the wandering has been to make songs. Like the road, the "last thing" is both literal and metaphorical. It is the last thing he will say in the song, which ends by suggesting that Dylan is a character in a Guthrie song because of his "hard travelin'." Yet it also carries a moral valence. The *last thing* I would ever say is that I've been hitting some hard traveling, because I haven't. The double register of the last line both claims Dylan's uniqueness and acknowledges that, like Joyce rewriting Homer, he is a modern reworking of an earlier original.[11]

Dylan's copping of a line from "Hard Travelin'" for "Song for Woody" is only one of a number of moments in his early work where he accesses that particular song, which seems to be a useful resource for him. His second album, *The Freewheelin' Bob Dylan*, offers a reworking of the folk song melody of "Hard Travelin'" in the form of a jokey love-problem song called "Honey, Just Allow Me One More Chance." Here the third line of the verse of "Hard Travelin'" ("I been doin' some hard ramblin' / Hard drinkin,' hard gamblin'") turns up as "Lookin' for a woman need a worried man / Is just like lookin' for a needle that's lost in the sand" (p. 85). Dylan's quick string of monosyllables breaks up the tumble of Guthrie's crowded line and sounds even more like a freight train rhythm than the original (tak-a-tak-a-tak-a-tak-a-tak-a), a feature that Dylan's bumpy harmonica solo emphasizes.[12] The melody and rhythm of the song simultaneously recall Guthrie and send an implicit message to listeners who know their Guthrie: that looking for a good woman is harder work than riding the rails or running a steam drill. So much for the proletariat; this is "Night and Day" for the new folk community.

Yet the rambling persona that Dylan invents does more than project a new type of space in song. It is also a conduit for social commentary. We can see this in an appropriation of Guthrie's recording with Sonny Terry called "We Shall Be Free." Guthrie's song exposes the hypocrisy of the clergy: "Here's the preacher, you shall be free / He's a singin' you shall be free / Takin' up c'llection you shall be free / When the good lord sets you free."[13] In Guthrie's version hypocrisy, salvation, personal liberty, and money all hang on the ambiguity of the same phrase. Dylan's first use of this form on *Freewheelin'* is called not "We Shall Be Free" but "*I* Shall Be Free" (my emphasis). Here, again, collective struggle becomes personal odyssey. Dylan gives us a group of satirical set pieces that remind us of the conventions of the talking blues, and we watch his persona run afoul of various authority figures. We start in bed:

> I took me a woman late last night
> I was three fourths drunk, she looked alright
> She started peelin' off her onion gook,
> Took off her wig, said 'How do I look'
> I's high flyin' bare naked out the window (p. 86)

Like a character in a movie farce, Dylan's persona takes his leave. Guthrie's somewhat conventional take on the grasping clergy — in a tradition dating back to Boccaccio — gives way to a fable of a self that may be naked but that is at least honest.

Here we see the emergence of a theme that Dylan will go on to adapt in powerful ways over the next five years. This is the theme of unmasking — of the unmasking of institutional authority, of hypocrisy, of psychological and erotic power. In "I Shall be Free" this consists of a series of humorous anecdotes about sameness and otherness. Race is not far away: Dylan's persona falls in a can of black paint, he is seen "shadow boxing" with Cassius Clay, and so forth. In each instance he cuts through some form of hypocrisy or fakery, often barely escaping unharmed. The persona filters social outrage into humorous adventure. His mobility keeps these stories from turning tragic, as he can always move on. Thus, in addition to his self-presentation as a wanderer, Dylan's template of identity also depicts him as a puncturer of the illusions set up by others. Both of these features of his persona — the wanderer and the unmasker — will undergo a transformation in the mid-1960s. At that point Dylan will recast himself, not as a dispeller of illusion, but as a weaver of illusion, as a shapeshifter and tale spinner, caught in a world of mirrors, unable to move.

Dylan's use of the vehicle of the talking blues will be short-lived. As he leaves his early adaptations behind, he will move toward more open-ended balladlike forms whose simple, almost chanted, melodies alternate between a simple pair of chords on the guitar, the tonic chord and the dominant, or V, chord. This form lends itself to sequences of narrative action. It does not require the moralistic or humorous commentary imposed by the talking blues (and somewhat awkwardly deployed, as we saw, in "Talkin' New York"), but it provides space for comment when needed. In "I Shall Be Free," every time Dylan hits the chord on the fifth scale degree (as he does to open the song), a new adventure unfolds, or a new scenario is announced. At the end of each line he returns to the tonic chord to establish the narrative significance of what has just been announced. He tells us what he did; then he tells us what it means. The V chord "opens up" the structure and imposes the expectation of eventual harmonic resolution. So, "I took me a woman late last night" comes over the dominant chord, resolving to the tonic, "She looked alright." This simple movement between the dominant and tonic chords, tension and release, will generate a number of Dylan songs. The form is expandable, enabling narrative elaboration, insight after insight, scene after scene. In "I Shall Be Free" he uses the looseness of the form to interject whoops, comments ("half-price!" "the country'll grow!"), and grunts that reflect ironically on the rest of the action.

More Rough Weather

I have been arguing that the energy of Dylan's earliest songs comes not only from his pasting together of different bits of language, but also from his manipulation of entire structures and genres. There are some patterns that we can discern: He characteristically turns songs about social experience into personal meditations and vice versa. These defamiliarizing techniques project his singing persona as a figure who is both recognizable and alien or evasive. The play of proximity and distance helps him work out a relationship to his audience that remotivates long outdated tropes of mobility and experience ("hard travelin'") and makes them pertinent for a newly mobile, college-educated listening public. Dylan evokes rural and ethnic experience — experiences that might even have been within the family memories of many of his listeners — but only to indicate that he has wandered away from them. Dylan is like The Kingston Trio, but rougher. He's like Big Bill Broonzy, but not as rough (and not black). He sounds like an Okie from the country — until he starts talking like a college kid. His songs sound old in their diction, but their themes are contemporary. His is a wandering persona, but he wanders to make songs about his wandering, not actually to do any work. In the age of the automobile, that pose is both absolutely accessible to Dylan's audience and strange enough to elicit curiosity. These contradictory impulses, which play themselves out at the very level of the poetic and musical line, mark out his template of selfhood.

Dylan's early songs both chronicle the disintegration of the communal forms depicted in Guthrie (the large farm family, the union), and begin to project a new relationship to audience — often by turning Guthrie's forms against themselves. Like Borges's Kafka, he makes Guthrie into the harbinger of new forms of communal experience in art that will reach fruition in Dylan's own immeasurably more expansive work. He explores this new reach through the ways in which he evokes, creates, and addresses his audience on his second and third albums, the breakthrough *Freewheelin' Bob Dylan* (1963) and its follow-up, *The Times They Are a-Changin'* (1964). *Freewheelin'* contains three of Dylan's signature songs, two of which, the anthem "Blowin' in the Wind" and "Don't Think Twice, It's Alright," became radio hits for the commercially successful (and politically progressive) folk trio Peter, Paul and Mary. Also included is Dylan's first major songwriting breakthrough, the quasi-allegorical "A Hard Rain's a-Gonna Fall."

Yet if much of Dylan's early writing focuses on scenarios of unmasking, the problem remains of who the character is who is doing this work, and why we should be interested. As Dylan declared in "With God on Our Side," he was really no one, "my name it ain't nothing." Certainly, what we can say about this persona is that he wanders and that he is — paradoxically, it would seem — in a hurry. And it is here that we can place the song that is, in a sense, the answer to "Girl from the North Country." This is the lover's kiss-off "Don't Think Twice, It's Alright." It is a striking piece of work when set against the conventions of popular love songs at the end of the 1950s, and even when set against the canon of songs within which Dylan and his fellow folksingers (Joan Baez, Dave Van Ronk, et al.) were working. This is no story of doomed desire, jealousy, or betrayal (say, "Lily of the West" or "Delia"). Nor is it a story of two star-crossed lovers kept apart by parents or clan (Baez's recording of "Silver Dagger"). Here we have two perfectly modern young people, both in control of their own destinies, who just can't seem to get along. They sound like something out of a Cole Porter song, not an old murder ballad. They rarely talk; when they do it gets them nowhere. The flagging of their desire for each other, signaled by the woman's failure to "turn on her light," becomes the link to the narrator's rambling. He is first metaphorically "on the dark side of the road" (p. 78), and then literally gone, "all the way down the road."

The form of the song mirrors the disharmony of the lyrics. Dylan may have learned the basic template from a traditional song done by his friend Paul Clayton as "Who's Gonna Buy You Ribbons When I'm Gone?" Here is Clayton's lyric:

> It ain't no use to sit and sigh now, darling
> And it ain't no use to sit and cry now
> T'ain't no use to sit and wonder why, darling
> Just wonder who's gonna buy you ribbons when I'm gone[14]

Dylan speeds the song up, introducing a beautiful picked guitar part that contributes to the delicacy and intimacy of the performance. He offers the characteristic, Guthrie-like major chord sequences we pointed to a moment ago, but he complicates the situation by landing on a minor chord at the end of the first and third lines ("why, babe"), which helps create some of the song's melancholy. He moves between these progressions until the fifth line. This is where he opens up the harmony of Clayton's simple four-line version. The only narrative action in this song about stasis occurs in the middle section of each verse, where three rhyming lines unfold across a single unit of musical tension and release:

When your rooster crows at the break of dawn
Look out your window, babe, and I'll be gone
You're the reason I'm a-travelin' on (p. 78)

This section is built on an interesting interplay of harmony and melody. The first two of these lines repeat the same melody figure, suggesting that nothing is happening, just as the two lyrical units rhyme, suggesting no movement. By contrast, the harmony presents a sequence leading from the I chord (E major) through a passing chord (E7) to the IV (A major). Many popular songs would then turn the A major into an A minor, to add drama. However, Dylan's melody, which dwells on a repeated G♯ note, leads him to a slightly discordant F♯7 chord on the second scale degree. In other words, the harmony suggests movement and change underneath a melody that stays mostly the same. Together they enact a musical manifestation of the emotional dilemma being narrated. Only after this movement does a third line, rhyming with the first two ("You're the reason . . ."), appear and harmonically recall the cadence of the very first line in the song. This is then resolved in the refrain, which rhymes, through assonance, only with itself ("twice" / "alright") and closes the harmony by landing back on the tonic E major chord at the moment that the singer delivers his concluding, dismissive comment. Thus, Dylan expands Clayton's repetitious lyric and the simple major-to-minor harmony of the traditional song into an entire drama of tension and release, discord and resolution. Along the way, the third line picks up yet again the third line rhythm of Guthrie's "Hard Travelin'" and Dylan's own "Honey, Just Allow Me One More Chance": "When your rooster crows," tak-a-tak-a-tak. In a trick that Dylan will use at later moments in his career, a half-remembered rhythm from one song is repurposed to animate the structure of another.

"Don't Think Twice" brings us beyond Dylan's own self-construction to the question of his evocation of the listener — both of the "you" to whom he sings and of the audience that overhears his reflections.[15] The invention of a purposeful yet vagabond persona on *Freewheelin'* goes hand in hand with Dylan's emergence as a singer of moralistic, often politically themed protest songs — songs deeply conscious of their audience and rhetorical effect. Yet what is striking about his most famous examples of this subgenre is the care with which he effaces the very persona he has elsewhere so carefully created. In his most powerful and popular protest songs, songs such as "Blowin' in the Wind," "A Hard Rain's a-Gonna Fall," and "The Times They Are a-Changin'," his ironic, madcap Okie persona vanishes. This disappearance is, of course, not completely consistent; "Masters of War," another major song from the same period, features an outraged singer-persona who appears as an actor in the story. But the general erasure of the singer's presence is made manifestly clear in Dylan's most famous song, "Blowin' in the Wind." Based on a song of slave defiance, "No More Auction Block for Me" (which Dylan probably learned from Paul Robeson or Odetta), the song lends itself perfectly to the new type of hybrid "folk song" that he was elaborating across his first three and a half albums. What matters here is not the singer, come back, like Lazarus, to tell us all what he has seen, but the audience, called into being as a new kind of virtual community. This is clear in the refrain, "The answer my friend / Is blowin' in the wind" (p. 70). We listeners are invoked individually, like the messenger/friend of "Girl from the North Country," yet we are also a group, as the song's main theme touches on collective topics — racism, war, and middle-class indifference. The audience is present in the song, but not as a "we" that assumes — in Seegeresque sing-along fashion — some participation. The singer is only to be found in the intimate vocative, "my friend," which implicates us in the questions being asked simply by virtue of the fact that we have now listened our way to the refrain. Having heard the questions, we are primed for the answer, ready to listen to the wind.[16]

"No More Auction Block" foregrounds individual defiance and laments the suffering of a community through the phrase "Many thousand gone" at the close of each verse. Dylan's song simply picks up where the model leaves off. It turns the comment about the "thousand" into a question: "How many?" In the process it moves beyond the mode of the lament, as if lament and its evocation of personal suffering were not enough. Yet this same gesture involves an abstraction. And it produces a whole string of questions, which make up the body of the verses. What follows is a "protest" song that doesn't protest anything at all but rather functions as a kind of shell — a template of sorts — for building community through shared acknowledgment of problems. Every listener can insert her or himself into it, and the contrast between the collective and the individual is mediated by its interrogative nature. The problems that are adduced demand collective action, yet the song calls to the listener individually.

"Blowin' in the Wind" seems to be about a whole set of themes, which are mutually elucidating, like a set of lenses trained on each other. It is introduced by an ambiguous opening question: "How many roads must a man walk down / Before you call him a man?" At one level, this is a question about the status of black people in America, long legally relegated to counting as three-fifths of a "man," and later still denied full moral presence. But seen against Dylan's other work it is also a question about wandering youth, trying to grow up. How much must he ramble before he is no longer a kid? Or, more grandly, when will the country grow up? At still another level it takes us back to Dylan's interest in masking and surfaces, since the question is, literally, about language. When will things be described with their correct names — by "you," the audience — instead of with false labels? Peter, Paul and Mary's megahit version of the song changed the opening words to "before *they* call him a man," thereby pointing blame at someone other than the singer and his listener, projecting generational solidarity. This keeps it political, and simplifies Dylan's multifaceted message, which links racial injustice to violence to a kind of moral immaturity. The song weaves these themes together, with each theme casting light on the others.

The overarching schema is about time. The key word is "before," which is repeated seven times. The first line might be about race, or it might be about growing up and time. From this ambiguity we segue into a question about birds, about flying doves and when they can rest. What does this have to do with anything? Well, we find out when the third question comes, about flying cannonballs, which suggests in retrospect that the dove is the symbol of peace. A resting dove and a ban on flying cannonballs offer two statements of the same problem, one allegorical, the other literal, like the two uses of "road" in "Don't Think Twice." Temporal progress reappears in verse two, when we get questions about geology (how to move mountains — with time, or with faith?), race relations (a people trying to be free), and willful indifference to injustice. By now Dylan has at least three thematic balls in the air. From here, in stanza three, he goes philosophical with a set of questions about the senses. And as the song becomes more abstract, it drifts toward excessive generality. First a question about sight: "How many times must a man look up / Before he can

see the sky?" Why, for heaven's sake? And why is looking up neces-
sarily good? "Looking around" might be more pertinent. But then a
question about hearing: "How many ears must one man have?" Can
one have more than two? We're using ours right now to listen to this
song. And we end with a strikingly vague question about how many
deaths are required before "too many people have died." The answer
to this — which very distantly echoes the lament, "Many thousand
gone" — can only be that everyone dies and there are always at once
too many, not enough, and just enough deaths to go around.

I don't mean to be overly literal or snide about these lyrics, which
have had such a powerful impact on many listeners. But it is impor-
tant not to overlook their vagueness and the looseness of the compo-
sition if we are to understand Dylan's poetics. We could, in fact, con-
trast Dylan's loosely linked collection of questions to a much more
artful "question song," Irving Berlin's "How Deep Is the Ocean,"
from 1932. Berlin's lyric is a dense labyrinth. It offers a question as the
answer to every other question: "How much do I love you? / I'll tell
you no lie. / How deep is the ocean? How high is the sky?" Berlin's
questions are tightly woven into a semantic knot intended to evoke
the intensity of erotic obsession. Dylan's questions are more of a
laundry list.[17] "No More Auction Block" was built on a list of specific
tortures rooted in an historical catastrophe: "No more auction block
for me," "no more driver's lash," and so on. By contrast, without a
controlling persona or a narrative direction, "Blowin' in the Wind"
flirts with disintegration into a set of grand queries about the nature
of everything from the cosmos to current events. This looseness of
structure is doubtless the reason for the insistent, countrified "Yes'n"
that Dylan interjects to introduce each question (and that cover ver-
sions generally omit). The questions that make up the body of the
song are cast in correct, even elegant, modern American grammar.
Yet here, between the lines, Dylan turns to his hobo voice, pulling
up an "authentic" Guthrieism at the moment that the machine starts
to slow down, urging it forward. On the recording, Dylan seems
to sense the tension between the seriousness of the lyric and the
elegance of the melody. His guitar part ends the second verse with a
neat cadence on the top strings that buckles up the verse cleanly, as
if it were an old ballad. But then he sets out again with a "Yes'n," only
to end the song with a ritard and a swatch of rapid strumming that
suggests the urgency of the topic at hand, telling us to pay attention.

As with "Don't Think Twice," Dylan turns a stately prototype into a song marked by movement and insistence. In lieu of the train of even quarter notes in "No More Auction Block," the new song produces an effect of syncopation through the interplay of longer and shorter units of time, moving up and down a set of major chord tones. Metrically, the song is built out of units of three beats, one long, two short: "How many" (- //) "roads must a" (- //), a pattern that is punched forward with the abbreviated, eighth-note insistence of "Yes'n" on the pickup beat heading to the next line. The chorus replaces the sad acknowledgment of tragedy in the prototype, designed to silence us into contemplation of the catastrophe of slavery — "many thousand gone" — with a cadence that moves through major chords to land on a minor chord with "wind," before opening up toward a resolution. Where the original ends with the definitive "gone," Dylan's reworking concludes on "wind," which blows us, so to speak, forward.[18]

And yet the loose logical and thematic connections between the questions that make up the song are counterbalanced by its sonic richness. Here, I think, is the true innovation of the song in terms of Dylan's technical development, since this is the first time he explores the sounds of words. Working as a counterweight to the listlike thematic disjunctions are the beautiful uses of alliteration and rhyme that set up the key terms: "How many roads must a man walk down?" preparing us for "call him a man," as if the repetition of the m sound were lending gravity to the presence of the "man" when he finally appears (and answers the "many" of the opening query). The technique becomes even more significant through the placement of the s-sounds in "How many seas must a white dove sail / Before she sleeps in the sand?" These alliterations balance out the beginning and ending of each verse in an almost symmetrical fashion. They are the raw material of anthemic song writing. The technique intensifies as the song unfolds, from the surprise of "before" and "forever" to the intensity of "hear" and "ear" in the third stanza (the difference between these last two being an aspirated h-sound, which Dylan helpfully sneaks back in at the chorus, by his pronunciation of "wind" as "whind," when he hits a melancholy minor chord on the guitar). And the final lines are punctuated by the fricative sounds of t and d presented in an elegant chiasmus ("deaths" "take," then "too many" and "died") that balances the structure. This gives way to the liquid flow of the n-sounds across the refrain: "The answer, my friend, is blowin' in the wind / The answer is blowin' in the wind." The rhyme of "friend" and "wind" includes us as listeners in the cosmic mystery of the song (which takes us back to the mysterious wind of "Girl from the North Country"). Dylan's own somewhat affected pronunciation of "the" as "thee," ("blowin' in *thee* w[h]ind") on his officially released recording underscores the power of the image, as it renders discernible the sonic echo between "in" and "wind," in a way that would not happen through slurring all of the last syllables together, as a more conventional pronunciation of "the" would tend to do.[19]

The resonance of Dylan's own voice is produced in the nasal cavity of the mouth. However, more important than his famous "nasal" sound—lamented by many critics accustomed to smoother singers—is the relationship between diction and musical structure. Here in this first of his many canonical performances of a canonical song Dylan does not, in fact, conform to or "follow" a melodic line. It is not as if he wrote a melody and then sang "to" it, as Peter, Paul and Mary would do. Rather, he sings over it, in proximity to it. He sings the song, not the melody. What matters is the story he is telling. This is an important feature of the performance, since it takes us back to the question of Dylan's self-invention and his relationship to the "music business" at the moment of emerging consumer culture. The distance between the implicitly understood or "underheard" melody of Dylan's songs—that version that would be written out, published, and sold as "product"—and his own dramatic performance of those same songs opens a critical perspective on the commodity itself. Musical transcription cannot capture the nuances of performance. Even when singing his own compositions, Dylan seems unable to color inside the lines. In the process, he points to the fact that the lines themselves are a construct.

The recorded and released performance of "Blowin' in the Wind" is intensely rhythmical, as Dylan hits the third syllable of each metric unit for maximum emphasis ("can a MAN turn his HEAD and pre-TEND"). Yet against this regularity he manipulates his intonation. There is a clear contrast between his pronunciation of the final words in the first and third lines of each verse ("walk down," "white dove sail," "cannonballs fly"), where he seems to back off of the articulation, sinking almost to a resigned whisper, on the one hand, and the endings of the first and fourth lines ("call him a man," "sleeps in

the sand," "forever banned"), which he holds out to their full dura-
tion, on the other hand. The alternation between the two approaches
makes the performance unhurried, almost offhand, as if the singer
himself didn't matter. This technique is particularly effective forty-
three seconds into the official recording, in the first chorus, where
Dylan hurries his second delivery of the phrase "in the wind," mur-
muring it a millisecond before his hand hits the picked bass note that
the rhythm dictates should be simultaneous to it. That is, he throws
out — almost throws away — the key phrase, "in the wind," a hair
early, as if suggesting that the song's pulse and its message are only in
temporary proximity, blown about. This is a technique of rhythmic
anticipation, of course, that he will use to great effect later in the
1960s, when his singing will play increasingly against the direction
and pulse of the rhythm track. It will become an easy target for those
wishing to parody his singing style. Yet here, in its earliest manifesta-
tion, this miniscule rhythmic disjunction goes to the essence of the
song, which it reminds us is both crucially important and infinitely
fragile. It helps generate the effect of intimacy hinted at in the voca-
tive call to "my friend."

The sonic effects of sonority and alliteration give the song a kind
of classical equipoise that compensates for the loose logic of the lyric.
Sound provides the structural scaffolding that sense only imperfectly
achieves. The interplay between sound and sense is underscored by
Dylan's delicate harmonica interludes — the first and perhaps great-
est of many such solos — which remind us that the song spinning out
in our ears is itself wind. Air is condensed into voice; voice is elevated
into the pure sound of the mouth harp. *There* blows another kind of
wind, in the performance itself. When we combine the effacement
of the singer's presence from "Blowin' in the Wind" and the active
inclusion of the audience (through the interrogative rhetoric) we end
up with a song that seems almost to sing itself.

The strategy of self-effacement, moreover, saves "Blowin' in the
Wind" from the trap that awaits most songs sung about political or
social justice — the trap of sincerity. Rhetorically, the song doesn't
protest. You need take no position for or against it. All it does is ask
a set of questions. They are legitimate questions, no matter how you
may choose to answer them. It matters not whether the singer is
"sincere" or "authentic" in his performance. The questions remain,
as questions, divorced from the voice that asks them. We are enjoined

to pay attention, if we will. This is pure song, needing no "identity" to sing it, beyond the audience. It is not quite the radical modernism of the poet Stéphane Mallarmé, who strove for poems that could exist on their own internal logic, freed of the presence of readers. It brings us closer to the poetics of the German dramatist Bertolt Brecht, of whom I will say more in a moment, and whose own brand of high modernism involved a mobilization of audience, both politically and sensorially.

Confrontations

Dylan's evasion of the trap of sincerity is developed with even greater complexity in the longest song on *The Freewheelin' Bob Dylan*. This is "A Hard Rain's a-Gonna Fall," which, as Dave Van Ronk pointed out in his memoirs, was recognized by the folk music community as a major work and an important step forward in writing song.[20] Here Dylan takes the scenario of an English ballad, reprinted by the collector Francis James Child, called "Lord Randall." Dylan would doubtless have heard Harry Belafonte's affecting recording of this song. In it, a mother asks her son why he looks so ill upon returning home: "O where have you been, Randall, my son? / Where have you been, my handsome young one?" are the first lines. He reports that he has been to the home of his true love, who has poisoned him: "I'm sick to heart / And fain would lie down."[21] It's a sad tale, to be sure, and Dylan exploits it to generalize the theme of betrayal and offer a visionary account of contemporary society. The rhetoric is biblical and mythical: "I've stumbled on the side of twelve misty mountains," sings Dylan, in good wandering-knight style. "I've been out in front of a dozen dead oceans." Like the Battle of Gettysburg, which is both past and not past, the plagues of the Old Testament are here before us, in the form of war, injustice, and ecological disaster. We are all Lord Randall, poisoned by politics and social hierarchy. The mode is allegorical, though not particularly opaque: "I saw a white man, he walked a black dog"; "I saw guns and sharp swords in the hands of young children" (p. 76). And, as should be obvious from the passages just cited, Dylan's new mastery of alliteration and internal rhyme is very much on display: "*s*even *s*ad fore*s*t*s*," "*t*en *t*housand *m*iles in the *m*outh of a graveyard," and so on. It culminates in the powerful refrain, which moves through the repeated *r* of "ha*r*d *r*ain's" to the strong ending on "fall," which does not rhyme with or echo anything else in the song ("hard" is pronounced "hard-uh" for emphasis). In a nice touch, the rhetorical "fall" at the end of the line — its cadence toward resolution — corresponds exactly to the falling of the allegorical deluge that awaits us.

It is important to note, here, as in the case of the other songs that we have studied, that the original scenario of "Lord Randall" resonates through "Hard Rain." The evocation of the antiquated theme of the "darling young one" ("my pretty one," in the original) who has been out a-wandering distances the language of the song from the modern listener. It makes it strange, the Dharma Bum as Ancient Mariner. This in turn creates a space for the juxtaposition of a set of very powerful, if often oblique, images (the "twelve misty mountains" and the "black branch" of lynching). That is, we know we are not in a modern setting — except that we are. Just as the personal defiance of "No More Auction Block for Me" is refracted in the liberation rhetoric of "Blowin' in the Wind," so here the theme of betrayal is generalized. Dylan reverses here what he did in "Song to Woody," where collective experience was reconfigured as personal odyssey. In "Hard Rain," private tragedy in the model becomes cosmic disaster in the adaptation. Randall is sick, Dylan's narrator is not, except that his society is sick, and Randall's sickness resonates through Dylan's song.

But no less important is the presence of the dialogic setup, of the questioning of the child by the parent. For here the wanderer has come in from the road. If much of the music around Dylan consisted of earnest young people criticizing war, racism, and social conformity, Dylan's song brilliantly includes two voices, the voice of the parent and the voice of the child. The "generation gap" is refracted into conversation. We might think, by contrast, of Nicholas Ray's 1955 film *Rebel without a Cause*, where the square middle-class parent, played by Jim Backus, asks his sullen son, played by James Dean, "Jimbo, where have you been?" when he comes home late. And yet this dialogic moment is saved from sentimentality in Dylan's song precisely through the strangeness and "distance" of the setting made possible by the archaic diction taken from "Lord Randall." The faintly medieval vision of the young man on a quest removes the conversation of parent and child from any present context, turning it into myth, even as it remains contemporary and recognizable. What is more, the conversational structure solves the problem that plagues many of Dylan's early songs — the problem of the relationship between personal experience and collective political action. The rambling loner now speaks for and to everyone, not because he's a loner or even much of a sage, but because *he's been asked to speak* by a voice from the older generation. The dialogue makes it possible to inject the claims of idealistic youth (don't mistreat people, don't destroy the environment, don't draft people who are too young to vote, and so on) with a cosmic importance, as the simple forest to which young Lord Randall had repaired in the old ballad now becomes one of the legendary "seven sad forests" on one of the "twelve misty mountains." The numerology and the mythical landscape invest the singer's act of witness with a rare grandeur, turning him into a combination of the Old Testament Jeremiah and the questing Lancelot.

The song stages its own message by setting social and political critique as the answer to a question by the listener/parent, who asks, in effect, to be educated by the young, by the "darling young one." A parent asks where his kid has been. In response he gets a lesson in geopolitics and moral philosophy. The dialogic aspect is reflected, at the level of performance, in Dylan's alternating attack on his guitar, which moves between strumming only the lowest strings following the "question" section, and then reintegrates the treble notes for the rest, until after the second "hard," at which point Dylan hunkers down for a moment more on the bass strings. The guitar enacts the dialogue, whereas the timbre of the voice does not vary. Dylan activates his "Okie" register with such pronunciations as "oshin" (for "ocean") and "waddrrr" (for "water") across both voices. As in "Blowin' in the Wind," there is an affecting contrast in the performance, between the final punchy delivery of the almost-spoken monosyllable "son" in the parent's question and the final "sung" bisyllabic word of each of the son's answers ("mountains," "highways," etc.). The dialogue enables the song to deliver its powerful message about a society out of whack without sounding preachy or naive. After all, the listener/parent wants to know what is happening, so the child simply tells what he has seen. And when the song ends the parent seems to approve as the young wanderer announces his intention to return to the fray. It concludes with a teaching moment. "But I'll know my song well, before I start singin'" is the penultimate line to the last verse, before the final turn to a Christlike self-sacrifice: "I'll stand on the ocean until I start sinkin'." This song, of course, is the song that we have just heard. Along with the curious parent, we have asked to be taught.

Dylan's early experiments with such open forms as the talking blues paint a persona who stoically tolerates indignities, a kind of Everyman in search of purpose. As he expands his range to include heavier themes, this figure is eclipsed and replaced by more impersonal structures (in "Blowin' in the Wind") or, in the case of "Hard Rain," a dialogic approach. Dylan begins by singing for a group of adepts who already know, more or less, what he will say. But the popularity of songs such as "Blowin' in the Wind" and, a year later, "The Times They Are a-Changin'" means that his songwriting impetus must begin to account for a larger audience.

"The whole wide world is watchin'" (p. 116), sings Dylan in the 1963 song "When the Ship Comes In." The line appears in one of two songs that rewrite the "Pirate Jenny" song from Bertolt Brecht and Kurt Weill's *Threepenny Opera*. Dylan takes on the individual parable of revenge, "Pirate Jenny" (where a hotel maid imagines a pirate ship sailing in to kill those who disregard and insult her every day), and turns it into a reflection on larger political change. What is being destroyed is the old order, those whom Dylan calls "the foes." Yet the final line, cited earlier, refers both to incipient political upheaval and to Dylan's own growing popularity, to the sense that he and his work are becoming spectacle. Whether that watching world will actually act for change, or whether it will simply watch the show that is the song, is the challenge faced by every politically committed artist.

Dylan speaks in *Chronicles: Volume One* of his encounter with the songs of *The Threepenny Opera*.[22] His girlfriend at the time, Suze Rotolo, was working with group of actors and singers who were mounting a review of Brecht songs. Dylan mentions the "Pirate Jenny" song as a work that made a particular impression on him. "What is important about the song is the way it implicates the listener. As it condemns the social order that oppresses people like Jenny, it also condemns those who sit in the audience and watch. For they are of the class that exploits her" (p. 275). Brecht's work brought Dylan into contact with a version of left-wing art that was quite different from the labor songs and topical music he had experienced in the Greenwich Village folk music houses. It featured an appropriation of "popular" or proletarian forms for an avant-garde sensibility. However we might understand the "influence" of Brecht on Dylan (as conscious imitation or mere osmosis), Brecht's work offered a model of art as confrontation. This was not music that sought to communicate campfire community, union solidarity, or anthropological information about the Other. It went full on in the face of the listener/spectator, who was projected as the antagonist of the art work itself. It was art that spoke to art's enemies and aimed, through some type of political education and incitement to praxis, to turn the enemy (as listener, spectator, or reader) into an eventual ally. Our concern here is not with whether Dylan ever read any of Brecht's theoretical writings on theater. The basics of Brecht's approach are clear enough from the songs — and, indeed, central to Brecht's poetics was the notion that the technique should be easily discernible to even the casual spectator. What is important is that Dylan's exploration of Brecht's confrontational approach would become one of the distinctive features of his songwriting over the subsequent five years.

The idea of writing from the perspective of a proletarian protagonist is not, of course, something Dylan gets only from Brecht. We could trace it back to any number of folk songs, including many by Guthrie. But it becomes linked to the question of form in "The Lonesome Death of Hattie Carroll," which Dylan himself has suggested is built out of "Pirate Jenny." Here we can see a proper Brechtian poetics begin to emerge. In this song, which was loosely based on an actual event, we witness an act of violence:

> William Zanzinger killed poor Hattie Carroll
> With a cane that he twirled round his diamond-ringed finger
> At a Baltimore hotel society gathering
> Then the cops were called in and his weapon took from him
> As they rode him in custody down to the station
> And booked William Zanzinger for first-degree murder (p. 118)

The debt of "Hattie Carroll" to Brecht extends beyond the plot device of shifting the viewpoint to the downtrodden figure.[23] Brecht's aesthetic took direct aim at the traditions of familiarity and ease associated with the conventional "realistic" bourgeois drama of the day. His art was confrontational, not comfortable. His radical modernism aimed to spell out its antagonism to the interests of much of its audience. This was achieved through various strategies of alienation designed to spur reflection on the part of the audience. Far from becoming "absorbed" in the action, the theatergoer was encouraged to reflect constantly on what was being shown, to realize that the representation before her was both a story to be followed and a commentary on social relations. Technically, Brecht sought to generate this response through a radically self-conscious performance style, including signs or "supertitles" that commented on the action as it was unfolding. That is, he offered *both* story and commentary on story at the same time. And this dialectical model extended to his songs. Brecht stresses that songs in the theater should not emerge "naturally" from the action, as is often the case in Broadway musicals or operetta, where the hero speaks his heart by suddenly breaking into song: "In no case should heightened speech represent an intensification of plain speech, or singing of heightened speech," writes Brecht.[24] There should be a clear distinction between different forms and levels because they are in tension with each other. The song is not the spoken play; it is a commentary on it, and vice versa.

From his earliest efforts at performance, Dylan's style involved gestures of self-conscious enhancement that called attention to what he was doing. His tics of whooping and laughing as he sings, interrupting his harmonica breaks with shouts and grunts, and gesturing toward his own performance ("That's nothing, just something I learned over in England" [p. 146]) point to the performance as performance, breaking the illusion of the fiction that is being presented in the lyrics. However, in "Hattie Carroll" he goes beyond this type of gesture to manipulate the form of the song itself. He uses the chorus of the song as a moral commentary — like Brecht's supertitles — that cements and shapes his relationship to his audience.

Dylan's songwriting has always had a somewhat uneasy relationship with the chorus. He generally prefers, in his early work, the one- or two-line refrain. This permits him to offer a brief interpretive comment that can stand in contrast to (or reinforce) the lines that precede it. "Don't think twice, it's alright," for example, sums up and evaluates all that we have just learned about the young lovers. "Hattie Carroll," by contrast, offers a full-scale chorus. And here Dylan confronts his audience. The strange courtly setting of the party is evoked through an archaism ("William Zanzinger, who had just twenty-four years"), and the densely abbreviated evocation of the setting as "a Baltimore hotel society gathering." The verse is presented over a ringing guitar accompaniment (no muted strings here) in 3/4 time, almost as if it were a waltz — imitating, perhaps, the music of the "gathering."

The voice begins high up in Dylan's register and rhythmically hits each key word in time with the meter ("William Zanzinger / killed poor Hattie Carroll / With a cane, that he twirled round"). This pattern then shifts when he turns to the chorus:

You who philosophize disgrace
And criticize all fear
Take the rag away from your face
Now ain't the time for your tears (p. 118)

The melody changes slightly, moving, in the first phrase, from an E down to a D♯, instead of from an E to a C♯, as it does in the verse. "You" and "who" are hit directly, as if in confrontation with the audience. The endings of lines two and four are not held out, as they are in the verse, but fade, in a diminishing cadence, most powerfully in "away from your face," where the melodic fall (as in "Blowin' in the Wind") suggests a kind of resignation. With these lines we shift levels, away from the sad story of the murder, onto the level of interpretation. How should we react? Not by weeping, says Brechtian Dylan. Wait until the end. This expectation — much more than the "Yes'n" that links the questions of "Blowin' in the Wind" — propels the structure forward. What in the earlier song was a rhetorical urging is now a structural tension. We have narrative suspense, but the suspense is not generated by the destiny of the characters in the story. We know that from the first line: "William Zanzinger killed poor Hattie Carroll." The suspense involves what it means *for us*. It involves the listening experience, the relationship between song and audience, between the grooves on the plastic disk and our ears. We are written into the structure of the song. Here we see a new development in the shifting relationship between Dylan's singing persona and the audience that he is simultaneously addressing and creating. The answer comes only in the final moment, when we learn that the judge has failed to punish Zanzinger appropriately. The real scandal is not the murder — which is bad enough — but the miscarriage of justice. You come not to bury Hattie Carroll, but to "bury the rag deep in your face" at what has ensued. This secondary narrative implicates us as listeners. We cannot do anything about the murder, which is long past. But we can change the justice system. "Now is the time for your tears," says Dylan in conclusion, thereby directing our response after the song ends. Whether this shift to a more abstract

74

level of outrage — rage against the machine, as it were — can preserve
the human tragedy of Hattie Carroll's death, or whether that death
will itself be effaced and forgotten in the general weeping, remains
an ethical problem that Dylan's formal experiments will have to con-
front as his work develops.[25]

"The Lonesome Death of Hattie Carroll" thus raises the struc-
ture of song to a new level of complexity. In contrast, both to "Hard
Rain," where the singer states that he will simply keep singing, and
to such anthems as Pete Seeger's "If I Had a Hammer," where we are
all left with "a song to sing," we now get a precise idea of what to do
and of who is really to blame. Moreover, and even more important,
we are enjoined to act, not in response to singular events, but in
response to institutionalized abuses of power. This is one of the main
features of the songs on *The Times They Are a-Changin'*. These songs
protest not events or incidents but institutional practices. "Only a
Pawn in Their Game" adopts the same limited, microscopic per-
spective as "Hattie Carroll" and "Pirate Jenny," only now the shift
is even more challenging to a liberal audience, as Dylan evokes the
experience of the white man who killed civil rights leader Medgar
Evers. The condemnation is not of the killing, but of the structures
of power that make his motivation seem legitimate to him. It asks us
to understand a murderer. Similarly, "With God on Our Side" offers
an account of American history from the perspective of those who
fight, die, and are sacrificed. But it ends with a turn to the listener:
"I can't think for you / Only you can decide / If Judas Iscariot / Had
God on his side" (p. 108). It's not an easy question, in fact, when we
consider that Christ's betrayal was predicted and understood to be
part of a divine plan. "What shapes history?" is the question asked by
the singer. This means that Dylan doesn't offer messages so much as
he asks us to consider institutional structures and how they work.
In this regard we can say that his work touches on the morality
of forms.

At a particular moment in the history of the folk song, between
an increasingly outmoded model of union solidarity and an emerg-
ing consumer culture, Dylan uses form to shift audience attention
away from mere complaint about injustice to a critique that would be
both practical and theoretical. Moreover — and perhaps most impor-
tant — the questions of "authenticity" and "authority" that I earlier
located in Dylan's persona as rambler have now been displaced onto

the relationship between singer and audience. Dylan is "authentic" because "we" are implicated in his songs.

The institutional critique comes together with confrontational poetics in what is perhaps the most obviously "protesty" moment in Dylan's entire body of work, the title cut of *The Times They Are a-Changin'*. Here the singer calls a community of listeners into being. He builds on folk song rhetoric stretching back to such models as "Come All Ye Bold Tarriers." But now the call is to everyone: "Come gather 'round people" (p. 104). And those who have been wandering like Dylan ("wherever you roam") are implicated as well. Unlike his models for this type of song, however, this composition aims, not to celebrate a jolly company, but to attack its members and warn them that, like the "gentlemen" who hear the story of Pirate Jenny, their days are numbered. As in "Come you masters of war," from the *Freewheelin'* album, the injunction to "Come gather round" is the prelude to a drubbing. For a flood is coming. And the focus is on institutions: the press, Congress, the family. The song is a warning and perhaps even a curse; "the curse it is cast," runs the final verse. Most of the song involves telling people what to do. The only actual information offered is the assertion that parents can no longer control their children: "Your sons and your daughters, they're beyond your command."

This is a quite different vision of generational dialogue from what we saw in "Hard Rain." The singer offers no account of his own experience — thereby abandoning the model of reporting from the road that Dylan had perfected from his very earliest compositions. The song alternates between prediction and description. It works through the balancing of commands ("admit," "accept it," "don't speak too soon") and warnings ("he that gets hurt will be he who has stalled"). These two operations stand in tension with the futurity that the song constantly projects through its image of time. It imputes change, not to actors, but to "the times," some grand historical force. Yet to mediate the distance between "the times" and actual human people ("wherever you roam") it infuses the mere fact of generational change with pseudo-biblical language ("the curse, it is cast"). Much of its power derives from the fact that we are left not knowing whether the simple changing of generations — a natural phenomenon, after all — is the effect of a cosmic plague, or its cause.

As with "Blowin' in the Wind," the structure is loose. It could go on forever, as the singer calls in more witnesses ("come all you

76

lumberjacks," "come bus drivers," "come anthropologists," etc.). At the same time, as the final lines tell us, the names of things are about to change: the first will no longer be first; it will be last. We are back to the theme of calling things by their correct names, which we saw addressed in "Blowin' in the Wind." Groups are invoked only to be told that some new language is in the offing.

The irony of the song is, in part, that the "list" approach doesn't generate much movement forward, even as the title suggests that time is passing and things are changing as we listen. This may be linked to the song's inability to provide an actual explanation of change. It is as if change were being willed into existence by the piling up of detail, filtered through Dylan's hectoring diction. The tension between a kind of logical stasis in the lyric and the urgency of the delivery is reflected in the harmony of the song. The first two lines are built on commonplace chord changes, leading to a dominant chord at the end of the second line. The melody of the fifth line ("So you'd better start swimmin'"), which recalls that of the first line, would appear to require a return to the tonic chord heard in the opening (the solution offered by most cover versions of the song, including those by the Byrds and Simon and Garfunkel). Dylan, however, stays on his dominant chord, which he holds a bit, as if suspending time. We can see an extension of the problem of time, when we consider the conclusion. "Changin'" rhymes through assonance with a whole set of other verbs about change and stasis ("fadin'," "savin'"), yet whereas those words are quickly dispensed with ("to you is worth savin'"), the key word in the song, "changin'" — the word that names change — is held out, "cha-a-a-ngin'." Dylan could have easily clipped off the last word. Dragging it out both delays and calls attention to the predictions of rapid change found elsewhere in the lyric. Obviously, he holds the note to resolve the verse and offer a memorable concluding line. But the performative gesture links as well to the very process he is talking about, the process of change. Unable to explain how all this change is going to work, Dylan simply performs it.[26]

Conversations
I have been arguing that Dylan's early love songs and protest anthems may be read as a set of experiments that try to reinvent the relationship between folk song and its community. They shape the relationship between the post-Guthrie, post-beatnik rambler and a new,

increasingly sophisticated and engaged audience. They do this by inventing a new imaginary space into which to insert the dramas of everyday life, and by bringing the audience into the very structure of the songs, not as "sing-along" partner, but as dialectical adversary. Dylan manipulates a set of formal elements — the turn to the listener, the rhetorical question, the dialogue, the anecdote, the proverb or "moral" — to give his own limited experience larger political or ethical significance.

Yet even as Dylan develops his persona and voice out of appropriations of songs known to many others, he begins to run up against a problem that is inherent both in the concept of the commercialized "folk song" and in the social ideas being presented. This is the question of how "Bob Dylan" — or whoever we invest with that name — might differ from the rest of us. Dylan's claim to be one of a special fraternity — "here's to Cisco, and Sonny, and Leadbelly too" — runs counter to the egalitarianism of a leftist political ideology and of the communitarian ethos of folk music.[27] Indeed, as Dylan's encounter with Mike Seeger (discussed in the previous chapter) showed, there were potential doubles everywhere. Moreover, the increasing conformity of consumer society, which consistently tells us that we can both stand out and fit in if we all buy the same commodities, raises questions about the status of the nonconformist or artist figure in a community born to shop. Social homogenization mimics and distorts communitarian ideals.

Dylan addresses the question of who is who in humorous terms in "I Shall Be Free No. 10," a talking blues from *Another Side of Bob Dylan* (1964), his last fully "acoustic" album of the early 1960s.

> Well, I'm just average, common too
> I'm just like him the same as you
> I'm everybody's brother and son
> I ain't different from anyone
> Ain't no use in talking to me
> It's just the same as talking to you (p. 146)

Here we see the limits of the theme of unmasking. What if we peel off our "onion gook" and say "how do I look," and we all look alike? What if "Bob Dylan" looks like everybody else? Another song on the same album, "To Ramona," puts the problem more delicately, touching on the personal consequences of political egalitarianism:

I've heard you say many times
That you're better than no one
And no one is better than you
If you really believe that
You know you have nothing to win and nothing to lose (p. 148)

Difference — here figured as some kind of social inequality — now appears to be essential to growth. Dylan has made comments about racial inequality (including a joke about having a can of black paint fall on him and having to sit "in the back of the tub" [p. 86] as he washed up) and class difference. But now, with *Another Side*, he begins to write about the question of difference more generally, and about how hierarchy and conformity are calibrated in social relations. These new themes put pressure on the figure of the wise rambler who can bring together country and city, north and south. The mystery that informs that figure — his experience of the road — begins to evaporate.

The aesthetic solution to this crisis of otherness and sameness, mystery and familiarity, is developed in the group of songs Dylan begins to write in and around the *Another Side* album. A structural dilemma emerges, a kind of crisis in the representation of the singer as rambling truth teller. In response to this dilemma, Dylan begins to explore a new kind of power, beyond social satire and political slogans. This is the power of the artist, as artist, to shape feeling and generate fictions. The songs on *Another Side* begin to address the consequences of this, and the interpersonal dynamics between the singer and those around him. "To Ramona" reverses the formulas of such songs as "Don't Think Twice," with Dylan's persona now no longer the wanderer but a counselor, and the "cracked country lips" belonging to the woman who is on the verge of rambling away. As the narrator counsels Ramona, who prepares to head back to "the South" (instead of to the "North Country fair"), he stresses that her melancholy stems from the conformity of the group in which she circulates: "They'll hype you and type you / Making you think / That you have to be just like them" (p. 148). Community is not empowering, as it is for Guthrie and the union song movement. It is deadening. The only consistency here is the consistency of fate. The song ends with the singer pointing out that they might be doubles of each other: "Someday maybe, who knows, baby / I'll come and be crying to you" (p. 148). Dylan's consistent juggling of communitarian social themes with radical individualism on his early albums begins to give way to a charting of his own situation as artist or "spokesman." *Another Side* is full of rejections, from the opening line of "All I Really Want to Do," "I ain't lookin' to compete with you" (p. 138), to the individualist's sendoff in the last song, "It Ain't Me, Babe." All Dylan wants is to "be friends with you." The problem, however, is that Dylan *is* "lookin' to compete" with some of us at least.

"I Shall Be Free No. 10" both evokes Guthrie's "We Shall Be Free" and Dylan's own earlier "I Shall Be Free" (one of many self-citations). It returns us from Guthrie's melodic template to a talking blues. Even if the title suggests the problem of writing the same damned thing over and over again, it also suggests Jimmie Rodgers's "Blue Yodel #10" and modern paintings like Jackson Pollock's "Number 1, 1948." It contains a moment of triumph, of sorts. At the end Dylan, who was by now dubbed a "genius" and many other equally grand things in the press, sings, "Yippee! I'm a poet and I know it / Hope I don't blow it" (p. 146). The ironic double register of the phrase suggests the ambiguity of the situation at hand: The singer is making a self-important statement, he's saying what everyone else is saying about him, but he does so with doggerel verse. He thus both acknowledges his genius and undercuts his claim to serious purpose at the same time. He asserts individuality and questions the mechanisms that construct that individuality. As Brecht noted of the actor, he must "act in such a way that the alternative emerges as clearly as possible, that his acting allows the other possibilities to be inferred."[28] Nowhere is Dylan's status as artist, media figure, pop hero, and political spokesperson evoked with more self-awareness or complexity than in these lines. They foreshadow struggles to come.

The swerve into a focus on the special status of the artist is both a political problem and an aesthetic problem. It is political to the extent that it constitutes a break with the collective issue-oriented politics of the folk music world. All men may be brothers, but it turns out that not every brother is equal to every other brother. By grasping the limits to orthodox left-wing communitarianism under the pressures of consumer society, Dylan reveals his own political insight — at the very moment that he seems to be least "political." But the problem has an aesthetic dimension as well, to the extent that it asks us to think about the special status of the singer in the do-it-yourself culture of folk music. Anybody should be able to sing this music, it would seem, since we are all more or less equal and these songs belong to us all. Music is just work, as Guthrie put it in *Bound for Glory*. And the songs have been patched together from songs that we already know. Yet not everybody enjoys the special status (social as well as, increasingly, financial) of the rambling folksinger. Thus, following his first three albums, Dylan's work begins to run into a set of interesting new problems. Having milked the resources of the wandering bard and the unmasker of hypocrisy, he must work out new models of writing. He must find a source of authority for his songs that comes from somewhere beyond the pose that he's been out on the road, working for the carnival, hitting some hard traveling.

CHAPTER THREE

Absolutely Modern:

Electric Music and Visionary Song

Following the first visit of The Beatles to America and the resurgence of rock and roll, Dylan begins recording and performing with a backing band. At the Newport Folk Festival in 1965, he causes a stir by playing "electric" music instead of the acoustic folk music many fans were hoping for. He releases a set of three recordings, Bringing It All Back Home *(1965),* Highway 61 Revisited *(1965), and* Blonde on Blonde *(1966), that draw on the plugged-in guitar and organ sound of Chicago-style, urban blues. These records, which include his first radio hit, "Like a Rolling Stone," establish him as the major songwriter of his generation and an electrifying performer. They also turn him into a darling of the countercultural Left. His personal appearance changes dramatically, as he sheds his workingman's garb for the clothes of an Edwardian dandy. He grows his hair out. He embarks on a world tour with the musicians who will later be known as The Band. The response to his increasingly confrontational music is itself confrontational, as fans boo and heckle him. In July 1966 he crashes his motorcycle on a back road near Woodstock, New York, and retires from performing. He will not tour again for seven years. Meanwhile, living with his family in Woodstock, he begins to produce a more countrified, relaxed set of recordings, released as* John Wesley Harding *in 1967. He meets frequently with The Band to jam and write. Their work together is soon circulated as* The Great White Wonder, *the first rock bootleg recording. Years later it will be reissued as* The Basement Tapes.*

In Chapter 2, I traced how Dylan's pose as a "rambler" or wandering bard is more than a simple self-portrait. It also provides an aesthetic resource through which he responds to the changing relationship between folk music and a new, post-1950s listening audience. Through the fiction of his mobility, updated from figures such as Woody Guthrie, Dylan is able to play the role of mediator and reporter, moving between the subworlds of rural music or blues culture and the market space of his increasingly vast record-buying public. At the level of content or theme, this makes it possible for him to shift between grand questions of justice and morality and the private world of interpersonal relations. At the same time, I suggested, his increasing interest in political and moral issues opens new and increasingly confrontational ways of manipulating form and rhetoric. As his corpus develops, he introduces expansions and innovations in the uses of the stanza, the chorus, and the address to the listener. But these innovations in turn lead to a slightly different set of problems, as the poet or singer's self-invention becomes entangled in the paradoxes of individuality and community: How can I be just like you and be completely unlike you?

Dylan's mid-1960s work, his famous "electric" albums, offer an attempt to work through those paradoxes. As Dylan confronts the changing relationship between community and artistic individuality, his early interest in the naming and shaming of hypocrisy modulates into the rhetoric of the put-down; he pens an influential series of compositions that involve humiliating or unmasking individual antagonists. This approach may also be read in terms of the larger problem of the scope of protest music. Dylan's earliest work targets certain very specific social problems: racism, injustice, corruption. The power of those songs, as I noted in Chapter 2, comes in part from the fact that they do not target specific people or events — though they usually begin there — but focus instead on institutions and practices that have gone awry. However, as Dylan further widens his scope in the mid-1960s, the target of protest, scorn, and satire extends from corrupt politicians and false-hearted judges to include society itself. Protest against the mistreatment of black people turns into protest against squareness. We know what a protest song against racial discrimination would sound like. But how can one "speak out" against the unhip?

"Poetry Will Not Accompany Action, but Will Lead It"
Dylan's authority as witness and critic of social ills during these years is linked to a new approach to writing. Beginning as early as *Another*

Side of Bob Dylan, he begins to develop what I will call a "visionary poetics." This new approach solves some of the problems around identity discussed at the end of Chapter 2, since it makes possible a self-description in song through which the poet or singer's authority is linked, not to his "experience" as rambler, but to his *vision*. Dylan's work in the middle years of the 1960s involves a fundamental recasting of song, shifting the nature of sensory experience and the type of information that it transmits to listeners. While much has been made of Dylan's gesture of "going electric" at the 1965 Newport Folk Festival, the expansion of Dylan's songwriting palette during this period involves much more than the medium of transmission. Imagery, lyric form, musical structure, and even the dynamics of performance are recalibrated through new strategies that emerge to replace the earlier interest in topical song.

Let us begin with a benchmark event. In December 1965, Dylan gave a news conference in San Francisco. Following the stir caused several months earlier at the Newport Folk Festival, he was beginning an extensive tour. The goal, he announced, was to play neither folk, nor rock, nor folk-rock, but something called "vision music."[1] What would that be? The idea of a "visionary music" places Dylan in a tradition of poetry reaching back as far as Dante. More pertinently, as I will show, Dylan's development during this period takes shape through his dialogue with artistic modernism. For mid-60s Dylan, the visionary is the modern.[2] What interests me, here as elsewhere, is less the notion of "poetic inspiration" (often assumed to be part of some generational zeitgeist) than the development of the specific literary techniques and musical innovations through which Dylan broadens his songwriting range.

Certainly, Dylan's expansion of his lyric vocabulary owes much to the work of the Beat Generation, and, in specific, to Allen Ginsberg, who was seated prominently at the San Francisco news conference. Ginsberg's great poem "Howl" had offered an effective demonstration of a long-form composition that piled up images in order to evoke a society out of balance. So it was no accident that the San Francisco visit included a pilgrimage to the beatnik mecca of City Lights Books, where Dylan was photographed in the alley behind the store with Ginsberg, Lawrence Ferlinghetti, and Michael McClure. This was the already aging royalty of the Beat Generation, who had, in their own time, rejected the collective activism of the Old Left to pursue individual beatitude or "beatness." Dylan was bringing Greenwich Village intellectualism to the epicenter of the developing sensory-based West Coast counterculture, casting himself as the heir to an earlier visionary generation.[3] Yet Ginsberg had been working in a visionary mode from his very first published poems. Dylan now had to *make himself* into a visionary; he had to develop a new poetic vocabulary and graft it onto the limited formal capacities of the popular song.[4]

To think about the process of visionary self-creation in the modern age, we must thus turn, not to Ginsberg, nor to Ginsberg's idol William Blake, but to the French Symbolist poet Arthur Rimbaud (1854–1891). It was Rimbaud who had given first voice to the brand of visionary modernism that Dylan would embrace. It was Rimbaud who had announced that the poet "makes himself into a *visionary*."[5] It was Rimbaud who had codified, in his letters about poetry, the procedures and limitations of the visionary mode. Rimbaud's reflections on modernity and poetry provide a critical gloss for Dylan's own development of new modes of writing and performing, after the fading of folk music.

Dylan's work during the mid-1960s, including his turn to an electric or rock-based sound, might be seen as a search for a set of forms that would keep faith with Rimbaud's famous axiom, "One must be absolutely modern" (*Season*, pp. 88–89). As John Ashbery has glossed this phrase, Rimbaud's investment in the present moment involves "for him the acknowledging of the simultaneity of all of life, the condition that nourishes poetry at every second."[6] Dylan's version of Rimbaud's modernism involves the processing of an entire phantasmagoria of raw material previously unexplored in American songwriting — movies, history, literature, legend, travel, exotica, and so on. This new raw material helps shape Dylan's response to the paradoxes of self-creation and authority I outlined earlier.

Rimbaud was canonized in the San Francisco news conference when, partway through the conversation, the topic of literature was raised: "What poets do you dig, Bob?" someone asked. Dylan struggled for a moment to recall the names of the Flying Wallendas, the family of circus acrobats, but he was on firmer ground when fixing the main figures in his canon: "Rimbaud," he answered without hesitation, then, "Smokey Robinson, W. C. Fields, Allen Ginsberg, Charlie Rich." The association of poetry with vaudeville comedy, circus acrobatics, soul music, and country can only come under the sign of Rimbaud. For Rimbaud, poetry is only loosely linked to words on a page. As he writes in one of his often-cited "manifestos" on poetry, "The future will be materialistic. . . . Always filled with Number and Harmony, these poems will be made to last. . . . Poetry will not accompany action but will lead it" (*Illuminations*, p. xxxii). This axiom reverses the relationship between writing and the world. Here art doesn't "represent" the world; it makes it. This formulation gives impetus to a whole set of modernist innovations, from Dada performance to the "happening"—innovations that break with traditional forms of consumption (the private ritual of novel reading, the bourgeois concert hall) and project art into action. For Rimbaud, as poet, the shaping of action comes materially, through the poetic resources of *rhythm* and *form*. The visionary experience overtakes the entire sensorium, recalibrating how we process phenomena. As Rimbaud put it in "Alchemy of the Word," "I prided myself on inventing a poetic language accessible, some day, to all the senses" (*Season*, p. 51).[7]

"The Poet Makes Himself into a Visionary"

Rimbaud has been an exemplar for a whole tradition of quasi-popular American artists, from the mid-twentieth century to the present. The case of the precocious adolescent from the provinces who, through force of will and talent, rises to artistic eminence offers a model of self-fashioning for any number of postwar American figures who come from outside the corridors of power, the halls of academe, or the ranks of the privileged. This exemplary influence is clear as early as Henry Miller's 1946 monograph on Rimbaud, *The Time of the Assassins*, and it grows in scope through the writing of Jack Kerouac and the work of such figures as Dylan, Jim Morrison, and Patti Smith. If you are a poor white American kid and you want to be an artist, a turn to the French modernist avant-garde—and to Rimbaud in particular—would seem to be the way to go.[8] He is an alternative to Woody Guthrie.

There is good evidence to suggest that Dylan encountered Rimbaud's work quite early on, at the very beginning of his writing career. Dylan's Greenwich Village mentor, host, and friend Dave Van Ronk attests that Dylan's seeming indifference to literary culture was simply part of his pose as an untutored Woody Guthrie imitator and that he was reading modern French poetry "very carefully."[9]

Certainly Rimbaud can serve us as the measure of Dylan's modernist aesthetic by the way his work makes certain things legible in Dylan's work that other poets do not. In contrast to many earlier figures in the tradition of visionary literature, Rimbaud stresses the close relationship between vision and work. Visionary experience is not something that overtakes you, as it seems to have overtaken Blake, or Saint Teresa; it is generated through a planned askesis, through a systematic technological exploration of the limits of the self. Rimbaud is the first great nonmetaphysical visionary. His visions are not presumed to come from God. Nor are they mediated through the Romantic notions of "imagination" and "fancy." They are generated out of work on the self and arise from the body. This "study" of the self, as Rimbaud calls it, involves the famous "rational disordering of all the senses" (*Illuminations*, p. xxx) that is central to the generation of poetry. But it also includes Rimbaud's powerful ambition and thirst for both fame and, later in life, fortune. The themes of labor and ambition link Rimbaud's self-study to Dylan's massive professional ambition and deep work ethic.[10]

Rimbaud's work blends braggadocio and self-doubt. Daring images of triumph give way to abrupt gestures of retreat. Expressions of discovery and exhilaration flip over into moments of abjection and despair. These vacillations are traced out in his constant experimentation with form, from his early use of the Baudelairean sonnet, through the long hallucinatory lyric "The Drunken Boat," to the dense prose poems of *A Season in Hell*, which evoke Rimbaud's travels and the love affair with the poet Paul Verlaine that Dylan would mention a decade later in "You're Gonna Make Me Lonesome When You Go" ("Situations have ended sad / Relationships have all gone bad / Mine have been like Verlaine and Rimbaud" [p. 506]). Finally, there are the brief, lapidary prose pieces called *Illuminations*, published by Rimbaud's friends after his abandonment of France and poetry. The fragmentation of Rimbaud's poetic corpus, marked by self-citation and self-revision, offers a material parallel to the emotional extremes visited in his self-examination. As Fredric Jameson has argued, this work is the consequence of the "shock" of "a world drawn together by colonization," in which new forms of economic exchange set in circulation unfamiliar or previously "exotic" objects, now available for contemplation and consumption.[11] So, we might suggest, does Dylan, in his own, later, pop modernist moment, expand the sensorium of the songwriting self to include the diverse material put in play by the new media culture issuing from American political and economic ascendency in the postwar years. The difference between the two is formal. Whereas Rimbaud can explode the rigid structures of French verse by venturing into the prose poem, Dylan, whatever his approach, must still work, however uncomfortably, within the limited structure of the popular song.

The visionary mode involves a break with the brute phenomena of everyday experience, as it recombines or transforms elements from the sensorium into some new artifact. For Dylan, the leap into hallucinatory abstraction required a studied break with the earlier tradition of political protest music that had made him famous. At the level of performance, this process of abstraction would become ever more pronounced. As the 1960s rolled on, Dylan's singing would begin to hover above the musical accompaniment, as if he were singing, not a melody, but some abstracted version of a melody that the listener could seek to reconstruct through the interplay of instrument and voice.[12] But we can see the visionary break with the past worked out already in Dylan's 1964 album *Another Side of Bob Dylan*. Midway through the collection comes the long retrospective song "My Back Pages," which narrates Dylan's break with the past. We link it, as well, to a major Rimbaud text. In "Alchemy of the Word," one of the long prose poems from *A Season in Hell*, Rimbaud recounts his own poetic development as a series of steps and a series of crises. He began in total confidence, he tells us, "possessing every possible landscape" and holding "in derision the celebrities of modern painting and poetry." He dreamed of "crusades, unrecorded voyages of discovery, [and] untroubled republics" (*Season*, p. 49). Yet this liberation from convention resulted in a questioning of both self and language. His development led, not to mastery, but to self-doubt; it was a parable of antigrowth. Only when he came to live as a "gold spark of *pure* light," "brush[ing] from the sky the azure that is darkness" (p. 61) — that is, reimagining the essence of things — could he reach some point of illumination from which, as the last line has it, to "salute beauty."

"My Back Pages" marks out a break with the past in analogous terms. At an earlier moment, Dylan says, he was certain of where he stood, using "ideas as my maps." As Rimbaud dreamed of "unrecorded voyages of discovery" and drew upon archaic language, Dylan has dreamed of "romantic facts of Musketeers," and wasted time "memorizing politics of ancient history." Now, however, he has moved to a new consciousness which involves, not chronological youth, but a newness of vision; as the refrain puts it, "Ah, but I was so much older then, I'm younger than that now" (p. 152).

The dialectic articulated by the break with the past is expressed in the complex spatial imagery of the title. On the one hand, the "back pages" would seem to be the past, the rigid categories of pro-test music that are here being rejected. At the same time, however, the "back pages" suggest the less current portion of the newspaper, the personals or the want ads. The political headlines ("front page news") are recast as a literary genre that must be sloughed off for a focus on the "back pages" of personal experience. Thus the "back pages" are simultaneously rejected (as "my past") and celebrated (as "my *personal* vision"). Here Dylan describes his break with the past not as a musical conversion (some "new song") but as a form of awak-ening in which a new consciousness can undo the process of aging.[13]

"A Long, Prodigious, and Rational Disordering of All the Senses"
Dylan's break with earlier work enacts, on the level of literary his-tory, a theme that comes increasingly to inflect some of his best work during the mid-1960s. This is the focus on the "moment," on the experience of a single instant of illumination in which time seems to stop. The "moment" is, of course, a modernist topos, from the time of Baudelaire's 1857 poem "To a Woman Passing By," and familiar to modern readers from the Joycean notion of the epiphany, from Proust's conquest of time through the ingestion of the madeleine, and from Virginia Woolf's essay "The Moment." As Rimbaud says in the closing of *A Season in Hell*, "All the noisome memories are fading.... My last regrets take to their heels. No hymns! Hold the ground gained..." (*Season*, pp. 87, 89). What is gained from the vio-lence of the trip through Hell is a heightened awareness of the harsh-ness of the present: "The new hour is at least very severe" (*Season*, pp. 86–87). And a sentence later comes the famous phrase, "One must be absolutely modern." Modernity lies in welcoming the intensity of the "new hour," for better or worse.[14]

Dylan explores the modernist topos of the moment by manipulat-ing both language and form in one of the high points of *Another Side*, "Chimes of Freedom." Here we find Dylan in full Rimbaldian mode. He seems to be taking direct aim at the tradition of topically oriented protest music, but he does so formally, rather than thematically, as in "My Back Pages." "Chimes of Freedom" has the anthemic feel of a protest song, but it recasts the moralistic refrains of such tunes as "The Times They Are a-Changin'" as personal vision. As he says at the end of each long stanza, "And we gazed upon the chimes of free-dom flashing" (p. 144). The performance is stately, backed by Dylan's beautiful, chimelike guitar strumming, as he slides up and down the neck, offering a sonic variety unexplored in the earlier recordings.[15]

But what is a "chime of freedom"? Rimbaud gives voice to a mod-ernist axiom when he notes that single words and even letters pos-sess a sensory and associative power that can overwhelm the reader or observer.[16] Language thus works through resonance, as much as through reference. We can see this demonstrated in the fifth and sixth stanzas of Rimbaud's long lyric, "The Drunken Boat," where the boat experiences the initial thrill of liberation from all connec-tion to the past. Since the poem also provides a thematic and poetic matrix for a whole series of mid-1960s songs, beginning with "Chimes of Freedom," it is worth quoting:

> Sweeter than sour apples to a child,
> Green waters seeped through all my seams,
> Washing the stains of vomit and blue wine,
> And swept away my anchor and my helm.
> And since then I've been bathing in the Poem
> Of star-infused and milky Sea,
> Devouring the azure greens, where, flotsam pale,
> A brooding corpse at times drifts by. (*Season*, p. 95)

The expression that sour apples are sweet to children evokes the dif-ferent sensory experiences of individual tasters (and readers). A sour apple is called a sour apple because of its taste, but it is sweet if it is stolen from the tree before picking time. Thus, its name contradicts the experience of its consumption. "Sour" actually means "sweet," if you are a child. The image also contaminates the image that follows it, that of the "green waters" that seeped through all my seams, since, as we know, "sour apples" are sour because they are green. Similarly, the "star-infused and milky Sea" would seem to evoke the foam of the ocean, which looks like milk. But how can the sea be both milky and "star-infused"? The milky foam suggests that it is not smooth enough to reflect the light of heaven (a Romantic image, anyway). In fact, the sea can be at once milky and astral only when we recall that the astral constellation most evocative of ocean foam is that formation known as the Milky Way. Thus, Rimbaud's images radiate in different directions, evoking different elements, splitting names from things and stressing the subjective experience of the individual. The technique of evoking two different senses and two different elements at the same time is what makes possible the expansion of the experience of the boat, as the sky and the sea become one with each other and with the poem, "The poem of the sea," "Le poème de la mer."[17]

These details of Rimbaud's poetry foreshadow the associative poetics that Dylan uses in "Chimes of Freedom." The singer and a friend are caught in a violent rainstorm late one night and hear church bells intertwined with the experience of thunder and lightning.

> Far between sundown's finish and midnight's broken toll
> We ducked inside the doorway, thunder went crashing
> As majestic bells of bolts struck shadows in the sounds
> Seeming to be the chimes of freedom flashing (p. 144)

What, we might ask, are "majestic bells of bolts"? How can you strike "shadows in the sounds" when sound is sonic and shadow is visual? At one level, these effects seem to be generated out of alliteration, through the sonic repetition of the *b* in "bells of bolts" and the *s* in "struck shadows in the sounds." We have seen Dylan's mastery of alliteration elsewhere, in "Blowin' in the Wind." Here, however — in keeping with the visionary mode — it not only anchors the composition, but it also generates a new experience. Conceptually, bells and bolts are linked by the idea of the blow, by the fact that lightning, clocks, chimes, and bells are all things that "strike." Dylan is thus able to give form to an experience that, like Rimbaud's astral "poem of the sea," is completely artificial, residing between two conventional sensory experiences. Moreover, like Proust's madeleine, Virginia Woolf's lighthouse, or the green light at the end of Daisy Buchanan's pier in *The Great Gatsby*, the artificially induced "chime," generated out of synesthesia and punning is also the vehicle of redemption. This is a classic modernist moment.

It is important to notice the role of form in this articulation of the visionary experience. "Chimes of Freedom" is built of six eight-line stanzas. Each stanza features four lines that evoke the storm and the church bells, and four lines that interpret that experience. So, after the initial evocation of the "bells of bolts" that seem to be "the chimes of freedom flashing," we get an explanation:

Flashing for the warriors whose strength is not to fight
Flashing for the refugees on the unarmed road of flight
And for each and every underdog soldier in the night
And we gazed upon the chimes of freedom flashing (p. 144)

The beautiful alliterations continue and migrate across the line, from left to right: "flashing for" / "flashing for" / "each and every" / "freedom flashing." These powerful lines gesture back to the protest song tradition that Dylan was trying to discard. They gloss personal vision as social vision. The tension between personal experience and interpretive gloss is mediated by form, in the contrast between the first half of each stanza and the allegorizing second half.[18] This is reflected in the musical harmony, which shifts at the midpoint to a set of lines built around the dominant chord before returning to the tonic in the last line. The complexity of the melody and the long stanza form (in contrast, say, to the repetitions of a song like "Hard Rain") suggest Dylan's increasing mastery of more complex song forms. Here we see an important moment in Dylan's emergence as a maker of songs—a moment that points toward his great long-form compositions of a few years later.

The authority of the interpretive response in the second half of the stanza is the consequence of the linkage of the music of the bells and the violence of the thunderstorm, which I noted in the first lines. For that linkage makes it possible for the violence of nature to become one with the bells of redemption. A song limited to describing the ringing of bells would take on communal or religious connotations—something like Pete Seeger's "If I Had a Hammer," which Dylan almost seems here to be rewriting ("If I had a bell . . ."). On the other hand, if we eliminate the bells we are stuck with a song about the weather. Only when the two figures—the trope of the bell and the trope of the storm—are blended can they enable the vision of cosmic and social disorder, crying out for redemption, mediating personal experience and political outrage.[19]

And yet, seen against the background of our earlier discussion of Dylan's changing relationship to audience, the paradox of "Chimes of Freedom" is that, despite its ethical impulse, the "freedom" evoked is a freedom of vision. It is the freedom of the singer to break with

conventional categories of experience and see all of Creation stand-
ing naked in its beauty and contingency. In this regard it becomes
a song about its own power to envision the world. We can see this
by contrasting it with the previous Dylan song to which it bears
the greatest similarity, "A Hard Rain's a-Gonna Fall." Whereas the
earlier song, for all of its power, relied on crude allegory ("I saw a
white man, he walked a black dog," and so on [p. 76]) and the folk song
topos of the singer as messenger, we now have private vision blended
with a strategy of allegorical rereading, made possible by the form of
the stanza.[20]

"Chimes of Freedom" hooks the moment of illumination to a set
of scenarios of redemption, the story of the refugee, the lonesome-
hearted lover, the misdemeanor outlaw. These mini-narratives keep
the moment of vision from degenerating into a diary entry. Other
songs from the same period confront this structural problem by elid-
ing the present at the very moment they are describing it. Thus, "Mr.
Tambourine Man," to take a masterful example from *Bringing It All
Back Home*, is built around the liminal moment between waking and
sleep, through a dreamlike journey on a Rimbaldian "magic swirling
ship" (p. 184). Yet two things are especially noteworthy about the
song. The first is that it interweaves a subjective visionary experience
and an objective description of fatigue and setting. What "Chimes of
Freedom" does through stanzaic structure, "Mr. Tambourine Man"
does in virtually every line. The second is that the experience of the
present is built on an extended gesture toward the future. The open-
ing verses describe a moment of stasis, of neither dream nor waking.
But the song is an invitation: "Sing a song for me," "Take me for a
trip." The song projects its present as a future that is unfolding as we
listen. It is a future that is also a present.

The double-layered depiction of time is played out in the form
of the song. Noteworthy is the way it works through a repeated
sequence of musical phrases at the center of each verse. Dylan's guitar
shuttles back and forth between the tonic D major chord and the sub-
dominant G major, repeating over and over again a melodic phrase
consisting metrically of two units of two short beats followed by a
long beat: "My senses have been stripped; My hands can't feel to grip;
My toes too numb to step; Down the foggy ruins of time; Through
the smoke rings of my mind; Out to the windy beach; Circled by the
circus sands; Silhouetted by the sea" (p. 184). This sequence of brief

lines — rhyming with each other as they do in "Chimes of Freedom" yet varying in number according to the verse — is what generates the dreamlike or hypnotic experience of the song. The lyric suggests that we are moving forward, even as the melodic line does the same thing over and over again.

The dreamlike mood of the harmony is given forward movement by yet another poetic technique that works to generate the concluding scene — somewhat like the artificially created "Chimes of Freedom" we saw earlier. This emerges in the last verse where the singer invites, "Take me disappearin' down the smoke rings of my mind." This description of the descent into the self then shifts back outside the self, to a landscape. Inside and outside merge (as in Rimbaud's inebriated boat scene) via the multipurpose image of the (internal) smoke ring, which turns effortlessly into (external) fog ("down the foggy ruins of time"). The image of the ruin, with its Romantic associations, takes us into a landscape that is both objective (that is, natural) and subjective, "far past the frozen leaves, the haunted frightened trees." A winter landscape becomes a gothic nightmare. We are then led to an everyday image, the image of the sea, "out to the windy beach, far from the twisted reach of crazy sorrow." The frightened trees now fade into the "twisted" reach of sorrow that is left behind. Having left fog and smoke, we've arrived at the end of the road. The fog has blown away and the sky has cleared. "Yes, to dance beneath her diamond sky, with one hand waving free / Silhouetted by the sea / Circled by the circus sands." The ruin and the dead tree in the fog now give way to the silhouette of the singer himself. Yet the "circus sands" of the beach also recall the very first image of the song, "Though I know that evening's empire has returned into sand / Vanished from my hand." The vanished sands of time are now recaptured and become the setting for celebration of the moment: the "circus" that "circles" the dancer (the words are linked, etymologically) takes form through the singer's gyrating dance itself.

The density of this journey is linked to the final image of the dance on the beach. This is one of Dylan's characteristic gestures, which we have seen before, in "Girl from the North Country" — the gesture of presenting an "unusual" or "exotic" landscape that expands our horizon, but nevertheless communicates with the world of the listener via some commonplace experience accessible to all. We cannot all, perhaps, venture into the visionary landscape of the haunted mind, but we can all recognize a joyful dance on the beach. Thus, the land-scape of the song is at once completely unfamiliar and totally familiar to the listener. The final image of the dancer, like Orpheus return-ing from the underworld, brings us back to shared reality, after the metaphorical smoky forest of the mind.

These modulations of setting — from inside to outside, from met-aphorical to literal — are paralleled in the manipulation of time. The future evoked in the fantasy of the dance on the beach is immediately welded to the past with the concluding wish, "Let me forget about today until tomorrow" (p. 184). The past has been elided, but so has the future. The point may be that any turn to memory in the present would diminish the intensity of the moment. Yet to push memory to the future is also to diminish the potential intensity of future moments like the one being evoked now. Here we see the struggle of poetry to seize in language and form the unique moment of vision. Dylan's solution to this struggle in "Mr. Tambourine Man" is eva-sively to bleed the present moment into a future that never comes and then to recast that future as a past that cannot be recaptured. The song moves beyond "My Back Pages" and "Chimes of Freedom" by gesturing toward an unfolding story and then eliding any sense of time that could link that story to some larger social vision. This is the poetry of the moment.

"I Is Someone Else"

The rise to dominance of rock and roll during its great growth phase in the mid-1960s was as much about the manipulation of images — made concrete in album covers, posters, and so forth — as about the manipulation of sound. Modernist art had long insisted on the fragmentation of the self, adrift in the disorienting world of the city or living in exile.[21] Here, again, possibly because of his precedence, Rimbaud offers the most influential formulation: "To each being it seemed to me that several *other* lives were due. This gentleman does not know what he is doing. He is an angel. This fam-ily is a litter of dogs. In front of several men, I talked out loud with one moment of one of their other lives." This multiplicity is an elabo-ration of Rimbaud's famous phrase, "I is someone else," "Je est un autre." "It is too bad for the wood which finds itself a violin" (*Illumi-nations*, p. xxvii), writes Rimbaud to his teacher Georges Izambard. And to Paul Demeny, "For I is someone else. If brass wakes up a trumpet, it isn't to blame" (*Illuminations*, p. xxix). In Rimbaud's own poetry this multiplicity of selves is often a source of difficulty for readers, as different voices appear and disappear without explanation in the middle of poems or stanzas. In Dylan's historical moment, the multiplicity of identity hinted at by Rimbaud has been appropriated and distorted in the material culture of the recording industry itself. The very machinery of the star system, with its multiplication of images, involves a perverse literalization of the insight that "I is someone else."

For Rimbaud, this multiplicity of vision is the result of work, of the famous process of self-knowledge and discipline that he describes in his 1871 letter to Paul Demeny as a "long, prodigious and rational disordering of all the senses" (*Illuminations*, p. xxx). "I became an adept at simple hallucination," he writes. "In place of a factory I really saw a mosque, a school of drummers led by angels, carriages on the highways of the sky, a drawing-room at the bottom of the lake; monsters, mysteries" (*Season*, p. 55). "I brushed from the sky the azure that is darkness," he writes, "and I lived — gold spark of *pure* light" (*Season*, p. 61).

Dylan's mid-1960s work, including his so-called "novel" *Tarantula* and several filmed sequences, shows him deeply interested in mixing up meanings of words and senses.[22] Indeed, at one level, we can note that the dynamic blending of idioms that characterizes the earliest songs (Dylan the hobo next to Dylan the potential graduate student) gives way, by the mid-1960s, to a collage of images, names, and cultural references. With the exception of the contraction "Ain't," Dylan's earlier hobolike diction largely vanishes by about 1964. His earlier pasting together of different linguistic registers is replaced by an equally strategic manipulation of collections of images. Songs become lists of literary and pop culture references, mosaics of cultural noise. By piling up images, Dylan marshals their power and constructs his persona as their master. He is no longer the hobo off the road, with a new message; he is the person who hangs out with a set of characters who seem to dwell just beyond our ken.

On one level, of course, the question of the multiple manifestations of "I" offers a simple explanation of the mutability of the self, including Dylan's own changes of style, from rugged proletarian to refined dandy. But it goes deeper into the language and forms of the songs. As I have noted, from his earliest songs, Dylan's lyrics are often built on a rhetoric of unmasking. Thus he unmasks power ("Come you Masters of War . . . I can see through your masks" [p. 72]), or hypocrisy ("She started peeling off her onion gook" [p. 94]). When it is applied to larger social themes, the unmasking gesture is capable of generating breathtaking insights into how power works. Songs such as "It's Alright, Ma (I'm Only Bleeding)," with its assertion that "Even the President of the United States must sometimes have to stand naked" (p. 188), get at the dynamics of mystification through which power functions. The "I" of the president is an "other"—a naked man.

Yet, at the same time—along the other edge of this particular knife—the unmasking impulse yields a series of songs aimed at breaking down identity. When it is given direction, aimed at a specific target, the unmasking gesture of finding the multiple "others" inside the self turns into the language of the putdown. *Bringing It All Back Home*, *Highway 61 Revisited*, and *Blonde on Blonde* are all sprinkled with songs that describe or confront various characters—mostly women—whose "masks" are systematically dismantled, or who are depicted as having lost the trappings that gave them their standing in society. These include Queen Jane (in "Queen Jane Approximately"), Mister Jones (in "Ballad of a Thin Man"), "Baby" (in "Just Like a Woman"), and—most famously—"Miss Lonely" (in "Like a Rolling Stone").

Dylan's gesture of confronting and instructing his characters about their changing positions in society emblematizes the dramatic incompatibility of public art and private experience as we move into the middle years of the 1960s. The language used by a progressive youth culture to critique power—a language that Dylan's songs had helped to form—loses its suppleness when applied to the intimate world of friendship and love. As the 1960s wear on, the rhetoric of protest will become counterbalanced by the shift to a more intimate form of examination. In Dylan's work, scenes of personal wounding—erotic betrayal, broken friendships—often shade into attacks on the personal integrity of the Other. At one level, these excavations of identity and interpersonal tensions reflect a tendency of much modernist writing, which turns from the grand frescoes of nineteenth-century art (Tolstoy, Cooper) to small communities (Faulkner's small towns, Joyce's "dear dirty Dublin," the circle of the Impressionists, the Beats). And much of Dylan's work during this period projects an image of a coterie or club within which the singer moves—the world of Mona, Louise, and Ruthie, where "it's people's games you've got to dodge" (p. 188), where "they'll hype you and type you" (p. 148). These controlled small-group dramas stand, at the level of plot and psychology, as the counterweight to the centrifugal, swirling proliferation of opaque "hip" characters ("Fifteen Jugglers," "Louie the King," "your Persian Drunkard") that decorates the surface of the lyrics.

Dylan casts the themes of multiplicity and hallucination as a drama of erotic fascination in one of his most often-covered love songs. This is the tune called "She Belongs to Me," from *Bringing It All Back Home*, recorded a few months before the famous appearance at Newport: "She's got everything she needs, she's an artist, she don't look back," sings Dylan. "She can take the dark out of the nighttime / And paint the daytime black" (p. 174). Dylan would appear to be translating Rimbaud here. When Rimbaud says that he has taken the "the azure that is darkness" from the sky, we must understand "azure" not as a shade of blue, but as shorthand for "the ideal" or "the essence" of things.[23] So, to remove the "azure" that is black is to take the essence out of the night—in Dylan's terms "to take the dark out of the nighttime." The artist remakes reality. The unfaithful lady manipulates her lover's very vision of night and day.

"She Belongs to Me" dramatizes the contrast between the idealized artist and the narrator/lover, who is depicted as not being able to keep up with her. Whereas she is "absolutely modern," to use Rimbaud's famous phrase, "you are a walking antique." Whereas she collects hypnotists and magical stones that sparkle when she speaks, the "you" addressed by the singer can only offer her military musical gifts, a trumpet and a drum. Whereas she remakes the very color of the sky, the "you" of the song "will wind up peeking in through a keyhole down upon your knees." Just as "My Back Pages" reflects on historical understanding, so does "She Belongs to Me" probe the nature of vision. Who sees? Who sees what?

This fracturing of experience into a multiplicity of perspectives is reflected in the structure of "She Belongs to Me." The song consists of a set of three-line stanzas, with the first two lines of each stanza repeated. Thus, the opening line, "She's got everything she needs, she's an artist, she don't look back," is repeated and then answered by the third line, "She can take the dark out of the nighttime / And paint the daytime black." Obviously, this verse form evokes the blues.

In the simple blues structures on which Dylan cut his musical teeth, the verse conventionally consists of one line, repeated, followed by an answering line. Musically, the traditional form of the blues requires three chords: the tonic chord, for the first line, the subdominant chord, for the second line, and a third line divided between the domi-nant chord and the subdominant, resolving to the tonic. Here, how-ever, the musical harmony pushes against the traditional blues form. For the third line, Dylan uses an unconventional chord sequence. Instead of going to the expected dominant or V chord, he turns to a major chord on the second degree of the scale, thereby introducing a note of tension. This has the effect of lifting the entire structure and pushing against the expectations of the blues, lending the blues lyric a pop inflection (which may account for its afterlife).[24] It generates a blues that, musically, seems headed elsewhere, even though lyrically it evokes that form. The wonderful detail is that at the very moment that Dylan sings "she can take the dark out of the nighttime," he is himself moving into a chord sequence that is complicating the blues structure that his own lyric points to. Or, to put it more playfully, at the very instant that his heroine is removing the dark from the nighttime Dylan is pushing against the blueness of the blues. The performance of the song thus enacts the argument of its own lyric.[25]

"Sweeter Than Sour Apples to a Child"

When seen from a distance, Dylan's confrontations with those around him during this period often seem somewhat vicious.[26] Unless, that is, they are redeemed by artistic form, which can reshape them to mediate our responses. And this is what happens in two of Dylan's signature compositions, "Like a Rolling Stone" (1965) and "Just Like a Woman" (1966). Both songs depict women who have lost their sheen. "Miss Lonely" of "Like a Rolling Stone" is now forced to live on the street; "Baby," in "Just Like a Woman," has lost "her ribbons and her bows." The consequences of these changes are written into the form of the songs. The verses of each song depict, step by step, a reinven-tion/criticism/emancipation of the character.

Following the famous snare drum hit that propels the first notes, "Like a Rolling Stone" opens with strummed electric guitar before shifting gears, as the lyric kicks in, to move up from one diatonic chord to another against a repeated melody note. You can feel it move up the scale, from C, to D minor, to E minor, until it reaches the fourth tone, F major, and then opens out onto a dominant or fifth chord ("didn't you!"). The sequence builds in intensity across each phrase, suggesting a progress toward some type of crisis. This chord sequence is then exactly reversed in the middle of each verse, when the progression slides its way back down to the opening C major tonic ("Now you don't / Talk so loud"). This up-and-down movement in the harmony (reflected lyrically in the contrast of "once upon a time" and "now") gives the narrator plenty of time to build his case against the "princess" who is reduced to invisibility by the last verse. Miss Lonely is unmasked, but also revealed to be what she was all along. Unmasking is the discovery of who you are. I is someone else.

The process of dismantling and revelation is counterbalanced, as it were, by the powerful groove of the chorus. For the chorus suggests, miraculously, both lyrically and rhythmically, that an identity crisis can also be a personal liberation. In this final insight the split between public experience and private experience is momentarily bridged. To be "like" a rolling stone (and we note the softer language of simile, rather than the more violent rhetoric of metaphor) is to be free. Thus, we are told and shown; Miss Lonely's fall is a fortunate fall. This is made possible by an affirmation of personal choice — a central concept in the emergence of affluent middle-class youth culture. Working stiffs and peasants lack the opportunity to turn their backs on school and job. Woody Guthrie *had* to ramble. Not so Miss Lonely. To seal the deal on this generational and class-based triumph of individual desire — triumphant even in moments of humiliation — Dylan recycles, for the chorus, a much-used rhythmic and harmonic groove taken from "La Bamba," "Twist and Shout," "Wild Thing," and "Louie, Louie," among other places. It is a groove that all listeners will immediately recognize. Self-discovery presents itself as the absolutely modern alternative to dancing the twist or stomp (*bamba*). This brings us listeners back to familiar territory (after the foray into the junglelike modernist atmosphere of the verses). It also liberates us harmonically, since the final groove could potentially go on forever, freeing us to dance our way into a future of self-discovery. It simultaneously projects us back in music history and forward into some new territory that will be picked up by any number of later artists who will cite the same groove: from The Beatles, on *Let It Be* (who include part of a jam on the "Rolling Stone" chorus) to Paul Simon's *Graceland,* which uses South African versions of the same groove.[27]

"Like a Rolling Stone" is the aesthetic counterpart to "My Back Pages" and "Chimes of Freedom." Where the earlier songs used vision and form to break with the past, "Like a Rolling Stone" provides an initiation that occurs, literally, as it unfolds. From the opening fairytale phrasing of "Once upon a time" (p. 206), it moves through two verses of fairly straightforward narrative development, before shifting to the evocation of such mysterious characters as the "diplomat" with the "Siamese cat" on his shoulder and "Napoleon in rags." This is the unsettling world of modernity, first evoked by Charles Baudelaire and suggested in Rimbaud's visions of "other lives." The break with an earlier moment of certainty is articulated, not through the sketching of some new ethics, but simply through the deeply ambiguous shouted question, "How does it feel?" that ushers in the chorus. "It" feels bad if you've lost everything, but good if you can give yourself over to the pulse of Dylan's groove. So much for Greenwich Village intellectualism. We are now in the sensory regime of self-discovery as rhythm.

Something analogous happens in "Just Like a Woman." The elegant structure of the opening lines, with its picked guitar figure, offers a stately background for the unmasking of "Baby," who needs to learn (another version of "I'm just average, common too") that "she's like all the rest." Here the small-group dynamics are handled with a concision that is remarkable. We begin with "Nobody feels any pain," which is surely ironic, since obviously the singer is in deep pain. He stands in the rain, having been excluded, either metaphorically or literally, from the company of his love. "Nobody" then gives way to "Everybody knows," which constitutes the small group within which the two protagonists move. This inside/outside spatial structure is then disturbed by being flung into time, into a before/after relationship with "Lately, I see her ribbons and her bows / Have fallen from her curls" (p. 249). And with that insight Baby's inclusion in the group is over. She now becomes outcast — and we are only four lines into the song. Baby's lack of self-knowledge will be mockingly affirmed in verse two, where the opening "Nobody" will return, as "Nobody has to guess" (meaning, again, "everybody knows") that Baby's sense of her own specialness is self-delusion. In the space of a few seconds a world has been evoked and set into crisis. Meanwhile, in the cadence supporting "Lately, I see her ribbons and her bows," the harmony deploys chordal movement up and down the first four steps of the diatonic scale in ways not unlike what we saw in "Like a Rolling Stone," recorded a year earlier. It suggests the rise and fall of destinies, if not of empires.[28]

Baby's loss of her "ribbons and her bows" may recall such stock songs about femininity as Dinah Shore's "Buttons and Bows" (from 1947) or the 1959 hit "Scarlet Ribbons," recorded by both Harry Belafonte and The Kingston Trio. Now, however, these traces of an earlier age of innocent song and wholesome girlhood are modernized when they are juxtaposed with the "hip" images of amphetamines and "fog." Yet the undoing of the Other is countered by the chorus, which reminds us of the fragility of the formerly pretentious "Baby," by telling us that she's now just "a little girl." The before/after structure is mediated by the ambiguity of "Baby," which wavers between metaphor and literal description. Indeed, in a sense, the whole drama of the song spins around the multiple meanings of "Baby." In conventional pop culture speak the word connotes an object of desire. But literally it refers to a child, a "little girl." The structure is held together sonically by the final word of each verse: "curls," "pearls," "world," "girl." These nouns stand out from the other rhyme words in each stanza, and rhyme between themselves, linking the structure together and telling the story in little. (This is what poeticians call "tail-rhyme"; it goes back to the Middle Ages.)

The movement through the bridge effectively recalibrates the scenario of the song. Dylan had introduced the bridge or "middle eight" into his songs only a year earlier, on "Ballad of a Thin Man," so this structural feature is a true innovation for him. Now, as across *Blonde on Blonde*, he deploys it to great effect. The singer acknowledges that his own pain in the relationship is such that he must leave: "I just can't fit." The image of exclusion that opens the song ("tonight as I stand inside the rain") is now replayed in yet another attempt to move that results in no change. "It was raining from the first," opens the bridge, suggesting that the opening downpour may be allegorical more than literal. No blue skies in this relationship. This is post-Guthrie Dylan. Instead of wandering away, he simply leaves the room. Even more important, the final stanza turns the drama back against the singer, presenting him, no longer as the accuser, but as a sadder but wiser comrade looking back discreetly on old struggles:

And when we meet again
Are introduced as friends
Please don't let on that you knew me when
I was hungry and it was your world

As Charles O. Hartman has pointed out, the last lines work through
a brilliant formal ambiguity. "When" may complete the idiomatic
expression, "you knew me when," resulting in a completed line.[29]
Or it may link up to the following line through an enjambment, "you
knew me when I was hungry." For our purposes, what is important
is that the two readings offer different visions of the position of the
singer. The singer projects a future meeting. In one version ("when
I was hungry") he hopes that she will not mention that he was once
scuffling, poor, down and out. This is literal hunger, and it suggests
that the singer may be as interested as the lady is in surface finery — a
good meal, clean clothes. Yet the rhythm of the performance marks a
break after "knew me when," which comes at the climax of a grand,
march-like sequence of chords up and down the scale. In this read-
ing, "you knew me when," means, "it was all a long time ago, when
we were both different." "I was hungry" becomes a metaphorical
comment on the whole story, and "hunger" may be a figure for sex-
ual desire, ambition, power, or simply the need to belong. Together
these readings emphasize the ambiguity with which Dylan conveys
small-group experience, as characters fade in and out, moving from
catastrophe to redemption, to fond recollection. The semantic rich-
ness of the final lines, coupled with the chorus, makes this one of
Dylan's most generous songs. As in the case of "Like a Rolling Stone,"
a formal innovation, powered by an infectious major-chord groove
in the chorus, reestablishes the relationship to the listener after the
somewhat disturbing drama of the verses.

"I Witness the Emergence of My Thought"
I have been suggesting that Dylan's expansion of his range over his
"electric" period is empowered through a poetics of vision. Rimbaud
offers the most useful partner for understanding this development,
both in terms of how Dylan explodes the restrictive conventions of
protest music and in terms of how that same explosion poses a set
of new problems, both aesthetic and ethical. New forms generate
new questions. In "My Back Pages" and "Mr. Tambourine Man" we

witnessed Dylan's attempt to be "absolutely modern," through a sev-
ering of present from past. Then, in "Chimes of Freedom," a vision-
ary aesthetic experience was generated out of sensory distortion,
only to be harnessed and interpreted by poetic form. In "She Belongs
to Me," we saw an exploration of the artist's unstable identity, as
both object and subject of the song. "Like a Rolling Stone" uses musi-
cal form to turn abjection into emancipation. "Just Like a Woman"
includes the narrator in the drama of unmasking.

We should note both the importance of the chorus in these
canonical mid-1960s tunes and the problems that it raises. Dylan's
technique of varying the chorus as a way of isolating the singer from
the listener is a central feature of the performances, especially on
Blonde on Blonde, with such songs as "Stuck Inside of Mobile with the
Memphis Blues Again," where no two choruses are sung the same
way. The phrasing and timing are constantly altered, even as the lyr-
ics stick in the mind, so that you cannot ever quite sing along with the
record. The long love song titled "Sad-Eyed Lady of the Lowlands"
uses this to great effect, as Dylan consistently sings ahead of the beat.
The modulations in time work to pry the vocal performance away
from the steady pulse of the backing track, leaving the vocal floating,
like a veil in the breeze, as if the singer were only temporarily visiting
the rest of the song, as if it were a momentary vision.

This dismantling of the role of the chorus may be Dylan's most
powerful rejection of the folk song tradition. It comes, however, not
at the level of theme or psychology, but at the level of performance,
and in the tension between performance and formal structure. Put
differently, that structural element in song that is generally assumed
not to vary becomes precisely the element that he varies most. Not
only are you not urged to join in: you couldn't if you wanted to.

Yet this increasing mobility in the timing of the performance
stands in contrast with the development of a new positioning of the
singer persona. Dylan's intensified engagement with a visionary
poetics goes hand in hand with an increasing sense that the "I" of
his songs cannot move; all it can do is watch. The themes of ram-
bling and travel that I discussed earlier (still distantly operative in
"Like a Rolling Stone") now give way to scenarios of immobility
and claustrophobia, from the narrator of "Stuck Inside of Mobile,"
who cannot leave Alabama and get to the home of the blues in Ten-
nessee, to the "stuffy room" of "Pledging My Time" and the "frozen

traffic" of "Absolutely Sweet Marie," to the singer of "Desolation Row" who "looks out" on the scene but later "can't read too good" (pp. 241, 246, 252, 221). Biographically, this sense of immobility may be a consequence of Dylan's own popularity and of the proliferation of his image in the popular music mediasphere. But it also has a poetic function. It stands in tension with the dynamic imagery and vision-ary intensity evoked by the singer. It raises the question — already broached in "Chimes of Freedom" and "She Belongs to Me" — of how the poetic or lyrical self establishes its own authority over a visionary material that often threatens to swallow it up.

These concerns come together in dramatic fashion in the third song from the *Blonde on Blonde* album, "Visions of Johanna." It is one of Dylan's most extraordinary compositions, and it places us clearly, not least by virtue of its title, in a tradition that we can trace back to Rimbaud the visionary.[30] As a counterweight to the grand sweep of Dylan's 1965 masterpiece, *Highway 61 Revisited*, with its flood of generalized vitriol aimed at everything that is "square," most of the songs on *Blonde on Blonde* concern themselves with intimate dramas marked by the dynamics of obligation — with promises given and bro-ken, pledges offered and refused, debts paid and unpaid. "Visions of Johanna" is no exception. It blends the heightened vision of "Chimes of Freedom" or "Mr. Tambourine Man" with the ethical concerns of Dylan's best early songs — What do I owe someone? — now recast as a private drama of responsibility and choice.

The scene is the dead of night. The narrator evokes a group of people, possibly three, in a room. As in "She Belongs to Me," the scene features a "you" who is the listener, but who is also the singer: "Ain't it just like the night," he sings, "to play tricks when you're trying to be so quiet / We sit here stranded, though we're all doing our best to deny it" (p. 242). Then temptation enters, in the form of a beautiful woman: "And Louise holds a handful of rain, tempting you to defy it." The rain, an important image in all of Dylan's writing, is also a slang term for heroin. The closer Louise gets to the singer, the more she seems to fade. And as the song unfolds, her physical presence evaporates under pressure from the absent Johanna, who eventually conquers the will and agency of the narrator himself:

> Louise, she's alright, she's just near
> She's delicate and seems like the mirror

But she just makes it all too concise and too clear
That Johanna's not here
The ghost of electricity howls in the bones of her face
Where these visions of Johanna
Have now taken my place (p. 242)

The temptation of sensual pleasure is overcome by a presence from afar, experienced as a vision — such that we are never certain whose "face" is being glimpsed here, Louise's or Johanna's. The wavering between illusion and reality, between internal fantasy and dramatic scenario, which we saw in the final sections of "Mr. Tambourine Man," here motivates the drama. The moment of temptation takes on an emblematic status, reminding us of any number of moments of temptation in art, going back, say, to the classical choice of Hercules between vice and virtue.

To articulate the contrast between the presence of Johanna and the scene before the narrator, Dylan sets up — here, as in "Chimes of Freedom" — a careful stanzaic scheme. He divides each stanza into three parts. An initial three-line unit of five anapestic feet (two short syllables, one long) then gives way to a four-line unit of three-foot lines that all rhyme:

Lights flicker from the opposite loft
In this room the heat pipes just cough
The country music station plays soft
But there's nothing, really nothing, to turn off (p. 242)

Musically, this second section consists of a simple up and down progression between the subdominant and the tonic chord in the key of A major. It recalls the middle section of each verse of "Mr. Tambourine Man." In "Mr. Tambourine Man" the repetition generates a hypnotic effect. In "Visions of Johanna" it produces the claustrophobia that permeates the atmosphere. There seems to be no escape from the repeated movement — up, down, up again, down again, and so on. These middle lines are where we learn that the "little boy lost" is "useless," "muttering small talk," that the "jelly-faced women all sneeze," that the "lights flicker from the opposite loft." This monotonous four-line unit then breaks, as we move to the V, or E, major chord, which takes us to the third moment in the stanza, the triumphant release in a concluding five-foot couplet. Here is where the most arresting images of the song appear: the "ghost of electricity," "the jewels and binoculars" that hang from the head of a mule, the harmonicas that play "skeleton keys," and where we learn how the visions of Johanna have taken over the dramatic space of the song.

The song unrolls across a series of mini-scenarios of sterility and immobility, featuring characters who cannot act or move. And the carefully defined stanzaic structure holds until the last verse. Here things change, both in the form of the song and in its very performance. Dylan introduces the figure of the peddler, who speaks to a countess who reminds him that no one is self-sufficient; everyone is a parasite. Then he shifts again to the middle section:

> And Madonna, she still has not showed
> We see this empty cage now corrode
> Where her cape of the stage once had flowed
> The Fiddler he now steps to the road
> He writes everything's been returned which was owed
> On the back of the fish truck that loads
> While my conscience explodes (p. 242)

This final verse of the song differs from the others. Here, instead of a four-line central unit, we get seven lines.[31] And that formal expansion sets up two possible endings. We are given both a moment of writing and a moment of performance. In the figure of the writing Fiddler (the image should already alert us that something strange is happening), the debt to Johanna seems to have been paid off. "Everything's been returned which was owed." The Fiddler exits. Yet things don't end there. For this is followed by the unforgettable final lines: "The harmonicas play the skeleton keys and the rain / And these visions of Johanna are now all that remain" (p. 242). With this, the vocal performance ends, to be followed by a harmonica solo — language giving way to pure sound ("harmonicas play"). However, this figure of haunting suggests that the debt to Johanna has not been paid after all. Whereas the Fiddler can walk away, the "I" who sings must remain, with his exploding conscience. A more conventional song about being obsessed by a lost lover — say "Blue Velvet" or "Help Me Rhonda" — might offer a solution via catharsis or distraction. By contrast, the visionary mode imposes the experience on the narrator in overwhelming fashion. The possibility of moving "outside" of the vision — of finding a position that enables an allegorical or moral interpretation of the type we saw in "Chimes of Freedom" — has now been foreclosed.

It may be no accident that the figure of the artist in this parable of subjective disarray is a fiddler, the character evoked by Rimbaud's famous description of how "I is someone else." "I give a stroke of the bow: the symphony makes its stir in the depths," to recall Rimbaud's elaboration of the idea. "I hold the bow in my hand, I begin" (*Illuminations*, p. xxxi), he notes a moment later. Dylan channels Rimbaud. And his own turn to the Fiddler as poet figure may explain why the evocation of the song's title and performance features the images of the skeleton key and the rain. The rain appears to have lost its function as narcotic temptation and become a generalized image, covering everything. More important, the skeleton key recalls an earlier mention of a keychain tossed around by the "all night girls" in a game of blind man's bluff. Initially an image of play and exclusion, the skeleton key now becomes, like the rain, an image of expansion. For the skeleton key brings together all of the main themes of the song: the spectral Johanna, the nightingale who has been unlocked from her cage, the spooky "ghost" of electricity that overcomes Louise, and the singer's own search for proper form — for a *musical key* that would be all musical keys, opening all doors, accessible, as Rimbaud put it, to all the senses.

Thus, the song seems to waver between two types of closure: the moment of writing — the figure of the Fiddler — and the moment of performance — the figure of the "I" who stays behind with his harmonica. The contrast between the two is registered in the performance itself. At six minutes and thirty seconds into the studio recording, at the precise moment when Dylan sings, "The Fiddler, he now steps to the road," the bass player plays an unexpected note. On the strong first beat of the measure, he hits the root of the dominant (E major) when he should be hitting root of the tonic A major chord. Coming after a sequence of strong cadences, each landing firmly on A (and doubled by the lead guitar line), the moment registers as a blip in the performance, where the bottom end of the track seems, for a second, to fall away. The reason for this instant of slippage, of course, is that the form of the song has changed. The middle section of the last verse, as noted, does not contain four lines. It contains seven. Line four is "The Fiddler, he now steps to the road." That is the moment when one part of the band, too, steps to the road for a brief instant.

The bassman heads for the exits by gesturing toward the dominant chord eight measures too soon, before quickly recovering.[32] The rest of the band waits for two more lines, until Dylan sings, "On the back of the fish truck that loads / While my conscious explodes." The contrast between these two moments, the moment of the exiting Fiddler and the moment of the exploding conscience, suggests the tension between a closure of the debt with Johanna, and the persistence of that debt as visionary haunting. As we saw in "Chimes of Freedom," vision requires re-vision, a rewriting that sets it in a frame. The poetic form, which stabilizes the visionary experience in "Chimes of Freedom," here seems to crack under the pressure of the moment.

At one level, we might suggest that the difference between writing someone off and remaining haunted by her ghost is nothing less than the difference between pre-Rimbaud Dylan (pre-"electric" Bob Dylan, if you like) and post-Rimbaud Dylan. For stepping to the road is precisely what Dylan's persona does again and again in those early songs, as he rambles his way here and there, like a young Woody Guthrie. It evokes the moment of the early protest songs, where big political and ethical problems can be addressed with parables of injustice and outrage. The whole point of "Visions of Johanna," however, is that the ethical landscape has changed. There is no place to go. And the difference between these two lines — called to our attention by the impatient bassman — signals nothing less than the splitting of Dylan's own subjectivity in song. The Fiddler becomes the embodiment of an earlier Dylan artistic persona. That persona can quite literally write off Johanna, but she persists to haunt the "I" of the song, whose conscience is said to "explode."

How we understand the "explosion" in the form and in the performance of the song may depend on how we read the final lines. The performance suggests that "conscience," an ethical quality, is also some kind of shorthand for "consciousness," the faculty of remaining awake and holding together all of the disparate sensory impressions being evoked. If we read "conscience" as conscience, the song is about the struggle to integrate a new artistic persona with the ethical demands of an older one. If it means consciousness, the song is about the sensory overload of the moment, the experience of being "absolutely modern." At issue is whether one of these can imply the other, whether a new ethics of personal vision can replace the morality and legalism of the earlier protest music.

Nowhere is the problem of the singer's relationship to his visionary experience more dramatically set out than in 1965's "Desolation Row." It is a companion piece to "Visions of Johanna" (though written before it), to the extent that both are extended records of the visionary experience: "As Lady and I look out tonight / From Desolation Row" (p. 220), runs the last line of the first verse, to set the scene. And Dylan goes on to provide an entire menagerie of characters from history, myth, popular culture, and literature, in the service of a nightmarish vision of a contemporary society and culture marked by violence and corruption. The song ends with an expression of simultaneous disorientation and artistic control that is analogous to what he would do a year later in "Visions of Johanna." The singer turns to a friend who has sent him a letter "about the time the doorknob broke," an image connoting the impossibility of escape or movement. He admits, "Right now, I can't read too good." And he notes that all of the people mentioned in the friend's letter, while known to him, have had to be rewritten: "All these people that you mentioned / Yes, I know them they're quite lame / I had to rearrange their faces / And give them all another name" (p. 221). This, of course, is precisely what he has been doing throughout "Desolation Row," by setting up scenarios populated by figures both familiar and unfamiliar to the listener.

It matters that Dylan's character warns his friend, in the final lines of "Desolation Row," not to send any more letters unless "you mail them *from* Desolation Row" (my emphasis). Everyone is in Desolation Row, and to try to escape it is to turn your back on the truth of experience. As Rimbaud had pressured himself: "Hold the ground gained. . . . The new hour is at least very severe" (*Season*, pp. 86–87). No less striking, for this powerful vision of chaos, is Dylan's remarkable development of melody. Whereas songs such as "Chimes of Freedom" and "The Times They Are a-Changin'" had featured insistence on a single note for the penultimate melody line, before the resolution, "Desolation Row" shows how far his approach has evolved from his earliest efforts. The beautiful leaps in the melody line, from the shouted high notes ("Right now, I can't read too good") to the pointed rhyme words an octave lower ("no more letters, no"), offer both a high-energy confrontation with the confusion of modern life and an implicit claim that it can be wrestled into some kind of order through the miraculous vehicles of rhyme, melody, and what Rimbaud called "Number" and "Harmony."

The strange fauna that peoples the world of "Desolation Row" shows both the resources and the limits of the visionary mode. Whereas early Dylan followed in the tradition of the protest song by creating mini-dramas of injustice and prejudice based on specific characters — Hattie Carroll, Hollis Brown, etc. — some of whom actually existed, his mid-1960s work shifts to a kind of montage technique, whereby names are snapped into place to suggest larger social and political identities. This generates a fresco effect, in which diverse figures jostle each other for our attention. Some are familiar names taken from popular culture or history (Bette Davis, Paul Revere). Others are less familiar or presented as if we were supposed to know their provenance (Mack the Finger, Angel, Napoleon in Rags). They create atmosphere through a kind of shorthand. The fauna of "Highway 61 Revisited" suggests blues or African American culture. "Desolation Row" is peopled by figures from mainstream white culture and Hollywood. On occasion, we seem to be witnessing the unfolding of a roman à clef, with the names changed to protect the participants. Yet at other times Dylan simply seems to be dropping names and references. This, of course, is one of the features of his style that will be most imitated by his contemporaries, for soon jugglers, clowns, wizards, and freaks will find their way into any number of popular recordings during the late 1960s and early 1970s.

Yet at the same time this naming technique produces its own political space. Thus 1965's "Tombstone Blues" moves through its final verse as follows:

> Where Ma Rainey and Beethoven once unwrapped a bedroll
> Tuba players now rehearse around the flag pole
> And the national bank at a profit sells road maps for the soul
> To the old folks' home and the college (p. 208)

There is no more powerful condemnation of the administered life than the final two lines just cited. Dylan sees into the workings of capitalism, its emptying of the spirit, and its reliance on slick patriotism, brilliantly evoked by the phrase "national bank." At one level, the first line might be a rewriting of Chuck Berry's "Roll Over Beethoven" (now we know who Ludwig was with when he rolled over!). But at another level there is a meditation here on history, fiction, and place. Dylan's clever linkage of "high culture" (Beethoven, 1770–1827) and "popular culture" (Ma Rainey, 1886–1939) to offer some vision of an earlier spirituality that has now been eroded is itself a fiction — a fiction, moreover, that can only come from his own particular moment. These two musicians can be in dialogue only in a world in which the riches of music history are being made available to the alert listener through the technology of the long-playing record. Dylan's establishment of a site ("*where* Ma Rainey and Beethoven") of some earlier cultural integrity is itself an act of the political and cultural imagination.

If there is ethical impulse in these visionary moments, it is no longer expressed through the evocation of the "misdemeanor outlaw" and the "mistitled prostitute" of "Chimes of Freedom." Most listeners cannot even identify figures such as Georgia Sam, Doctor Filth, or Poor Howard or point to them as the referential grounds for the songs. But they offer a kind of shorthand raw material for intrigues of love, betrayal, and cultural anger. In this regard, they offer the answer to the question, posed on *Another Side*, of who "is better" or "different" than whom. "I'm just average, common too," sings Dylan on that album, adding later that Ramona is a fool to say that she's "better than no one." Now Dylan's persona surrounds himself with half-imagined fictional characters. "You see, you're just like me" (p. 246), he snarls to the Tea Preacher in "Stuck Inside of Mobile." If many of the songs during this period are built on jabs at pretentious hangers-on and rivals, the targets of the singer's sarcasm are easy prey, since they bear names that you can't look up in the telephone book. He expands the critical impulse beyond the specific targets of the early work (racism, war, injustice) to include "straight" society itself. This is achieved by emptying characters of content and turning them into surfaces, ciphers for social types. Plot and scenario then come to dominate character.

This process reaches an apogee of sorts in "Desolation Row," where the singer creates his own private vocabulary of types — Romeo, the Fortune Telling Lady, the Blind Commissioner, and so on. And all he can do at the close of the song is to point to his own writing process: "I had to rearrange their faces / And give them all another name." Here, as in "Visions of Johanna," the writing self both acknowledges the chaos of being "absolutely modern" and underscores the writer's limited power over images. Visionary style mediates the struggle between the material and the hand that records it. Yet it is not clear whether the "lameness" of these faces was the cause or the effect of their rearrangement. "Chimes of Freedom" stressed the redemptive power of "rearranging," of visionary art as the response to injustice. "Desolation Row" is less clear about it.

Thus, the development of a visionary poetics necessarily places pressure on the limited song forms that Dylan deploys, and his work during this period dramatizes his struggle with form and vision. We move from vision, to an interrogation of the status of the artist, to an attempt to write illumination into the form of the song itself. The pressure Dylan's investment in being "absolutely modern" places on popular song involves not only a poetry that would grab all of our senses — visual, aural, tactile, olfactory (with that stinking "fish truck") — but also, on occasion, the very shaping of the performance itself. Dylan's work explores the fragility of that experience in song, while staging his own struggle to control it.

"To Each Being It Seemed to Me That Several Other Lives Were Due"

Dylan's work after *Blonde on Blonde*, following his motorcycle accident in 1966, withdraws from the edge of experience that I have been calling the visionary mode. These changes are developed across the songs on 1967's *John Wesley Harding* and on the influential *Basement Tapes* sessions that Dylan recorded during this period with The Band. Much has been written about these latter recordings, which have taken on importance for biographically oriented scholars of Dylan's work. Formally they mark no major departure from Dylan's other compositions during this period. A number are still about small-group dynamics ("Nothing Was Delivered," "This Wheel's on Fire"). Others, such as "I Shall Be Released," take us into the territory of the *John Wesley Harding* album, where we find the reestablishment of the relationship of subject and object that had been blurred in such songs as "Visions of Johanna" and "Mr. Tambourine Man."

John Wesley Harding returns to themes of vision, but now the poetic landscape has changed. This is most evident in "I Dreamed I Saw St. Augustine," a reworking of the old labor ballad, "I Dreamed I Saw Joe Hill," where the vision is now of a figure who imposes a clear moral injunction on the dreamer, an overwhelming feeling of guilt and eventual tears. After having gazed on Saint Augustine's glory the singer says, "I put my fingers against the glass / I bowed my head and cried" (p. 280). No such catharsis awaited the narrator of "Visions of Johanna."

The fauna of these songs is in large measure distinct from the name-dropping lists seen on *Highway 61 Revisited* and *Blonde on Blonde*.

In lieu of figures such as Mack the Finger, Louie the King, and Einstein, we now get a set of songs about clear social types: the Landlord, the Drifter, the Immigrant, the tempting Fairest Damsel, or Frankie Lee, the Gambler. It's almost as if Dylan had returned to his early 1960s interest in institutional power and pried loose a set of figures who function in different ways on the edges of those institutions. However, they are not actual people (Hattie Carroll), but rather types, or placeholders in a social equation. Dylan uses these figures to set up dramas of responsibility that are more accessible than the private intrigues of *Blonde on Blonde*, and more universal than the journalistic reporting of some of the early work. This allows Dylan to focus on plot, setting up narratives of hope and despair into which listeners can project themselves. In contrast to the immobilities of *Blonde on Blonde*, the stories now are about reconciliation, about being freed or gaining respect. The moral pronouncements or conclusions offered in much of the early work are also missing, leading one to think that there is some type of hidden (allegorical) message floating around in the world of the songs. What we learn from these songs is that certainties are hard to come by. "Nothing is revealed" (p. 282) says the end of "The Ballad of Frankie Lee and Judas Priest." "If you cannot bring good news, then don't bring any" (p. 291), says "The Wicked Messenger" in conclusion. What is presented in lieu of knowledge is a kind of generosity. "Please don't underestimate me" (p. 286), says the narrator of "Dear Landlord," "and I won't underestimate you."

These characteristics are on display in the album's most famous cut, "All Along the Watchtower," a minor-key, up-tempo tune that was reworked immediately as an electric jam vehicle by Jimi Hendrix. Here we can still see the metamorphic energy of Rimbaud's "I is someone else" at work, but in ways quite different from the masking/unmasking dynamic of the preceding three albums. The song presents two figures, the Joker and the Thief, who are overwhelmed by circumstances. They are robbed by "businessmen" and "ploughmen." We might well see here an allegory of the entertainment business, with artists exploited by managers. It is worth noting that already, from the get-go, we are dealing, not with characters we know, but with metaphors of . . . something. When the third verse opens, the scenario is rearranged, and the already allegorical characters change into something else. The swindlers reappear as "princes" watching from their fortress. The Joker and the Thief return as two mysterious marauders who have come to claim what is theirs: "Two riders were approaching / The wind began to howl" (p. 281) run the last two lines.

Rimbaud had explored similar shifts in scenography in the brief prose poems of *Illuminations*, where lapidary descriptions of scenes disclose hints that other scenes or scenarios lie latent inside them. Thus, for example, in a poem entitled "Bridges," a tangle of cables is also a tangle of musical strings — and a tangle of musical strings is a tangle of cables. One referential register resides inside the other; neither dominates; the relationship is bridged, as it were, by the double meaning of "Bridges," as architecture and music. These are two moments of the different "lives" that Rimbaud posits for all creatures: "To each being it seemed to me that several *other* lives were due." Similarly, in the Dylan song, no narrative mediation links the Joker and the Thief of stanzas one and two to the "two riders" of stanza three. It is not as if we begin with a "literal" Joker who turns into a "metaphorical" marauder. The Joker is already a metaphor, standing in for some other type, presumably an artist. In the song, neither identity is a figure of the other. Joker and marauder exist in equipoise, and it is not clear whether we are to assume that all artists are marauders, or vice versa. The claustrophobia of "Visions of Johanna" is now recalled: "There must be some way outta here," begins the lyric (p. 281). Yet it is resolved through an oblique metamorphosis of the characters into their doubles. "All Along the Watchtower" emblematizes the process through which Dylan's writing both inscribes and uncovers multiple layers of identity.

The density of figuration is replayed in the performance and in the harmony of the tune, which consists of two chords, C♯ minor and A major, that are very close in sound and construction. The only break in this dense structure is the one-beat passing chord, a B major, which, like a swimmer emerging for an instant to grab a breath, renders perceptible the otherwise murky alternation between C♯ minor and A. The repeated cycling of the guitar from one chord to another suggests the unresolved struggle that is set forth in the lyric. However, the apparent impasse of the harmony is finally broken open by Dylan's carefully controlled vocal performance, which rises in intensity and pitch to recast the melody as we move into the final verse. The dramatic vocal modulation ushers in the apocalyptic scenario in which the Joker and the Thief return to claim their due.

"All Along the Watchtower" points to how Dylan's work after

Blonde on Blonde begins to move past the poetics of vision that I have argued marks his work in the mid-1960s. Dylan's turn to "vision music," announced in the San Francisco press conference, was, as we have seen, not merely a substitution of an electric sound for his acoustic guitar and harmonica. It involved an entire recalibration of his use of imagery, his relationship to language, his self-description, even the tempo of performance. However, as visionary poetics expands the songwriting palette, it also imposes scenarios in which the narrative self is immobilized, limited in its ethical reach, forced to reflect on the processes of creation — on the rearrangement of faces.

"All Along the Watchtower," which narrates the evasion of that impasse, points toward Dylan's exploration of new territory in the late 1960s, when he turns, on such albums as *John Wesley Harding*, *The Basement Tapes*, and *Self Portrait*, to narratives of redemption or reconciliation peopled not by victims of injustice such as Hattie Carroll but by invented heroes and survivors — Quinn the Eskimo, the "gypsy" (of "Went to See the Gypsy"), the "drifter" (of "Drifter's Escape"), the miner Tom Moore (in the folk song "Days of Forty-Nine"), the outlaw Wes Hardin. This heroic strain in Dylan's writing would expand steadily through his work in the early 1970s, reaching its apogee on *Desire*, released in 1976, the same year as the American bicentennial celebrations.

Throughout this process Rimbaud would modulate from being a model of the poetic visionary to a type of the vagabond and a figure of memorialization. This is in part an exigency of Dylan's own career path. Rimbaud could reject the past in his poetry and then reject his poetry as the past by decamping for Java and East Africa. Dylan was compelled to stick around, having decamped only as far as Woodstock, and, later, Malibu. A 1974 album recorded with The Band, chronicling Dylan's return to live performance, was named *Before the Flood* — a nod to the first poem in Rimbaud's *Illuminations*, "After the Flood." A bit later, on 1975's *Blood on the Tracks*, Dylan evokes the doomed love of Rimbaud and Paul Verlaine as a model that he has left behind for a crimson-haired lady. Here Rimbaud makes a repeat appearance as an unhappy lover, as just another name to be dropped. Yet a year later, in the liner notes to *Desire*, Dylan will begin with the phrase, "On the Heels of Rimbaud."[33] No longer "walkin' a road" trod by Woody Guthrie, as he had claimed on his first album, Dylan has found new models. His style has diversified too.

CHAPTER FOUR

Tangled Generation: Memory, Desire,

and the Poetics of Escape

Seen against the background of his grandly chaotic mid-1960s work, Dylan's recording in the last years of the 1960s and early years of the new decade appears decidedly low-key. The stripped-down sound of John Wesley Harding *(1967) gives way to the warm glow of 1969's collection of country love songs,* Nashville Skyline. *Several other collections follow, including the ill-favored* Self Portrait *(1970), a collection of mostly covers,* New Morning *(1970), and the hastily recorded* Planet Waves *(1974). Dylan takes a small role in a film, does the soundtrack, and makes a few concert appearances. In 1974 he returns to regular touring, in the company of The Band. At the end of that year comes perhaps his most unified and polished album,* Blood on the Tracks, *followed by the elegant coauthored collection* Desire *(1976) and the larger, horn-backed sound of* Street Legal *(1978). He takes to the road with a group of friends to perform as The Rolling Thunder Review.*

"Demonstrators found our house and paraded up and down in front of it chanting and shouting, demanding for me to come out and lead them somewhere—stop shirking my duties as the conscience of a generation. The neighbors hated us. To them it must have seemed like I was something out of a carnival show."[1] So writes Dylan in *Chronicles: Volume One* about his life in the late 1960s. Having given up performing several years earlier following the motorcycle accident, Dylan was in semiretirement, raising a family. Yet, at the same time, in the larger public imagination, he was expected and assumed to be everywhere, including the famous Woodstock Festival that was associated with him because of his residence in the village of Woodstock at an earlier moment. Indeed, the more Dylan was absent in the late

1960s, the more he was present. His existence in the popular imagination was precisely that of a specter.

The personal consequences of this situation were clearly difficult, as Dylan's comment indicates. Yet Dylan's depiction of his situation also raises two related but distinct aesthetic problems that can help us grasp the poetics of his work in the mid-1970s. They involve both his relationship to his audience (which we considered back in Chapter 2) and his relationship to history—to, as it were, his sense of the modern. The first of these problems involves what happens when an artist is overcome or threatened by his own popularity. The response of Dylan's public to his work (or lack thereof) was the consequence of his having been pigeonholed as a particular kind of antiestablishment artist. In this regard, Dylan's fate is not unlike that of any number of artists who have had to flee their publics. We might think, for example, of J. D. Salinger, whose retirement from publishing novels seems to have been linked to his very success publishing novels. Perhaps the classic instance of flight from one's audience is the case of the French novelist Romain Gary, who invented an alter ego, Emile Ajar, under whose name he published four novels and won France's most prestigious literary award, the Prix Goncourt, in 1975. This prize could come, Gary wrote later, only because he had abandoned his identity and legacy. As Romain Gary, "I was an author who was classified, catalogued, taken for granted," he wrote. This process of "classification" by the public, he notes, is a recent phenomenon; we might locate it, I suggest, in the post–World War II era, since it reflects the rise to dominance of quickly produced media such as the long-playing record and the paperback novel.[2]

This brings us to the second problem faced by Dylan, which is his status as the "voice of a generation." His association with the so-called 1960s generation (evoked by his canny characterization of the fans outside his house as "demonstrators") poses the problem of how figures associated with particular generational moments may break free from those moments. In Dylan's case his outsized influence in the mid-1960s, combined with his retirement, had led to massive expectations surrounding any new work. Like the aging Lester Young, who had to suffer hearing his own jazz saxophone style played back to him by younger imitators, Dylan's own work had become frozen in time and its mannerisms appropriated by younger artists who currently dominated the scene. Thus, he had to struggle against the competition, as well as against his earlier self (or selves). This marked a step beyond his earlier adaptations of work by illustrious predecessors. Out of this situation came a kind of creative renaissance, in the form of a record entitled *Blood on the Tracks*, recorded in 1974, the year of Watergate, and released in early 1975, the moment of the fall of Saigon. It is perhaps Dylan's strongest album. It is also his elegy to and escape from the 1960s. It is followed, a year later, by *Desire*, which picks up on some of the same themes and explores their implications.

Both *Blood on the Tracks* and its companion piece, *Desire*, work out solutions to the weight of the past and the expectations of the "demonstrators." The first of these recordings I locate, not in post-Woodstock nostalgia, but, rather, in a denser and more archaic literary tradition that informs its poetics. Through the carefully considered use of earlier writers, among them Jack Kerouac and the Italian Renaissance poet Francesco Petrarca, or Petrarch, Dylan confronts the myth of the Sixties and effects a stylistic transition in his own songwriting. This transition, I argue, unfolds across these two seminal mid-1970s recordings, expanding in interesting, if limited, ways as we move from *Blood on the Tracks* to *Desire*.

Tracks
It is as both an escape and the record of a struggle that we might understand the ambiguity of the title of *Blood on the Tracks*, in which the "tracks" may refer to some image of a train that has run someone down, the tracks of a fugitive whom the singer either incarnates or is seen to pursue, or the tracks — the songs — of the record itself. This density of allusion motivates the several levels on which the album works. On one level, it would seem to be an account of Dylan's breakup with his first wife, Sara. Yet it is also a meditation on literary history and on the problem of poetry's relationship to political upheaval. It offers a poetic and musical engagement with the problem of the weight of the past — personally, politically, and artistically.

As an explicit reflection on the 1960s generation that Dylan had both inspired and fled, the album evokes a whole series of earlier generational pronouncements in American literature, from Horace Greeley's "Go West" to Hemingway's "Lost Generation" to Allen Ginsberg's "best minds of my generation" at the outset of "Howl." However, it is also deeply indebted to a slightly different "generational" text that rose to canonical status as a meditation on

American life just as Dylan was coming of age—a text that defined, as would Dylan's own work, not merely a cultural/historical category (as had, for example, the Spanish literary "Generation of 1927") but also a new form of social identity. This text is Jack Kerouac's "beat" novel *On the Road,* first published in 1957. *Blood on the Tracks* is Dylan's rewriting of *On the Road.* It marks a step beyond Dylan's earlier adaptations of various folk song prototypes, studied in our first two chapters.[3]

Kerouac, too, wrestled with his status as generational artist. For the very success of *On the Road* turned him into a popular icon of a particular "generational" moment. As early as 1960 he wrote in a notebook, "Realized last night how truly sick I am of being a 'writer' and 'beat'—it's not me at all—yet everybody keeps hammering it into me .... They're going to insist that I fit their preconceived notion of the 'Beatnik Captain.'" These lines prefigure the regret and anger that informs the lines from Dylan's memoirs with which I began this chapter. Both artists were pigeonholed by their own adoring publics. Kerouac was consumed by this dynamic. He spent the 1960s struggling with a variety of writing projects, many of which were closely related to and informed by time on the road. The model of the writer as anticonformist pilgrim was both essential to Kerouac's writing process and the machine that swallowed up his creativity.[4]

Central to the poetics of *Blood on the Tracks* is an appropriation of the topography of *On the Road. Blood on the Tracks* offers a set of narratives of pursuit and loss across Jack Kerouac's version of the American landscape, evoking all four cardinal points and several well-known landmarks. It is significant that Dylan should have chosen Kerouac's map of America, since it was that map—much more than, say, Woody Guthrie's—that had shaped the cultural mythologies of the 1960s, the very period on which Dylan was offering commentary. The album's topography pointedly marks a break with Dylan's earlier evocations of landscape and territory. As we saw earlier, the Guthrie-like "rambling" themes of the early albums give way, in the middle years of the 1960s, to several collections of songs about being stuck in space. This is most powerful on *Blonde on Blonde* (1966), where we hear again and again about figures who cannot move: "Visions of Johanna," with its characters "stuck here stranded" (p. 242); the singer of "Absolutely Sweet Marie," who is in prison after having been caught in "the frozen traffic" (p. 252); and, of course, the hero of "Stuck Inside of Mobile," who is, well, stuck. At one level, this paralysis reflects the ubiquity of the long-playing record itself. You can't ramble away down the road if your own picture meets your gaze from every shop window.

The immobility depicted on the mid-1960s albums then mutates as we move toward the end of the decade. *John Wesley Harding*, from 1967, the first post-accident album, offers a series of meditations on reconciliation and generosity toward one's neighbors, toward the immigrant, the landlord, the drifter. Yet, it is followed by a kind of sapping of dramatic energy. What stands out from such albums as *Nashville Skyline* (1969), *New Morning* (1970), *Planet Waves* (1974), and even the double album of mostly covers, *Self Portrait* (1970), is the sense of stasis. These records are noteworthy for the number of songs in which nothing happens. "All the tired horses in the sun / How'm I supposed to get any riding done" (p. 344), writes Dylan on *Self Portrait*. We see the singer involved in erotic dramas in which there is no drama at all; the object of desire is close at hand and seems to be ready for action. All that is required is to turn off the light, lock the door, or unplug the phone (see "To Be Alone with You," "I'll Be Your Baby Tonight," "On a Night like This," "Lay, Lady, Lay," "You Angel You," "Tonight I'll Be Staying Here with You," "Hazel"). In other songs, the point simply seems to be to acknowledge and celebrate the fact that things are already going well and that we're glad they are ("New Morning," "Winterlude," "Wedding Song" "Time Passes Slowly," "If Not for You," "The Man in Me," "Country Pie"). When things don't go well, what's needed is often simply a quick reset ("One More Weekend," "Tell Me that It Isn't True"). Certainly, on a biographical level, songs like these reflect aspects of Dylan's own situation—married, financially and professionally secure, away from the stresses of touring, raising a family. Notwithstanding the craft and beauty of many of these compositions, they are marked by an absence of the drama and irony that lent character to such earlier compositions as, say, "Boots of Spanish Leather" (1964), "She Belongs to Me" (1965), "Spanish Harlem Incident" (1964), and "Love Minus Zero/No Limit" (1965). "Stare straight ahead and try so hard to stay right" (p. 362), writes Dylan in *New Morning*'s "Time Passes Slowly." It's a fine rule to live by, but it seems a good deal less interesting than being stuck "inside the frozen traffic" (not to mention being "lost in the rain in Juarez" [p. 218]) back on *Blonde on Blonde* or *Highway 61*.

The mid-1960s work offers dramas of immobility and disorienta-
tion that are crises of self and commitment. The flip side of this coin
is domestic bliss. Domestic art assumes that the listener or reader
is already a fan, wanting to check in on what our familiar bard is up
to, to follow the foibles and pleasures of her or his interesting life. It
paints stories that unfold apart from the experience of the casual lis-
tener, with little universal or general relationship to larger collective
experience. So, in "Day of the Locusts," we learn Dylan has received
an award, but that the ceremony made him uncomfortable. In "Went
to See the Gypsy," he goes to meet someone famous, but the meeting
is a bust. In "Something There Is about You," a woman reminds him
of somebody he once knew. It's comforting art, but not very compel-
ling. This is why the emphasis on movement, crisis, and adventure
that marks *Blood on the Tracks* and *Desire* is so vivifying.

As noted, the scene changes with *Blood on the Tracks*, where Dylan
locates us in the fast-moving America of Jack Kerouac. The album
makes specific reference to the same literary terrain as *On the Road*.
Dylan's closing lament on side one of the original LP, in "You're
Gonna Make Me Lonesome When You Go," that, "I'll look for you in
old Honolulu, / San Francisco, Ashtabula" (p. 339), recalls the numer-
ous catalogues of American place names that lace *On the Road* (includ-
ing the narrator Sal Paradise's song "Home in Missoula, / Home in
Truckee, / Home in Opelousas, / Ain't no Home for me" [p. 208]).[5]
The album evokes the San Francisco where much of *On the Road*
takes place, the Tangier where William S. Burroughs (or Bull Lee,
as Kerouac calls him) wrote *Naked Lunch*, as well as the somewhat
surprising landmark of Ashtabula, Ohio, which is mentioned by Sal
as the first landmark on his westward journey ("countryfolk getting
on at one Penn town after another, till we got on the plain of Ohio
and really rolled, up by Ashtabula and straight across Indiana in the
night" [p. 13]). The "diamond mine" and "gambling hall" town of the
shaggy-dog tale "Lily, Rosemary and the Jack of Hearts" recall, if
anything, an important location on the maps of both writers — the
Colorado mining town turned tourist trap of Central City, where
Sal Paradise, Dean Moriarty, and their friends spend a wild weekend
early in the *On the Road*, looking for the romance of the Old West and
finding only curio shops. By a nice coincidence, Dylan's first profes-
sional singing job was in a honky-tonk in the same town, just after his
graduation from high school.

Trips

Beyond this common geography, *Blood on the Tracks* draws explic-
itly on a central motif of *On the Road*, which is the impromptu auto
journey of escape into adventure. The wild car journey followed by
breakdown is central to *On the Road*. It appears most vividly toward
the end of the novel, when Sal and Dean split up in Mexico City, leav-
ing a landscape of wreckage, both emotional and mechanical, behind
them. Dylan deploys this motif several times on *Blood on the Tracks*.
It is evoked in its genesis in "Meet Me in the Morning," the first song
on side two of the original LP, where the singer promises his love
that "We could be in Kansas / By the time the snow begins to thaw"
(p. 489). It is also evoked as a figure for doomed love in "Tangled Up
in Blue," the opening song on the album, where the singer steals his
beloved away from her disapproving parents only to run things into
the ground too quickly: "We drove that car as far as we could / Aban-
doned it out west / Split up on a dark sad night / Both agreeing it
was best" (p. 480). The escape on the road is both the sign of promise
and the sign of failure.[7] Later, on *Desire*, the motif of the journey is
expanded, as we are given songs about travel into magical landscapes
and exotic lands where characters seem to lose their identities and
from which they come back changed.

On *Blood on the Tracks*, all of these journeys are marked by a dense
relationship between literary allusion and self-mystification. The
journey of "Meet in the Morning" is to begin at "56th and Wabasha"
(p. 489). These are two streets in Minneapolis, where Dylan briefly
attended college before heading east to New York. It turns his escape
from the Midwest, a solitary journey in the winter, into a promise of
new life as "the snow begins to thaw." Just as "Lily, Rosemary and the
Jack of Hearts" reinvests the touristy mining town with romance,
these songs reinvent Dylan's biography through Kerouac's narrative
scenography and geographical motifs.

We can see this most clearly in the depiction of a slightly dif-
ferent journey — one that coincides with the action of entering
from quotidian reality into the special magical world of adven-
ture and travel. This involves travel by thumb. It is mentioned in
"Tangled Up in Blue," where we hear of the singer "standing on the
side of the road / Rain falling on my shoes / Heading out for the
East Coast / Lord knows I've paid some dues / Gettin' through"
(p. 480). There is an autobiographical dimension to this reference,

since Dylan left college in Minnesota for fame in New York by hitch-hiking in the dead of winter.[8] However, it also evokes the first journey of Kerouac's hero Sal Paradise. Dylan escapes middle America by thumb to discover New York. Sal leaves New York by thumb to discover middle America. Dylan's landscape on *Blood on the Tracks* is neither simple autobiography nor some "America" lost in the mists of time, but a self-conscious appropriation of the topography of another text, Kerouac's text, that lends personal reference generational resonance.

Yet, if Dylan's "generational" meditation is heavy with literary self-consciousness, what of Kerouac's? *On the Road* opens with the narrator reflecting on his initial meeting with Dean Moriarty. This, he says, was not long after the breakup of his marriage, and his "weary feeling that everything was dead. With the coming of Dean Moriarty began the part of my life you could call my life on the road" (p. 5). There is an influential literary model, set explicitly on a "road," that begins in death and passes back to life. This literary model is Dante's *Divine Comedy*, a text that we might assume is of some importance for a novel whose Italian American narrator's full name is Salvatore Paradiso. It will be remembered that the *Divine Comedy* opens with an allegorical scene of retreat. Lost on the path (or road, *cammino*) of "our life," stuck in a terrifying valley "that had pierced my heart with fear," Dante seeks to ascend to the mountain of illumination. However, he is repulsed by three allegorical beasts: a wolf, a lion, and a leopard. He then turns back and pursues his journey downward instead of upward, passing through Hell, Purgatory, and, eventually, Paradise.[9]

A similar failure of ascent marks Sal Paradise's excited departure, by thumb, for "the West." He sets out to hitchhike to California, heading north from New York City with the plan of catching Route 6, a road said to run from Cape Cod, via Ely, Nevada, to Los Angeles (the city of angels): "I'll just stay on 6 all the way to Ely, I said to myself and confidently started. To get to 6 I had to go up to Bear Mountain" (p. 12). But such is not to be, as, like Dylan's protagonist hitching east, our hero gets caught in a massive rainstorm: "It began to rain in torrents when I was let off there. It was mountainous. Route 6 came over the river, wound around a traffic circle, and disappeared into the wilderness... the rain came down in buckets and I had no shelter" (p. 12). Already we can hear echoes here of Dylan's song titles "Shelter from the Storm" and "Buckets of Rain." But what is most important is that this storm is more than a rainstorm. It is an allegorical deluge in which the landscape itself comes alive: "High up over my head the great hairy Bear Mountain sent down thunderclaps that put the fear of God in me. All I could see were smoky trees and dismal wilderness rising to the skies. 'What the hell am I doing up here?' I cursed, I cried for Chicago" (pp. 12–13). Like Dante's allegorical beasts on the mountain, Kerouac's mountain becomes an allegorical beast in its own right, a "hairy Bear" whose threats to his progress leave him stuck in the valley of "dismal wilderness" until he wises up, returns to New York City, and, like Dante going down through Hell, takes the low road to the West — via the Holland Tunnel. The modulation to his new life then begins a few pages later as he wakes up in a hotel in Des Moines (the city of monks): "Really I didn't know who I was for about fifteen strange seconds. I wasn't scared; I was just somebody else, some stranger, and my whole life was a haunted life, the life of a ghost. I was halfway across America, at the dividing line between the East of my youth and the West of my future, and maybe that's why it happened right there and then, that red afternoon" (p. 16). *Incipit vita nova*, writes Dante in the story of his own conversion to love, "the new life begins."[10]

The landscape of *On the Road* is both infernal and paradisiacal, blending moments of bliss and scenes of torment. Indeed, that ambiguity is one of the characteristics of post-Dantean literature, as the great metaphysical system of medieval Catholicism that Dante draws upon gives way to less rigid literary landscapes. Yet if the *Inferno* provides a narrative substructure for the opening passages of *On the Road*, for Sal's entry into the world of narrative adventure, Dante is no less important for the novel's end and his exit from that same world. At the end of *Paradiso*, Dante looks into the Godhead and is overcome by a vision that transcends his powers; his "high fantasy" or *alta fantasia* fails. This overcoming of the self is what makes possible the transformation of the pilgrim, the traveler whose adventures we have just been following, into the poet, who will write those adventures down.[11] Kerouac rewrites this moment of transcendent vision. "We had reached the approaches of the last plateau," recounts Sal as they pull into Mexico City. "'Man, man,' I yelled to Dean, 'wake up and see the shepherds, wake up and see the golden world that Jesus came from'... now we were about to reach the end of the road" (p. 246). And a moment later, as Dean and Sal prowl the streets of Mexico City, Sal acknowledges that the end has come:

This was the great and final wild uninhibited
Fellahin-childlike city that we knew we would find at
the end of the road. Dean walked through it with his
arms hanging zombie-like at his sides, his mouth open,
his eyes gleaming, and conducted a ragged and holy
tour that lasted til dawn in a field with a boy in a
straw hat who laughed and chatted with us and wanted
to play catch, for nothing ever ended. (p. 248)

Except that it does. The moment of vision with the boy-Christ breaks
as Sal suddenly collapses in the very next sentence: "Then I got fever
and became delirious and unconscious. Dysentery." At that point
Dean (whose last name, Moriarty, means "navigator" in Irish) aban-
dons him there: "Gotta get back to my life" (p. 249).[12]

Just as Dante's overwhelming vision provides him with the voca-
tion to turn around and place what he has just seen into art—Dante
the pilgrim becoming Dante the poet—so now, on the way back home
from Mexico after his collapse at the end of the road, does Sal meet a
mysterious pilgrimlike stranger who gives him a message that deter-
mines his literary vocation: "Go moan for man" (p. 250). This cryptic
message then provokes a change in Sal's relationship to his travels and
his friends—a change that involves literary genre as well as plot. A few
pages later we see him walking down a street in New York:

[I] called up to the window of a loft where I thought my friends were having a
party. But a pretty girl stuck her head out of the window and said, "Yes? Who
is it?" "Sal Paradise," I said, and heard my name resound in the sad and empty
street. "Come on up," she called. "I'm making hot chocolate." So I went up and
there she was, the girl with the pure and innocent dear eyes that I had always
searched for and for so long. We agreed to love each other madly. (p. 250)

Salvatore Paradiso would appear to have reached paradise, leaving,
for a cup of chocolate and a pretty girl, his Virgilian guide Dean back
on the road. And the name of this ideal woman, not coincidentally,
is Laura. That is, she carries the name of the beloved of Dante's most
direct literary heir, the greatest lyric poet of early modern Europe,
Francesco Petrarca. Petrarch's Laura is the girl Sal has always longed
for. He can have her and the spiritual/literary contentment he craves
if he leaves the epic journey of life on the road.[13] Like Romeo, Shake-
speare's greatest Petrarchan, all he has do to is call up to the balcony.

Having escaped the inferno, Sal can now write about it in the book we are reading. We move from experience to writing in the spiral structure of the novel, as we move from Dante to Petrarch in literary history. As Petrarch opens his *Canzoniere,* his great lyric collection, by looking back to the time "when I was in part another man from what I am now," so does Sal put an end to "the part of my life you could call my life on the road" (p. 5).[14]

Verses

It is worth reflecting for a moment on Kerouac's evocation of a literary historical shift from Dante to Petrarch. Through Petrarch Sal escapes the world of the road into which he had entered on Bear Mountain. If that journey marked the beginning of his "life on the road," the turn to Laura marks the way out of it. In the very last pages Dean reappears, but Sal and Laura reject him, encouraged by their friend Remi Boncoeur ("Remi" = rower; Boncoeur = "good-hearted," in French), and as the novel ends they drive off to listen to Duke Ellington, leaving Dean alone in the street, like Dante leaving Virgil at the end of *Purgatory*. By becoming Petrarchan, Sal can leave the "spontaneous" action of the road and the visionary Dantean poetics that inform the journey and turn to the work of imposing narrative structure on his past.

It is significant that the shift from Dante's world to Petrarch's world—from pursuit of beatitude to amorous passion—is a shift in genre, from narrative autobiography to lyric poetry. Dante had the advantage of a fixed metaphysical system through which his characters could pass as they moved toward the revelation of truth. Kerouac's poetics are based on the notion that the movements of his beat characters are spontaneous and always open to moments of visionary illumination. In literary terms this means that they are always threatening to disintegrate into aimless confusion—as any reader who tries to follow the plot of *On the Road* has noticed. However, the form of the loosely organized autobiographical lyric sequence—Petrarch's invention—responds to that narrative pressure. Petrarch's major collection of lyric poetry, the *Canzoniere* (or "Scattered Rhymes" as they are often called), offers an account, in the form of 366 sonnets, madrigals, and *canzoni,* of the poet's obsessive love for Laura. The *Canzoniere* possesses something of the retrospective autobiographical structure of the *Divine Comedy*—the poet looks back in the first poem and reflects on his doomed and wayward passion—but without the rigidity of allegorical narrative and with little of its visionary power. In place of Dante's model of a long journey through Hell toward his beloved Beatrice, Petrarch offers a series of sonnets and songs that describe the impact on him of a beautiful golden-haired woman who is both omnipresent and evanescent. The *Canzoniere* depicts the poet's first glimpsing of Laura, the impact of her beauty on him and his devoted love, despite her coldness. When she dies partway through the collection, it expresses his grief and evokes the memory of her beauty. Petrarch's constant punning on her name, Laura, which is homonymic with the Italian word for "breeze," *l'aura*, shapes the tension between her presence and absence throughout the collection. Never glimpsed entire, evoked only through the description of her body parts, Laura is never wholly present, yet she haunts the poet. Petrarch's fragmentation of her person powers his poetic fragmentation of the great Dantean visionary poetic model. That fragmentation in turn celebrates the poet's own power to sing of the love that he creates in song. The collection is marked by startling descriptions of the power of love over the poet. These are matched by ironic depictions of the lover's self-deception and blindness to his own folly—depictions generated by the sonnet form itself, with its multiple moments and angles of perception set in juxtaposition. Petrarch's poetic example, which shaped and dominated the history of the sonnet up to at least the nineteenth century, offers a literary phenomenology of the relationship of desire and memory through a series of discrete but related moments of intense lyric experience.[15]

This is the literary form that Bob Dylan picks up from the end of *On the Road*. It breaks with the visionary poetics of Dante and of Kerouac, as well as with what Dylan called his own "vision music" of the 1960s—that music we explored in Chapter 3. *Blood on the Tracks* is Dylan's evasive rewriting of Kerouac's visionary poetics, through the form of Petrarchan lyric, but set in Kerouac's very own invented American landscape.[16] It is a song cycle, the most unified of all of Dylan's myriad albums. It gives us a series of moments that appear to recount the genesis, flowering, and disintegration of a heterosexual love relationship between the singer and a woman with "red" or "crimson" hair. This affair corresponds, chronologically, to the 1960s. In the context of the larger cultural work done by the album, the question of whether or not it is an account of Dylan's marriage is of secondary importance. The biographical angle is of interest to the extent it puts Dylan, at the time of the breakup, at the same juncture as Kerouac's Sal Paradise, who takes to the road "not long after my wife and I split up" (p. 5).[17] What matters for us is that it is a modern Petrarchan lyric sequence, leading from the *innamoramento* or lightning-bolt falling-in-love scene of "Simple Twist of Fate," through the seductive promise of "Meet Me in the Morning," the bitter jealousy of "You're a Big Girl Now," the long, *canzone*-like political rant of "Idiot Wind" (with its denunciation of the fiasco of Vietnam), the mythography of "Shelter from the Storm" (where "shelter" offers a version of Laura's gift of hot chocolate to Sal, saving him from the "sad and empty street"), the self-deceptive lament of "You're Gonna Make Me Lonesome When You Go," to the resigned irony of the closing blues, "Buckets of Rain." Dylan takes his distance from Kerouac by appropriating his landscape and recasting it, without embracing its visionary, Dantesque, poetics.

In "You're Gonna Make Me Lonesome When You Go," Dylan points toward the new postvisionary poetics that *Blood on the Tracks* explores. There the singer evokes the homosexual poetic passion of the French poets Paul Verlaine and Arthur Rimbaud. The latter, as we have seen, is both the author of the Dantean *Season in Hell* and a Dylan influence during the 1960s. Together they offer the literary prototypes for Kerouac's Dean and Sal, the brilliant delinquent Dean/Rimbaud adored by the more sedate and literary Sal/Verlaine. "Situations have ended sad / Relationships have all gone bad," sings Dylan. "Mine have been like Verlaine and Rimbaud." Now, however, he rejects that paradigm: "There's just no way I can compare / All them scenes to this affair / You're gonna make me lonesome when you go" (p. 506). The pairing of the two great Symbolist seer poets yields to a heterosexual obsession of a Petrarchan poet who glimpses his evanescent love everywhere: "I'll see you in the sky above, in the tall grass, and the ones I love," says Dylan. "Thus," notes Petrarch, "I go searching in others, Lady, as much as is possible, for your longed-for true form."[18]

The entire sequence of *Blood on the Tracks* is overseen, as it were, by the powerful opening track, "Tangled Up in Blue." This song, one of Dylan's major compositions, recounts the disjointed story of two lovers who come together, then break up, then come together and break up again. The lyrics contain, in miniature, the entire scenography of the album. The narrative, however, is anything but chronological. It offers a series of moments or flashes of experience that, when taken together, give us a more or less coherent story. The characters pursue each other but become "tangled up" in the "blue" that may suggest the blues, as well as the "azure" that for Symbolist poets like Verlaine and Rimbaud was the embodiment of the ideal.

But "Tangled Up in Blue" resonates yet more deeply with the conventions of lyric in the Petrarchan mode. Most suggestive, for my purposes, is that the song contains an explicit reference to Petrarch. As the singer meets his lost love down in Louisiana, she gives him a book of poems, "written by an Italian poet from the thirteenth century" (p. 480). Dylan's chronology is, characteristically, a bit wobbly, since Petrarch died in 1374. Some listeners have taken this as a reference to Dante. However, when questioned later in an interview about the "Italian poet" Dylan slyly answered, "Plutarch. Is that his name?"[19] In any event, we are clearly in Petrarch's emotional and psychological universe, not in Dante's.

Yet even more important than the topical reference is the fact that "Tangled Up in Blue" takes the form of a sequence of sonnets. Here we can see the value of studying these songs for their formal features—their poetics. The song is built of seven stanzas, each of which consists of fourteen lines. Each stanza divides exactly after line eight—what in sonnet criticism is called the "turn" or "volta." And each stanza operates through the contrastive perspectivism of the conventional sonnet, in which the octave sets forth a situation upon which the sestet then comments—with, in many cases, a move toward some type of dialectical resolution at the close. Thus, for example, the central stanza of "Tangled Up in Blue" begins with a narrative slice. The protagonist is in New Orleans, where he meets his old lover working in a "topless joint" and picks her up:

> She lit a burner on the stove
> And offered me a pipe
> "I thought you'd never say hello," she said
> "You look like the silent type"
> Then she opened up a book of poems
> And handed it to me
> Written by an Italian poet
> From the thirteenth century (p. 480)

So much for the scene and the octave. No hot chocolate for this wanderer, only a pipe. This is then followed by a shift in perspective, with six lines describing the impact of that narrative moment on the narrator:

> And every one of them words rang true
> And glowed like burnin' coal
> Pouring off of every page
> Like it was written in my soul
> From me to you
> Tangled up in blue.

This sonnet structure is repeated across every stanza, with a break after line eight that changes the perspective ("She turned around to look at me," "And later on, when the crowd thinned out," "But me I'm still on the road," etc.). The stanzaic scheme, with its alternating rhyming endings culminating in the couplet that ends the verse, perfectly articulates the movement of the sonnet form. This structure is probably mediated through the English tradition. Petrarch, whom Dylan wouldn't have read in the original anyway, rarely uses rhyming couplets at the ends of his poems. But Shakespeare does. So do Wyatt, Spenser, Sidney, and Donne, as well as Dante Rossetti in his translations and adaptations of early Italian lyric.[20]

This sonnetlike movement is also articulated in the musical structure of the stanza. As noted, each stanza in the song is marked by a break after eight lines. The break is musical as well as discursive. "Tangled Up in Blue" is performed in the key of A major. However, the verse opens with a powerful sequence of two-beat alternations between the tonic chord, A major, and the chord built on the flatted seventh, the G major chord. The slightly discordant move from A down to G creates a sense of tonal instability. The bass guitar is playing an A throughout. The D note in the G chord is thus suspended over the A, creating an unresolved tension. This is followed, in measure eight of the melody, by a shift to a D major chord. D is the IV chord in A major, but the pattern of A to G to D suggests that we might, in fact, not be in A major at all, but rather in D major. The inclusion of a G natural in the melody (an accidental in A, but diatonic in D) underscores this impression. In other words, the song feels (and sounds) like it could be in two different keys. This fluctuation perfectly sets up the unstable mobility that is narrated in the lyrics, since it can never find a point of rest. The opening eight lines of each stanza unfold across this wavering musical structure: "Early one morning [A major] the sun was shining [G major] I was layin' in bed [back to A major]."[21] Then, at the breaking point, midway through each stanza, the melody and the musical vocabulary shift. We move to the V chord of A, which is E major. Dylan has been singing an E note over the D chord, which makes the shift feel natural to the listener. However, instead of a simple cadence of resolution back from V to I (E back to A)—typical of thousands of popular songs and conventional in Dylan's work—we get something quite different. The V chord powers a two-measure phrase over the long lyric line ("And every one of them words rang true / And glowed like burnin' coal") that runs from V (E) to VI (F♯ m) to I (A) but then continues on up to IV (D), leaving the line musically unresolved. The gesture of beginning the lyric phrase ("And every one of them words") on the V chord or E major, together with the repetition of the movement, temporarily shifts the song to a new tonal center, distinct from what preceded, with its own set of ascending chords. In this way the musical structure offers another "point of view," to use Dylan's phrase, on the basic pattern that structures the first half of each stanza. We now have a self-sufficient progression of chords, over the last six lines of verse, a recursive movement that seems to circle, with no point of rest, like the characters of the song itself, as they wander the country from "the great north woods," to "New Orleans," from "the East Coast," to "out west."

The harmonic resolution of this movement, bringing us back firmly to A major so we can move on to the next verse, only comes in the final phrase, which, like the closing rhyming couplet of the lyric, recalls the entire previous musical vocabulary of both halves of the stanza. The concluding refrain line, "Tangled up in blue," comes over a return to the play with A major, adding a suspended D note (hinting at the G chord): "Tangled Up in Blue," and we are back to where we started. In other words, the chord sequences of the stanza offer a musical articulation of the dialectical movement of the Petrarchan sonnet. An opening narrative slice or setting of the scene is later commented on by a different musical phrase, with a different chord sequence, and different discursive register, only to reach a dialectical resolution, musically and lyrically, in the final couplet. The song is, in effect, a condensed musical sonnet sequence.

This Petrarchan structure of conflicting perspectives in both lyric and music appears again in slightly less developed, though no less interesting, terms in the eighth song on the album, "If You See Her, Say Hello," which is the song most closely linked, thematically, to "Tangled Up in Blue." Here we have a sequence of five eight-line stanzas divided equally between two four-line units of meaning. After an intro in D that echoes "Tangled," the first four lines offer a narrative context: "If you see her, say hello / She might be in Tangier / She left here last early spring / Is livin' there I hear" (p. 492). This is sung over a simple sequence of major chords, punctuated by a brief dip down to the discordant C major chord, the exact same move into discord that opens "Tangled Up in Blue" (and the only other place on the album where it occurs). The second four lines then expand and comment, shifting, in the same way as do the sonnet-like stanzas of the earlier song, from the viewpoint of one person to another: "Say for me that I'm alright / Though things get kind of slow / She might think that I've forgotten her / Don't tell her it isn't so." The chords shift as well, to a minor chord, and the melody changes. This musical break, while conventional, perfectly reflects the tension between the two halves of the stanza. For the second half is a statement marked by self-delusion that contrasts with the straightforward longing of the first four lines. That is, if you are requested, in the last four lines, not to tell her that I haven't forgotten her, why would you, in the first four lines, "say hello" in the first place, and "say for me that I'm alright," since that very act would reveal that I haven't, in fact, forgotten her. This contrast between narrative romance and ironic contradiction, linked, moreover, to the act of communication itself, is repeated in every stanza of the song. Each verse ends with the singer mouthing a statement of deluded consolation that undermines the account of the events of the affair he has just offered. This ironic display of self-delusion marks a dramatic new stage in Dylan's songwriting. It is unprecedented in his work. It is Dylan at his most Petrarchan.

Visions

As we have seen, the great Petrarchan themes of loss, self-delusion, and fragmentation are inscribed into the very form of Dylan's songs, binding the articulation of the persona's character to the performance that unfolds before us. Yet the formal tensions I have described within the lyric stanza—articulated most powerfully in "Tangled Up in Blue"—have larger implications that take us back to the questions of literary history and "generational" identity with which I began. The movement of the sonnet form—and of Dylan's stanzas—works through a logic of perspective. Conventional to the Petrarchan sonnet is a formula in which, for example, the poet speaks in his first eight lines of one aspect of his experience before turning, at the midpoint, to reinterpret what he has just said. Thus, to take a couple of fairly random examples, in poem 133 of his *Canzoniere*, Petrarch offers up eight lines of questions about his love. How can he be so miserable and so happy at once? What kind of love can seize you, even if you don't agree to it? But then he breaks off, in line nine, to focus on his own situation ("I shiver in midsummer, burn in winter") describing his suffering and what the love he has just spoken of so abstractly does to his body. The shift from one half of the poem to the other involves a change of approach; it is a shift from philosophical questioning to the depiction of personal experience. In the following poem he reverses the approach: he describes what love is doing to him for eight lines ("I am hoarse, Lady, with calling for mercy"), then he backs up and offers metaphors for the woman's charms ("your angelic singing and your words . . . are the breeze before which my life flees"). The sonnet is a form that works by juxtaposing different perspectives on the same experience.[22]

This perspectival poetics underpins much of *Blood on the Tracks*, shaping both its depiction of time and its psychology. Thus "Tangled Up in Blue" opens "early one morning," when "the sun was shining." We meet the singer "layin' in bed," "wonderin' if she'd changed at all, if her hair was still red." Where are we? Is this the aftermath of the affair, or its very outset? The singer seems to think he's wondering about the girl's heart (has she changed?), but in fact his main focus is her appearance and how to identify her visually. The love object seems to be the "crimson"-haired girl whom we will meet five songs later in "You're Gonna Make Me Lonesome When You Go" ("Purple clover, Queen Anne lace / Crimson hair across your face" [p. 492]), the Petrarchan beauty who has replaced for the singer the unhappy loves of Verlaine and Rimbaud. Yet we don't even know if this lady was, or is, really a redhead. Is her hair still red? Perhaps she is like Lily in "Lily, Rosemary and the Jack of Hearts," who after the show in the gambling hall is over takes "all of the dye out of her hair"

(p. 490).[23] Now how will he find her? Petrarch's Laura vanishes in the wind, like her name. The lady in Dylan's songs dyes her hair. On the one hand, Dylan generates a cycle of lyric moments out of the encounter between his literary persona and a beautiful woman. On the other hand, that woman slips away by changing her hair color in the fourth line of the very first song on the album.[24] No less striking is the temporal displacement. The song opens with the hero "layin' in bed." A second later we learn that "I was standing by the side of the road / Rain fallin' on my shoes / Heading out for the East Coast." So much for the sunny morning. Yet when does this Kerouackian moment of meteorological unpleasantness occur? Are we at the end of the 1960s, or at the beginning? Did we just get out of bed, or are we thinking back onto earlier deluges from the safety of the covers? This narrative ambiguity mimics the disjointed nature of the sonnet sequence, even as it points ahead to the entire structure of the album that is unfolding before us.[25]

Dylan has stated that his technique in "Tangled Up in Blue" was influenced by art lessons he took with Norman Raeben in New York in the early 1970s. However, as we have seen, such shifting perspective is no less central to the discourse of the Petrarchan sonnet.[26] Whether Dylan chose the sonnet as the form to express a new perspectival alternative to the "vision music" of the 1960s, or whether the sonnet form imposed a new poetics on him, we cannot know. What is clear is that fragmentation and perspectivism, not Dantean or Rimbaldian vision, underpins these songs. And it is commented on. "Tangled Up in Blue" closes with a summary of the differences of perception that underpin both the sonnet and the generational experience here evoked. The narrator recounts the great aspirations of the 1960s generation: "There was music in the cafes at night / And revolution in the air" [p. 480]. Then he registers their disappointment: "Then he started in to dealing with slaves / And something inside of him died / She had to sell everything she owned / And froze up inside." The revolutionaries give up the cause and turn to less grand pursuits: "All the people we used to know / They're an illusion to me now / Some are mathematicians / Some are carpenters' wives / Don't know how it all got started / I don't know what they're doin' with their lives." By contrast, the singer is still traveling: "Me, I'm still on the road / Headin' for another joint." And he concludes with what appears to be a hard-won insight: "We always did feel the same / We just saw it from / A different point / Of view / Tangled up in blue" (p. 481). With this the song ends.[27]

Yet this concluding bit of wisdom, a distillation of the phenom-enology that has informed the song itself, is strangely tangled. For one thing, it comes at the only point where the metrical unfolding of the lyrics can't be made to fit with the rhythm of the melody. We get an awkward distortion of normal speech cadences: "We just *saw* it from / A different *point* / Of view." This rhythmic emphasis on the "a" in "a different point of view" is a rare, almost amateurish, infelic-ity in the work of someone who is an acknowledged genius at cre-ative phrasing. Dylan can evoke difference, he just seems unable—or unwilling—to fit the word "different" into his line. Not by accident does this uncomfortable gesture toward consolation and wisdom come in a line about sight. For the problem is that the concluding insight is backward. It is in fact not possible to say "we always did feel the same" unless you have access to the interiority of another person across time. And that knowledge is precisely what the character does not possess, as the whole song has demonstrated. The line should read, "we shared a set of experiences / we just ended up responding differently to what we saw." As in the ironic verse structures of "If You See Her, Say Hello," we end with an assertion of limited aware-ness, of a fragmented vision of reality—presented at the very moment that wisdom would seem to be forthcoming.

The implications of this logical reversal shape the question I began with, the problem of Dylan's relationship to his "genera-tion," and to the generational identity that earlier haunted Kerouac. For it is impossible to say for certain who "we" is in the lines just quoted—"we" who "always did feel the same." Is this about the lover and his lady and their busted affair? Or is this all of the characters just evoked from the 1960s, those who felt "revolution in the air," and for whom the biographical Bob Dylan ended up being, for better or worse, the "voice"? Either way, the ironic gesture toward insight that ends the song suggests that the revolutionary dreams of the Sixties are no more real than the illusory visions of the Petrarchan lover. The narrator presents the story, but he seems to be no less the dupe of history than anyone else.

We can understand more clearly the stakes of this contrast between "we" as Petrarchan love dyad and "we" as generation by returning to the evocation of Petrarch at the center of "Tangled Up in Blue." We recall again the moment at which the singer's beloved gives him a volume of Petrarch: "And every one of them words rang true / And glowed like burnin' coal / Pouring off of every page / Like it was written on my soul / From me to you / Tangled up in blue." The brilliant pairing of "From me to you / Tangled up in blue," brings the stanza to a rest, formally. But what is important is the way this concluding couplet effects a reversal of subject and object, of giver and receiver, in the scenario being described. The poems of Petrarch, which are given *by* the lady *to* the singer, now become an emanation *of* the singer: not "written on *your* soul from you to me," but "written on *my* soul / from me to you." The singer, as reader of Petrarch, now takes on Petrarch's voice, turning what he receives from the lady into his own song.

There is certainly an irony to the fact that we see the Petrarchan lady offering a volume of Petrarch's poems to her man so that he can become a Petrarchan poet. At one level, of course, one could say that this is a gendered power play, a seizure of authority. But such a response would reduce the complexity of what is happening. For the scene of reading Petrarch also constitutes the conversionary moment — the equivalent of Dante's acknowledgment of his poetic vocation, and of Sal Paradise's realization that he must "go moan for man." It is after this moment in the song — after the reading of Petrarch, that is — that the singer finds his way. Up to now he has been haunted by a paralyzing blend of desire and memory ("And I just grew / Tangled up in blue"). But he now learns that he must continue his journey, regardless of what happens around him. So in the very next stanza, the penultimate, as the revolution fades and the "bottom [falls] out" of the 1960s, the singer learns to "keep on keepin' on / Like a bird that flew." And then in the final stanza the singer describes himself as "still on the road / Headin' for another joint." This bit of folky wisdom — keep on moving — is repeated in different forms several times across the album and is reprised in the final stanza of the last song, "Buckets of Rain": "All ya can do / Is do what you must" (p. 496).[28]

Songs
The seizure of voice through the reading of Petrarch underpins the thematic emphasis on performance throughout the album. Despite all the journalistic hoopla about Dylan as "troubadour" in the 1960s, his dozens of lyrics from that time contain barely a handful of

references to musical instruments or the act of performance. This is of course completely unlike troubadour song (or Petrarchan song), which is obsessed with its own performative power. In *Blood on the Tracks*, however, that changes. Dylan stresses the power of his singers to perform. Many of the songs contain references to the singer as singer ("I'm just like that bird / singin' just for you," "headin' for another joint," "no one else could sing that tune"), and "Lily, Rosemary and the Jack of Hearts" stages a honky-tonk performance.[29] As the last lines of the album assert, "All ya can do / Is do what you must / You do what you must do / And you do it well / I do it for you / Honey, baby, can't you tell?" (p. 496). We end with a staging of the act of performance in a serenade. Not the voice of a generation, it would seem. Just a voice.

Dylan would seem to leave us, then, with an interplay of two scenarios. On the one hand, we have a formal insistence on fragmentation and limited vision that generates a series of figures who are caught in their own delusions, confused, tangled. This includes the singer himself, when he consoles himself about lost love or claims to speak for another by asserting "We always did feel the same." At the same time, we are given an insistence on the power of performance, on the singer doing what he must and trying to "do it well." Together these two facets give us a model of poetry and song that insists on its own aesthetic difference from the grand visions of vulgar activism symbolized by both the "revolution in the air" of "Tangled Up in Blue" and the "demonstrators" outside Dylan's front door in the quote with which I began this chapter. Through his use of Kerouac, Dylan grasps the problem of generational identity as a problem of collective illusion. Through his use of Petrarch, he then turns that generational fiction against itself, revealing the emptiness of its revolutionary clichés. Yet through the theme of performance he affirms the power of his own song as a special type of illusion, as fragmented lyric insight, self-conscious, oblique, even difficult. The record renews song with a series of poems that know themselves to be illusory, alive for the moment of their ragged performance, holding at the very center of their language a response to the totalizing vision of the "demonstrators."[30]

In the tradition of Dante and Rimbaud, Dylan's "vision music" from the 1960s had charted new territory for popular song. The technical innovations that had emerged from that experience (streams of images, insider jargon, historical and cultural name-checking, expansion of the length of the single track, and so on) had, by the early 1970s, become clichés. As we have seen, Dylan's response to this situation is to turn to older forms of representation, archaic models that can help power an ironic break with the recent past. Old forms reanimate and shape the poetics of Dylan's songs, offering formal and aesthetic resources that have literary historical consequences.

Replay

Yet, for all of Dylan's interest in the relationship between personal drama and collective memory, the solution to how political crisis and personal crisis intersect is not obvious. The challenge is perhaps best emblematized by a moment in "Idiot Wind" when we hear of the "priest" who "wore black" and "sat stone-faced while a building burned," before the singer laments that "I waited for you on the running boards / Near the cypress trees, while the springtime turned / Slowly into autumn" (p. 486). The public disaster of Vietnam and private disappointment—here evoked as yet another failed car trip—are set in simple juxtaposition, with nothing linking the two spheres of experience. We can understand the poetic challenges posed by this juxtaposition if we turn to the material history of the record. Dylan recorded two versions of the album, one in New York in September 1974, and one in Minneapolis a few weeks later. The second version, for the most part, is what was released to the public. The first version contains a number of bitter, autobiographical references to Dylan's marriage and his sinking career trajectory. Key among these is the first version of "Tangled Up in Blue," where, strikingly, the entire political context of the 1960s is absent. Instead, we have a picture of a failing marriage, haunted by an excess of "objects and material things," where the husband is always "too busy or too stoned" (p. 481) and the wife denied the chance to pursue her interests.

The domestic scenario hints at the difficulties faced by many successful 1960s-era popular artists as the long decade ended. One career move involved shifting toward a more intimate form of expression. As I noted at the outset of this chapter, Dylan's pre–*Blood on the Tracks* albums are characterized in part by this type of writing. One could think as well of the (increasingly irrelevant) "domestic" music of, for example, Paul McCartney and John Lennon during this period.[31]

Blood on the Tracks, too, falls into this category, as a fable of domestic misery—that is, until Dylan recasts the lyrics and rerecords it. When he does, he makes the singer's personal disillusionment into generational disillusionment.

In Dylan's songs people come and go, but the singer cannot forget his lost love, any more than Petrarch can forget Laura. Central to the poetics of Petrarchan style is the persona of a poet who is haunted by love. "With every step is born a new thought of my lady," writes Petrarch in the great *canzone* that begins "From thought to thought, from mountain to mountain." He goes on: "So long as I can hold my yearning mind fixed on the first thought . . . my soul is satisfied by its own deception."[32] Technically, on *Blood on the Tracks*, the coherence of vision—the sense of being "haunted"—is evoked through the repetition of motifs and hooks from song to song. Thus we are treated to images that reappear in vastly different contexts (the bird, Italy, the dyed hair, the rain, the sense of lateness), chord sequences that reappear, stressed, in multiple songs, echoes of guitar lines, and so on. You can even sing the lyrics of several of the songs over the melodies of several others, as if they were interchangeable, the same song sung again. "If You See Her, Say Hello" fits easily over "Tangled Up in Blue," for example. This technique of repetition across the songs lends them a loose stylistic coherence that loops collective memory and personal obsession together.[33]

The shift to a language of memory and erotic fixation marks yet another break in Dylan's work. By the 1970s he had written dozens of "love songs." Most were put downs ("Don't Think Twice") or expressions of short-term desire ("I'll Be Your Baby Tonight"). Now we are given a vision of a love that is both broken and grand, precisely because it is indistinguishable from the narrative of political disarray at the end of the 1960s. Indeed, the album's most bitter song, "Idiot Wind," almost feels like the answer to 1965's "Like a Rolling Stone," as personal emancipation has given way to disaster and a general acknowledgment of affective and political impotence: "We are idiots, babe," sings Dylan. "It's a wonder we can even feed ourselves" (p. 486). Yet memory endures. What holds personal crisis and political crisis together is the Petrarchan theme of fidelity across time, through memory. Dylan's singer is haunted. Like Petrarch's lover, Dylan's singer cannot escape from the image of the woman he has loved and lost. "Though our separation / It pierced me to the heart," he sings in "If You See Her, Say Hello." "She still lives inside of me / We've never been apart" (p. 492). The great dream of political renewal that Dylan evokes in his references to the 1960s was a bust, and Dylan's character may give himself over to wandering, yet, like Petrarch, he is in the same emotional place all along. The stylistic tic of repetition across songs gives form to the Petrarchan theme of erotic obsession. The persistence of memory—written into the very structure of the songs—counterbalances the poetics of fragmentation that we saw a moment ago.

This claim of continuity through memory links the content of the songs to the material and commercial history of the album itself. *Blood on the Tracks* is not simply the response to the collapse of political idealism and the breakup of the artist's domestic life. It is the response to a break in Dylan's own career as well. Not only were the projects directly preceding this one, as noted earlier, minor in nature, but he had left his record label, Columbia, for an ill-fated dalliance with Asylum Records that had recently ended. Now he returns to his first love, as it were. This sense of a return that is also an expression of fidelity is staged and thematized in the packaging of the recording, which features a lengthy essay by the journalist Pete Hamill reminding the listeners that, throughout the 1960s, Dylan had, as it were, been there all along, waiting on the running boards. Chaos had come and gone, but, as Hamill puts it, "He had remained . . . and remained true."[34] Even as Dylan's lyric voice is turning away from a 1960s that evaporates into "illusion," his long memory sutures together public and private experience. His memory is of a love, but also of an earlier moment that, through his rejection of it, he calls into being, as "generation," and shares with his listeners. Those who are "an illusion to me now" are still, one presumes, record buyers. The conventional circular relationship that links Petrarch's expressions of amorous obsession to his claims to artistic immortality is here played out in the dynamism of the long-playing record itself, as both an account of love through time and the material proof of the artist's unchanging commercial relevance. Through the material reproduction of the LP, Dylan's appropriation of the Petrarchan themes of memory and constancy is subsumed into brand loyalty.

Thus, when taken up by the quickly digested form of the popular song, the high-literary tradition of Petrarchan lyric enables a fictional mediation between personal crisis and political upheaval.

Dylan deploys the Petrarchan poetics of perspective and fragment to generate a loose dialectic of memory and experience that transcends the limitations of Kerouac's beatnik "vision." At the same time, precisely because of its absorption into the dynamics of popular stardom, that same Petrarchan poetic degenerates into a parody of its own mediating fiction, as the poet "singin' just for you" bleeds from troubadour lament into marketing ploy.

Spin

The evasive poetics of *Blood on the Tracks*, with their focus on fragmentation, movement, and regret sutured together by memory, are expanded by Dylan's next album, *Desire*, written mostly in collaboration with Jacques Levy, who had directed the 1969 theatrical review *Oh! Calcutta!* Having confronted and recast the journeys of the 1960s on *Blood on the Tracks*, the question would be, where (and how) to go next? "On the heels of Rimbaud . . . streaming into the lost belly of civilization at a standstill . . . Romance is taking over," wrote Dylan in his own liner notes to *Desire* (p. 512). The mention of "Romance" here is significant, as it suggests not only the themes of passion, seduction, and, well, *Desire*, but also the literary form of romance – stories of quests into enchanted worlds and battles against unknowable enemies. "Magical narratives" is how the critic Fredric Jameson characterizes the romance tradition, suggesting that romance has its roots in the medieval European aristocrat's attempt to make sense of a world of unknown menace, in which the Other was both familiar (another aristocrat) and threatening.

By contrast, the set of romance narratives that Dylan offers on *Desire* needs to be seen against the decidedly disenchanted background of the mid-1970s: after 1960s idealism, after Woodstock and Altamont, after Vietnam and Watergate. Even the return to the "country" that Dylan had chronicled at the turn of the decade had been sucked up into the machine of Madison Avenue, with its marketing of "natural foods." As Bob Dylan and Jacques Levy were composing these songs, in the year of the American bicentennial, popular music was dominated by sweet-faced "country-folk" singer John Denver. Springsteen was beginning to make his mark. Disco was on the rise. "Civilization at a standstill," indeed. Into this 1970s atmosphere of disillusionment and anomie, where, as Andreas Huyssen has suggested (channeling Dylan), "the vehicles of avant-gardism and postmodernism have come to a standstill," come Dylan's attempts to reinject mystery and delight.[35] Here the project is not to domesticate the unfamiliar, as medieval literary romance had done, but to find and explore experiences that haven't already been domesticated or commercialized. So, he offers a set of exotic adventures: songs set in Mexico, Africa, among gypsies, on distant islands, in the mysterious, dangerous "North" (not to be confused with the more accessible "North" of "Girl from the North Country" or "Tangled Up in Blue"). In contrast to the explicitly American topography of *Blood on the Tracks*, *Desire* is the first (and perhaps only) Dylan album that has a truly international cast. "On the heels of Rimbaud," wrote Dylan in his notes. Here is Rimbaud, not as the rebel poet of the senses seen in Chapter 3, but as adventurer, as African trader, as the boy who walked across Europe.

The problems raised by this new exoticism may be read, for example, in "One More Cup of Coffee." It features a haunting melody (descending, flamenco-style, from a minor chord on the sixth to a major chord on the third degree of the major scale) in which the narrator lingers in a gypsy camp with a beautiful woman. The denouement, however, is both ominous and banal: "One more cup of coffee, 'fore I go / To the valley below" (p. 520). The characteristic workaday gesture, another cup of coffee, is linked to some vague sense of adventure, a walk through the Valley of . . . something. Through the vehicle of the familiar request (already canonized in Buck Owens's 1965 hit "Truck Driving Man," with its refrain, "pour me another cup of coffee") the exotic and the banal are linked. This explains how the narrator can penetrate the secret world of the gypsies, "where no stranger does intrude" (p. 520). Initially, he was just asking for coffee.

The romantic foray into exoticism on *Desire* raises the question of whether the enchantment here being purveyed is coming from the journeys and landscapes themselves, or from Dylan's own claims that there is magic everywhere. Is he reporting on adventures, or is he simply imposing adventure through the force of his own artistry? This problem is especially clear on "Mozambique," a tune said to have emerged from a rhyming game played by Dylan and Levy.[36] The song was composed and recorded at the exact moment that Mozambique was being released from two centuries of brutal Portuguese rule. Yet we can also note that the title refers to a form of music, the Cuban "mozambique" or the Brazilian "maxixe" (which is, in fact, evoked by the musical groove on this recording).[37] Yet, whether we understand it as a celebration of emerging liberation, a callous cluelessness about real conditions in Mozambique, a sonic joke about rhyme patterns, or a song about itself, a gap remains between the song and its setting. The song sings the mystery of a land where "the sunny sky is aqua blue" (p. 518). But the characters are not Mozambicans. They are Western tourists, jet-setters. The setting could be anywhere—Malibu, Maui, Málaga. Mozambique seems, as the rhyming game suggests, to be an empty signifier. Yet the song is built on the idea that Mozambique, as place, contains some type of particular magic that is essential to it. The lyric effort needed to get beyond this paradox is revealed in the bridge or "middle eight" of the song—in that formal element whose job is to offer commentary on the rest and move the structure toward conclusion. There we hear: "Lying next to her by the ocean / Reaching out and touching her hand / Whispering a secret emotion / Magic in a magical land" (p. 518). The repetition of the word "magic" is the giveaway. For it is never clear whether the magic is generated by the erotic encounter on the beach (in which case we could be anywhere) or by some essential mystery of the land (in which case being in Mozambique, and nowhere else, actually matters). The repetition indicates that the scene is generated out of a kind of rhetorical overkill. Only by doubling down, by repeating the same word, can Dylan and Levy bridge the gap between sunburned tourist and Third World landscape.

A similar moment appears in the bridge of the only other song on the album to feature a bridge, the lovely "Oh, Sister."[38] Here the erotic adventure with a beautiful woman turns religious. The singer makes the unmotivated claim that he and the lady are both put on earth "to love and follow His direction"; therefore she should take him in her arms. And we get the explanation in the bridge: "We grew up together from the cradle to the grave / We died and were reborn and left mysteriously saved" (p. 522). It is probably wise not to inquire too deeply into the theology of this claim. As a pickup line, it certainly grabs one's attention. But what strikes us is the claim of religious mystery: "Mysteriously saved." The "mystery" is never shown or explained. It is simply asserted, in passing, like "magic," in the word that names the greater force it seeks to evoke.

Desire is full of such rhetorical excesses, where we are given more information than needed in order to create "atmosphere." We see this kind of overkill in "Romance in Durango," where we start with "hot chili peppers in the blistering sun" (p. 526). Are they spicy hot, or simply cooking in the afternoon heat? In the same song the hero gets *two* guitars, one for subsistence, to be traded for food, one for music, so that we can have the emblematic image of him strumming as he and his girl ride away—thereby blending both the literary and erotic senses of "romance." The image sets the desperado as folksinger, making him both exotic and familiar. And we are treated to a doubling of spirits and buildings, as the ghosts of the Aztecs and their bloody temples stand in juxtaposition with the "bells in the village steeple" and the memory of the "bloody face of Ramón," whom the hero has killed.

The problem here is that in 1976 romance is not, in fact, "taking over," as Dylan says it is. Rather, Dylan and Levy are working madly to inject it into the scenarios of these songs through rhetorical ornamentation. They do this by naming what they are trying to make happen—"magic!" "mystery!" "romance!"—as if they could conjure it up. In "Tangled Up in Blue" and "If You See Her, Say Hello," Dylan's reversals of logic were integral to the representation of a confused self, disordered by love and memory, struggling with the lost illusions of the 1960s. In "Romance in Durango," by contrast, phrases such as "hoof beats like castanets on stone" (which should be "hoof beats on stone sound like castanets") generate an onomatopoeic rhythmic effect that remains distinct from the drama of the murder and its aftermath, like piped-in music. The fact that castanets are Spanish, not Mexican, doesn't help, either. We can see this as well in the intermittent "ethnic" instrumentation—mandolin, accordion, trumpet, violin—that comes and goes to create mood. We are a good way here from the deeply symbolic exoticism of the boots in "Boots of Spanish Leather" (1964) or the disorienting import-export curiosity shops of the mid-1960s, with their "Arabian drums," "Chinese suit," or "Persian drunkards."

These tensions between surface and structure appear as well on the level of the narrative. The complex historicity of "Tangled Up in Blue," with its leaps in time and space, turns now, in the "Romance in Durango" version of flight and pursuit, into a narrative line where the hero is everywhere at once, initially depicted as "on the run" but later crying "Come, let us fly" to start the journey already in progress and then, almost in parody, "O, can it be that I am slain?" (before pointing out that there is a long night still ahead). Stylistically, in "Romance in Durango," we seem to be edging out of Dylan's powerful modernism toward a kind of pastiche. This is especially clear when we recognize that the story (with its nearly dead narrator) only makes sense when read against Marty Robbins's magisterial 1959 hit, "El Paso," of which it is a rewriting. That earlier song underpins this one, not as a countervoice (as was the case with Dylan's rewritings of Guthrie), but as a template, like the pop culture references in the knowing fiction of some postmodern novelist. Thus, rhetorical excess, now emptied of historical content, structures what appears to be a necessary poetic response to precisely the moment of the American bicentennial. Romance "takes over" as a semblance that both masks and mimics the flatness of the culture of credit-card tourism. *Desire* is a near-heroic attempt to reanimate, through language and sound, the "civilization at a standstill" that Dylan had mentioned in his liner notes.

Writing of the structural contradictions that haunt much modern art, the philosopher-critic Theodor Adorno notes that all artworks are constructed of heterogeneous elements. To the extent that the work can unify these elements, it creates what he calls a "semblance." Yet to the extent that it is masking contradiction and heterogeneity, that semblance is also inauthentic; it is a fiction with a bad conscience. The meaning of an artwork includes both of these things, the beautiful "semblance" and the deeper struggles and contradictions. The beautiful harmony of the work's surface is what enchants us, even as it only imperfectly resolves the contradictions between diverse bits of primary material.[39] Something like this seems to be going on in the exoticism of *Desire*, which wants to conjure up magic but constantly calls attention to its own conjuring. We can read this perhaps most clearly in the sonic texture of the album. Notable is Scarlet Rivera's beautiful violin playing, which is integrated into the mix, as part of the rhythm section. Rivera plays against and around Dylan's vocal as he sings. When Dylan's characteristic harmonica solos kick in, the two instruments create an interesting blend, as they negotiate the same sonic territory. Yet the intersection of the two instruments is in itself symbolic of the larger poetics of the album. The violin is precisely the marker of "local color" or "the exotic." Dylan's harmonica, by contrast, comes from a set of musical traditions—Guthrie's ballads, the blues—alien to the worlds of gypsies and Mexican *bandidos*. His harmonica's intervention in the mix introduces an emotional counterpoint to the rest of the atmosphere. Like the repetition of "magic" in "Mozambique," the dialogue of harmonica and violin mediates, at the level of sound, the clash between First World desire and exotic setting.

These forays into exotic territory contrast with a pair of sociological studies of the "American hero." These are the single "Hurricane," about the boxer Rubin Carter's unjust (and subsequently overturned) condemnation for murder, and "Joey," a strangely elegiac account of the career of the mobster Joey Gallo. "Hurricane" opens the album. The harmony of the song clearly recalls 1967's "All Along the Watchtower." Here the exploitation of the artist figures, "the joker" and "the thief," has modulated into injustice toward black men, and in particular toward the great boxer, who retains his dignity in the face of injustice. Just as "All Along the Watchtower" ends with a moment of expected apocalypse, as "the wind began to howl," here we end with an expectation of the end, "it won't be over till they clear his name" (p. 514). The anger expressed through the high energy performance and the rising intensity of Dylan's voice contrasts dramatically with the plodding logic of his early 1960s "protest" songs, where it was assumed that an exposé of the miscarriages of justice would lead to eventual social reform. By 1976, performative intensity has replaced journalistic logic, and the track simply fades out, with no closure to the story.

The different settings for the songs (exotic lands on the one hand and New Jersey and Brooklyn on the other) may, however, not be so far apart as they seem. Dylan's longstanding interest in the abuse of power is here blended with an attempt to romanticize these two heroes—perhaps, in its way, another kind of love affair. As was pointed out at the time of the album's release, Joey Gallo was a notorious thug, mostly known for his willingness to murder his rivals. Yet his story gets the same atmospheric mandolin and accordion accompaniment that graces "Romance in Durango," and the portrait of the crime family (with the "old man" or patriarch who mourns for his lost son) looks suspiciously like the gypsy clan of "One More Cup of Coffee," where that father of the beautiful heroine "oversees his kingdom" (p. 520). "Joey" uses the mob family to blend the praise of the workingman ("It's peace and quiet that we need / To go back to work again" [p. 524]) with the praise of the marginal. The problem, however, is that though Joey Gallo befriends black men in prison because they know "what it's like to be in society / With a shackle on your hands," the shackles are, in Joey's case, literal, not metaphorical. He is in the stir. The case of Carter is more complicated, since he was eventually released and exonerated. Yet at the time of the recording, despite the obvious corruption of the police investigation, his innocence was far from an accepted fact. Since Dylan and Levy had read books about both men, it may simply be the songwriters themselves who are prey to the "romance" of literature. Either way, the struggle to recast these lives in the mode of Guthrie's "Pretty Boy Floyd," or Dylan's own "John Wesley Harding," suggests the difficulty of finding heroes anywhere in sight in 1976.

The point here is that *Desire* builds on the poetics of *Blood on the Tracks* but also runs up against the limits of the tropes of movement, fragmented vision, and evasion. Indeed, if we recall the importance of Kerouac for *Blood on the Tracks*, the problems faced by *Desire* are not so far from the problems faced by the Beats, after *On the Road*. Where to go next? Whereas *Blood on the Tracks* depicted travel and escape through the lenses of personal history and generational memory, both memory and the "I" are largely absent here. This shift brings about a new type of irony in Dylan's work. This is no longer the Petrarchan self-irony we saw on the earlier album, which saved it from bathos. Now we have a kind of unintentional irony generated out of the pressure placed on the songs by the tension between plot and setting. It makes *Desire* particularly difficult to read. The fact that several of the structures seem to echo other songs ("Hurricane" echoes "All Along the Watchtower," "Oh, Sister" harmonically recalls the 1969 reworking of "Girl from the North Country," and "Romance in Durango," as noted, is a recasting of "El Paso"), suggests a new sense of the limits of form as well as theme.

Dylan seems to sense this generic difficulty. For two of the most innovative songs on the album explore the relationship between adventure and artistic forms. We can see this most explicitly in "Black Diamond Bay," a wild tale about an exotic, doomed, south sea island that is loosely based on Joseph Conrad's novel *Victory*. We are given all the tropes of literary and cinematic exoticism—a beautiful, mysterious woman, a casino, an old hotel, bits of French stuck into the dialogue, and so on. The kicker comes, however, in the last verse, where the obliteration, via earthquake and volcano, of the exotic

world into which we have just been immersed reaches the narrator
on TV:

> I was sittin' home alone one night
> In L. A. watching old Cronkite
> On the seven o'clock news
> It seems there was an earthquake that
> Left nothing but a Panama hat
> And a pair of old Greek shoes
> Didn't seem like much was happenin'
> So I turned it off and went to grab another beer (p. 529)

The whole tale into which we have just been drawn turns out to be a
snippet from a newscast. As Dylan had written way back in 1963, in
a different mediascape, "The whole wide world is watching" (p. 116).
In 1963 the world was witnessing social upheaval. In 1976 the narrator
turns off the tube and goes to grab a beer.

What is striking is the relationship between the narrated expe-
rience of the bulk of the song and the frame that appears out of
nowhere in the last verse. As listeners who have followed the story
of Black Diamond Bay close up, we see the events from the perspec-
tive of the doomed characters. Yet it is the singer / narrator, who has
not seen these things, who ultimately controls the story. He shapes
the narrative . . . by turning off the TV. His indifference undercuts
our experience. The contrast between these two viewpoints builds
on what we saw demonstrated in the poetics of *Blood on the Tracks*.
In songs like "Tangled Up in Blue," differences in perspective were
linked to the struggle to grasp history itself. Here, by contrast, Dylan
is playing with the problem of perspective, yet the meaning of events
is recuperated by the media, which reduces even disaster to trivia.[40]
Conrad's prose romance/novel *Victory* ends with an expression of
impotence in the face of violence: "There was nothing to be done
there. . . . Nothing," reflects an observer who has discovered the bod-
ies of the murdered protagonists. Dylan and Levy echo Conrad, but
for them the heavy hand of destiny is mediated by television, which
forestalls not only action but also speech: "There's really nothing
anyone can say / 'Cause I never did plan to go anyway / To Black
Diamond Bay."[41]

By framing the exotic inside the banal Dylan and Levy offer a
formal commentary on the rest of the album. Romance heroism and

the dangerous world of Rubin Carter's Paterson, New Jersey (where Kerouac's hero Sal Paradise had lived with his aunt and once hosted Dean Moriarty), all exist in the same mediascape. These songs are caught between, on the one hand, a vision of history in which all cultural memory—even the story of Hurricane Carter—is already a media creation and, on the other hand, a set of tales which longs to deny that fact. "Black Diamond Bay" reveals that such denial is futile. *Desire* moves beyond the evasive poetics of *Blood on the Tracks*, with their disenchanted account of 1960s idealism. Yet the album shows the limits of a cultural production that is merely spatial (geography, ethnography) without being truly historical. Only later in his career, as we shall see in Chapter 6, will Dylan return to history, to the pre-1960s world, through a deep reengagement with traditional folk song, on the albums *Good as I Been to You* (1992) and *World Gone Wrong* (1993).

Within a media-saturated world, what types of authenticity are available to the individual? The autobiographical/mythical register of *Blood on the Tracks* returns in several of the love songs on *Desire*: the lament "Sara," with its references to family trips to romantic places, and "Oh, Sister," which echoes the mystery of "One More Cup of Coffee," with "time is an ocean" (p. 522) recalling "your heart is like an ocean, mysterious and dark" (p. 520). Yet these sentimental moments pale next to what is surely the most aesthetically impor-tant song on *Desire* (and the mythic counterbalance to "Sara"). This is the adventure tale "Isis." It opens up a different perspective on Dylan's postvisionary, post-Petrarchan work. Here the literary sub-text would seem to be Jack London—himself a writer of romance tales in prose—as we meet a hero who leaves the woman he loves in search of adventure in the North. It opens with a marriage on "the fifth day of May," that is, Mexican Independence Day, an allusion that looks ahead to "Romance in Durango." Yet the song quickly turns into a parable about choices, as the protagonist heads out for the wild country "where I could not go wrong" (p. 516). He stops off in a "high place of darkness and light," where "the dividing line ran through the center of town." The exotic landscape shades off into allegory, where good and evil may—or may not—be obvious, depending on how you read phrases like "I could not go wrong" and "a high place of darkness and light." From here our hero meets a mysterious stranger who invites him on a trip to find fortune in the North. As the greedy hero and his companion make their way into the snows, the hero realizes that the companion is only looking for a body, either to bury it or to bring it back for bounty, and that any old body will do: "I saw that my partner was just bein' friendly / When I took up his offer, I must've been mad!" When the companion dies, our hero buries him and returns to find his beloved Isis, to whom he seems at last able to commit. He gets love, but not fortune.

One of the melodic motifs that echoes across *Desire* consists of Dylan closing or resolving a unit of semantic meaning with a quick cluster of notes all on the same tone. So, "went to grab another beer," or "Soviet ambassador" in "Black Diamond Bay," or the punch line "to the valley below," in "One More Cup of Coffee." This melodic motif is both recalled and exploded in "Isis." Driven by a repeated descending three-chord piano line in waltz time, "Isis" is built out of a series of four-line groupings. We begin with the same melodic motif, as the hero marries Isis and heads off for the wilds, "where I could not go wrong," with the last clause built on a repetition of the same note, the tonic Bb. But from there it goes in all directions, as every fourth line returns to that resolving tonic Bb in a different way, sliding down from a third interval above, up from a third below, down from a second, and so on, with different emphases in the lyric ("To wash my CLOTHES down"; "I HAD to go ON"; "I must've been MAD"; "I've EVER HEARD"; "how she thought I was SOOO reckless"). This turns the performance into a marvel of narrative singing, as the melody twists and mutates according to where we are in the tale. There seems, in fact, to be no "set" melody line, as each verse finds Dylan hopping around inside his chord tones according to the needs of the moment. Rhythm anchors the song as the melody changes from verse to verse. This marks a break from the fairly controlled singing on *Blood on the Tracks*, as well as from Dylan's games with rhythm and tone on his mid-1960s albums. Here narrative at last breaks free from fixed melody and takes the shape of story as song.

Given this dramatic innovation, where voice itself takes over, it may not be by accident that it is here, and nowhere else on the album, that we get a meditation on the nature of the self. The contrast between framed cliché and lived experience set forth in "Black Diamond Bay" is displaced in "Isis" into the splitting of the narrator. The protagonist confronts his own greed in the form of the companion who, in the end, is his own double. The story is of the death of the evil twin who leads him into temptation, and to the eventual recognition of the emptiness of his own greed. The insistent power of the temptation is punctuated by the repeated descending three-chord piano line, which in live performances from the same period turned into a swirl of noise. On an album fascinated with the exotic, the protagonist learns that adventure can be deadly, and that only a kind of self-purification can make him worthy of love. In the end, commitment is more interesting than adventure. This "inward turn" both questions the exoticism of the rest of the album and marks a striking departure in Dylan's work. It sets the vision of a divided self into a quest narrative, with the hero as both survivor and victim. For a writer not noted for self-exploration, this look inward, via the tropes of adventure narrative, marks a kind of transition. Precisely because his self is split, Dylan is able to retain his tough-guy persona while exposing his own weakness. Subsequent work will feature a number of such self-regarding songs and moments.[42]

"O Generation keep on working!" wrote Allen Ginsberg as the concluding exhortation in the notes he penned for *Desire*.[43] The preceding analysis has suggested that Ginsberg was a bit out of touch or behind the times when he wrote this nostalgic call to arms. Dylan had already bundled up the 1960s generation and moved on. His encounter with the idealism of the past on *Blood on the Tracks* could only come through his deep and insightful reading of earlier "generational" texts, most notably Kerouac's *On the Road*. Moreover, through his engagement with the seemingly archaic literary tradition of the Petrarchan love sonnet, which Kerouac alludes to at the end of his own romantic fiction, Dylan was able to turn Kerouac's topography to his own purposes, marking out the poetic discourse that enabled him to leave the cliché of the 1960s in the past as one more "point of view," like a bad love affair. All of the extraneous noise of the Sixties—the revolution, the fellow travelers, the betrayal of idealism—turn, on *Blood on the Tracks*, to smoke, "an illusion to me now," what Petrarch called "a brief dream."[44] What dominates the present is a lyric performance that points forward, beyond the generational poetics of Ginsberg and the Beats, even as it is subsumed into the dynamics of commercial rebirth. Visionary schemes give way to a poetics of fragmentation and performance, in which insight comes in shards and always imperfectly, thereby requiring yet another spin of the disk. *Desire* then expands the Petrarchan/Kerouackian poetics that Dylan had offered up as the alternative to his "vision music" from the previous decade. It attempts to regenerate romantic idealism beyond politics and personal reminiscence. It shows how the poetics of movement, when unmoored from a reflection on history and personal experience, run up against their own limits. Yet in response to this crisis of history and romance Dylan seems to open new possibilities that will be explored in the following half decade. The recognition in "Tangled Up in Blue" that "all the people we used to know are an illusion to me now," gives way to the awareness that the self is not merely split across time—between the naive revolutionary and the wise, ironic bard—but torn by instinct and desire at every moment, driven by evil twins. In a world where everything—even romance—is mediated through old Cronkite on the seven o'clock news, the confrontation with the persecutor within may be what remains of authentic experience.

Turn, Turn Again:
A Poetry of Conversion

Following The Rolling Thunder Review, a star-studded tour to support the
Desire album, Dylan releases Street Legal *(1977), a record that features,*
for the first time in his career, elaborate accompaniments, including backup
singers and horns. Dylan's vocal performances take on the mannerisms of
a rhythm and blues shouter. A film generated from The Rolling Thunder
Review, Renaldo and Clara *(1978), loosely based on Marcel Carné's* Chil-
dren of Paradise *(1945), is a flop. A concert album,* Live at Budokan, *fares*
no better. Dylan then releases a set of records reflecting his new interest in
evangelical Christianity. The first of these, Slow Train Coming *(1979), wins*
a Grammy for best vocal performance by a male on the single "Gotta Serve
Somebody." The other two, Saved *(1980) and* Shot of Love *(1981), are less well*
received. Dylan's stage show begins to feature powerful gospel performances,
punctuated by bouts of preaching from the habitually laconic performer. By
the early 1980s his interests seem to be shifting again. In 1983 he releases
Infidels, *a record that draws deeply on the language of religion but seems to*
be gesturing in other directions.

In "If You See Her, Say Hello," the lament from 1975's *Blood on the*
Tracks that we looked at briefly in the preceding chapter, Dylan pres-
ents a character who is trying to move past a broken love affair, but
remains haunted, no matter how much he protests to the contrary:
"I hear her name, here and there, as I go from town to town" he
sings. "And I've never gotten used to it, I've just learned to turn it
off / Either I'm too sensitive or else I'm gettin' soft" (p. 492). The last
plaintive line says the same thing twice: I'm letting something get
to me that shouldn't. However the two phrases seem to come from

different worlds, from different languages, almost. "Or else I'm get-tin' soft" (pronounced SAHHFFFFFT) is a line from a gangster film. It is what happens to tough guys who are over the hill; they get "soft." In tough-guy parlance, admitting to getting "soft" is one degree short of the expression of the worst form of manly weakness, "I guess I'm yellow, all right."[1] By contrast, the preceding statement, "Maybe I'm too sensitive," comes from a different sociolect. It is the current jargon of the early 1970s, when thoughtful singer-songwriters such as Carole King, Jackson Browne, and James Taylor were inventing a new vocabulary for adult male identity in the West. The male figure in classic rock and roll was either deeply wounded ("Only the lonely know the way I feel tonight," sang Roy Orbison in 1960) or joyfully in pursuit of another girl ("I'm a-gonna tell you how it's a-gonna be," ran Buddy Holly's 1958 "Not Fade Away"). "Sensitivity," which implies a median space, a world of nuance and shading, of give and take, was not a major value presented in these songs. Dylan's lines thus regis-ter a shift in the language of male identity. His old-fashioned hero is trying on a new vocabulary to see how it fits. And it doesn't fit neatly. Whereas Frank Sinatra had sung the word "insensitive" with consummate cool in his 1967 recording of Antônio Carlos Jobim's "How Insensitive" ("inn-senn-si-tive"), Dylan pronounces "sensitive" as "SENS-ahh-tif," as if it were unfamiliar, a big word he has overheard somewhere. This suggests that the narrator of the song is used to being a tough guy but is suddenly off balance.

Thus Dylan's lyrical world begins to register, if only obliquely, some of the shifts in social relations that characterized the mid-1970s. Under the pressure of the women's movement, following on the civil rights movement of the 1960s, new paradigms for talking about affective and social life were beginning to emerge. This meant that old clichés for writing about, for example, love came into contact with a newly refined vocabulary that made old postures of wounded machismo seem somewhat out of date. The questioning of the lan-guage of sentiment and of male power may be tracked across several Dylan compositions during this period. *Street Legal* (1977) features a set of bitter songs mostly about betrayal. It includes a snide mockery of the protagonist's ex-girlfriend ("Miss X") in "New Pony" (where the woman is compared to a horse), a scene of humiliation in which the protagonist is beaten up ("Just gotta pick myself up off the floor" [p. 551]) in "Señor (Tales of Yankee Power)," and an extraordinarily deft meditation on the confusion of modern life called "No Time to Think" ("Betrayed by a kiss on a cool night of bliss" [p. 550]). Woven into these tunes were moments where the autonomy and unity of the self were at issue, and where male confidence seemed to be ebbing. Thus the opening track, "Changing of the Guards," features the protagonist as a Christ figure who tries to redeem a scene of injustice ("Eden is burning" [p. 518]) before the onset of some new order. "Your hearts must have the courage for the changing of the guards," is the last line. The final cut, "Where Are You Tonight? (Journey through Dark Heat)" offers a set of mini-scenes of a character torn against himself and in confusion: "I fought with my twin / That enemy within / Till both of us fell by the way" (p. 557), he sings. And, a bit earlier, "I left town at dawn / With Marcel and St. John / Strong men belittled by doubt." One can attribute many different emotions to Dylan's various heroes in his songs from the 1960s and early 1970s, but "belittlement by doubt" is not one of them. Dylan even wrote a song, not used on *Street Legal*, called "Legionnaires' Disease," about a deadly form of pneumonia that mysteriously struck a group of veterans at a convention in Philadelphia in 1976. The song refers to Revolutionary War heroes, now struck down inexplicably: "Whatever it was, it came out of the trees / Oh, that Legionnaires' disease" (p. 561). Following the ironic focus on travel and romance set forth on *Blood on the Tracks* and *Desire*, in these later songs self-assurance seemed to be leaking away.

Prophecy

In 1979 Dylan revealed that he had had a personal encounter with Jesus. He proceeded to write several very moving songs about his relationship to the Savior, most notably "When He Returns," from the first of his "Christian" records, *Slow Train Coming*. But no less important than the personal experience was a general sense of disarray in the world. A number of songs over the next few years featured an angry, insulting protagonist. The anger was not only aimed at the self, for its sinful past; it was aimed at everyone. Thus, the title track from that album features the following bit of international policy analysis:

All that foreign oil
Controlling American soil

Look around you, it's just bound to make you embarrassed
Sheiks walking around like kings
Wearing fancy jewels and nose rings
Deciding America's future from Amsterdam and to Paris
And there's a slow, slow train coming up around the bend (p. 574)

This is a reference to the so-called Middle East oil crisis that roiled American life during the Carter presidency, as the OPEC nations raised the cost of petroleum on the world market. There were gasoline shortages at some service stations in the United States, and prices went up at the pump. Energy rationing was threatened, and the country seemed powerless to respond. Moreover, in 1979, fifty-two Americans were taken hostage in the U.S. embassy in Tehran as the Iranian Revolution broke out. Dylan registers the energy crisis, as did many people, as a threat to American identity and power. His account of it runs in parallel to his laments about the loss of personal agency and integrity. Thus "Slow Train" begins with a general expression of malaise:

Sometimes
Feel so lowdown and disgusted
Can't help but wonder what's happening to my companions
Are they lost or are they found
Have they counted the cost it'll take to bring down
All their earthly principles they're gonna have to abandon?
There's a slow, slow train comin' up around the bend

In Chapter 2 we noted that Dylan's complaints about social ills in the 1960s often took aim at institutions, at the miscarriage of justice, at official corruption or lying. Here the disgust is general. As the lines just cited suggest, even personal transformation is seen in economic terms — an important analogy in what was then an inflation-plagued economy. The awkwardness of the economic metaphor, which hints that one should calculate before converting, reveals that the analogy between personal malaise and social malaise has its limits. Personal transformation and political revolution may not go hand in hand. And yet the image of a judgment or an apocalypse, in the form of the "slow train" around the bend, mediates the relationship of private and public by sweeping into itself both international politics and personal spiritual crisis.

Representations of conversion in literature generally take the form of narrative, built on the opposition of before and after the conversionary moment. To represent conversion in lyric is more complicated. We will see that these songs operate within a kind of dialectic. On the one hand, here Dylan unmasks and reveals himself as nowhere else in his work. The biographical "Bob Dylan" seems to be hovering around these songs, sometimes even putting in an appearance. Yet the more Dylan reveals his own vulnerability, the more the songs themselves seem to celebrate the power of his voice as performer, as authority, as star, as artist. Indeed, the humiliation of the self in the rejection of sin is shaped by the fact that, at this point, Dylan was probably the most famous rock artist in the world, yet an artist who had just suffered, for the first time, several artistic failures in a row. Thus the debility of the self is implicated in the strength of his voice to speak weakness, and to turn old forms to new purposes. We will see a bit later how the paradoxical relationship between artistic authority and personal abjection reaches a resolution, of sorts, in a sequence of songs written in the early 1980s in which the status of the artist and the reach of art itself are thrown into question.

The most famous instance of religious conversion in the West is recounted in the *Confessions* of Saint Augustine, about whom, we recall, Dylan had written a song back in 1967, "I Dreamed I Saw St. Augustine." That song ended with the singer contemplating the Saint at his death, unable to do anything but weep. The *Confessions*, however, tell a different story, a story not of tragic catharsis but of transformation. Saint Augustine, the fourth-century philosopher and rhetorician, finds himself mired in vanity and lust. One day, sitting in a garden, he hears what sounds like children's voices saying, "Take up and read." Taking up the Bible and opening it at random, he reads a verse about turning away from his bad old ways: "Not in rioting and drunkenness, not in chambering and wantonness, not in strife and envying, but put ye on the Lord Jesus Christ, and make not provision for the flesh" (Romans 13:13, in the King James version). "Instantly," says Augustine, "as the sentence ended — by a light, as it were, of security infused into my heart — all the gloom of doubt vanished away."[2] Later accounts of conversion often correspond to this one, as reading a text or seeing a vision brings about some transformation of the self.

But there are multiple turnings in the process of conversion. As William James's seminal discussion of the phenomenon notes, conversion *to* something is equally a conversion *from* something, and more energy is often expended on rejecting the past than on embracing the future.[3] Saint Augustine's preparation for conversion, for example, consists of a series of scenes in which his hatred for his own weakness is described in great detail. No less important, moreover, when we consider the relationship between conversion and art, is that the expression or representation of the conversionary experience in language or image requires a return to the preconversion experience. We know this story well from the *Divine Comedy* of Dante Alighieri, whom we encountered in the last chapter, and whose journey through Hell, Purgatory, and Paradise is the account of how he came to be converted so that he could *write* his journey through Hell, Purgatory, and Paradise. To embrace the new bliss the horrors of the past must be confronted and discounted. Thus the aesthetics of conversion involve not only a "turning toward" something new. They involve a "turning away" from what is being rejected and a "turning back" to bear witness to where one has come from. "Turning to, turning away, turning back"; these positionings will be played out in different ways in Dylan's postconversion work.

Dylan's Christian songs involve the forging of a new artistic personality. This is certainly connected to his conversion. But just as *Blood on the Tracks* is sprinkled with personal references that are also literary tropes (with Petrarch and Kerouac providing the vocabulary), so does this work, whatever the biographical circumstances, respond to some of the problems raised by *Desire* and *Street Legal*. If those albums struggled with the place of art in a disenchanted world, the thematics of Christian conversion provide the opportunity to see the world as newly filled with magic. Personal humiliation and betrayal emerge as literary vehicles for exploring authorship. So how do genre and doctrine intertwine? If conversion implies "turning" from the old (*convertere* = Latin, "to turn"), how can a new art be invented that would give form to this rejection? And what about the "turning back" of witnessing in art? How is the general weakness of the age answered by a rhetoric of need that may itself be part of the problem?[4]

Dylan's song lyrics and titles during this period make repeated references to dramatic change, or to turning from one choice to another. "Gonna Change My Way of Thinking," declares one song. "Ye Shall Be Changed" and "You Changed My Life," declare two other later released songs from the same period. But figures of turning, spinning, and revolving are everywhere. "Slow Train Coming," which I just quoted, features Thomas "Jefferson turnin' over in his grave" (p. 574). "Felt around for the light switch, turned around for her face" (p. 628), says *Shot of Love*'s "The Groom's Still Waiting at the Altar," the chorus of which points to some new dispensation: "I see the turning of the page." This is a very different scenography from the static world of *Blonde on Blonde*, or the romance evasions of *Desire*.

"The Groom's Still Waiting at the Altar" points to the resources and limits of imagining collective change that would also be personal change. The chorus evokes the biblical trope of Christ as bridegroom to his church and presents images of Messianic expectation: "I see the turning of the page / Curtain rising on a new age / I see the Groom still waiting at the altar" (p. 628). Yet the verses tell a more modest story, a story about a "groom" in love who lives in a world where no one can keep a promise to anyone else. The song is filled with images of broken communication, of barriers and walls. The hero, like the protagonists in the songs on *Street Legal*, is persecuted and misunderstood. He drifts in and out of a relationship with a mysterious woman named Claudette, with neither of the two able to make a serious commitment: "Finally had to give her up about the time she began to want me," he says. Then, "I'd have done anything for that woman if she'd only made me feel obligated" (p. 628). Yet, between these two levels of deferred turning — between Messianic expectation and personal drama — the song also evokes images of political revolution, a violent form of overturning (*revolvo* = Latin, "to turn over"). Against the backdrop of the dirty wars in Latin America (the song makes explicit reference to Argentina) Dylan sings, "Cities on fire, phones out of order / They're killing nuns and soldiers / There's fighting on the border." The fact that Dylan acknowledges the soldiers as humans whose death means something (rather than singing a more morally comfortable line like, say, "nuns are killed by soldiers"), suggests the capacity of his moral imagination.[5] Within the problematic I have been tracing involving the relationship between personal conversion and general political disgust, it also suggests that while marriage, revolution, and salvation may all involve forms of turning, these conversions may not always unfold in consort. Indeed, it is within the context of fragile relationships, regret, and deferred conversions that many of these songs take shape.

The relationship between the new wine of Christian doctrine and the old bottles of popular music is raised by the first track on the 1979 album *Slow Train Coming*, "Gotta Serve Somebody." It is a very simple groove tune that evokes Memphis Slim's 1951 song "Mother Earth." Memphis Slim's tune, which he once called "Consolation Blues," lists a number of people who are proud or who have treated him badly.[6] At each verse, we are told that they're all going to go back to Mother Nature. It offers a universal vision of the cycle of life as a gentle form of revenge. Dylan's song, too, is a list song. It catalogues a group of potentially proud or self-sufficient people who are warned that they are in trouble because they are not powerful and self-sufficient after all. All will have to "serve somebody" at some unnamed point in the future.

Literary scholars have often noted that the Greek word for religious conversion, *metanoia*, was also used by early teachers of rhetoric to describe moments of turning or revision in language, what the Romans called *correctio*: "Not life, but love in death," is the line from Shakespeare's *Romeo and Juliet* that is sometimes cited to illustrate this rhetorical turn. But we can recall as well Augustine's conversion line, "not in rioting and drunkenness ... [but] on the Lord Jesus Christ." Dylan's lines in "Gotta Serve Somebody," "You may be a socialite with a long string of pearls / But you're gonna have to serve somebody" offer a version of the same rhetorical figure. Dylan's line activates both the religious and the rhetorical senses of *metanoia*.[7] The lyric sets forth a list of "A but B" phrases. You may be comfortable in who you are (A), *but* you don't see the bigger picture (B). Not in your pride, but in service — of either the Devil or the Lord. We touch here on Dylan's longstanding interest in the rhetoric of unmasking. However, here he does not unmask only the rich ("Masters of War"), the fancy ("Queen Jane Approximately"), or the corrupt ("Hurricane"). Everybody is now a target. Even the local tonsorialist gets called out: "You may be working in a barber shop / You may know how to cut hair ... But ..." (p. 568).

The process of unmasking continues into the last verses, where something striking happens. The singer and composer, the biographical Bob Dylan, shows up and names himself: "You may call me Terry or you may call me Timmy," Dylan intones. "You may call me Bobby or you may call me Zimmy." In a song about unmasking, Dylan drops his own mask. In 1965's "It's Alright, Ma (I'm Only Bleeding)," Dylan had unmasked the hypocrisy of straight society by placing himself as an observer whose pain is implicit but never dramatized in the ironic title phrase "I'm only bleeding," which is never sung. There, we learned that "even the president of the United States / Must sometimes have to stand naked" (p. 188). Now it is Dylan who stands, if not naked before us, at least willing to set aside his show business identity and reveal his birth name. Robert Zimmerman, born a Jew, ready, it would seem, for some new identity. The song is leading toward a moment at which Dylan himself will be included among the rest of us, those who "gotta serve somebody." Indeed, the very title of the song suggests the universality and ambiguity of service: "Gotta Serve Somebody" could be "(I) gotta serve somebody" (as in the expression, "Sorry, gotta go") or "(You) gotta serve somebody." However, a universal vision of service — which would follow Memphis Slim's lead — is not to be. For Dylan turns aside the threat toward which his own song is pointing — something like "I, too, Bobby Zimmerman, here known as Zimmy, gotta serve somebody." Instead it offers, "You may call me R. J., you may call me Ray / You may call me anything, no matter what you say / You're still gonna have to serve somebody." Dylan unmasks himself. However his goal is *not* to include himself in the crowd. He is who he is, but not as the subject of abjection and humiliation. Rather, he is the target of calumny who turns calumny back against his accusers.[8]

This reversal or turning in the rhetoric of the song suggests both the vulnerability and the defensiveness of the singing persona. You might think this guy is "getting soft," until he puts you in a place of weakness and reclaims the authority to judge you. It is a jiujitsu-like game of (un)masking and accusation that works through the unfolding of the musical structure. Harmonically, "Gotta Serve Somebody" may be the simplest song Bob Dylan has ever written. The verse unfolds over one chord, an A minor chord. Once the chorus arrives, it evolves into a simple blues form. The musical movement in the verse comes, not from chord changes (since there are none), but from the interplay between the hypnotic drum hits on the second and fourth beats and an A minor pentatonic riff on the first beat. Played on keyboards, the riff is basic blues harmony. It hiccups up from a C note to a D and then back to C and A, spelling out for a second the notes also in a D7 chord, which is where the band will end up a few measures later. The keyboard riff jerks in anticipation at the rest of the song. It powers the jumpiness of the lyric, as if all of the characters who are content in their false identities were being unsettled by Dylan's own harmony — as if the song couldn't wait to get to the chorus, which is where the action is. Because of this jerkiness, when the harmony finally ascends to the D of "Gonna have to serve somebody," it feels almost like a release. Any feeling of comfort would be a mistake, however, since that is the exact moment at which Dylan delivers the bad news to whoever thinks he or she is doing fine: "You're gonna have to serve somebody" after all.

The twitchy musical groove underpins a lyric through which Dylan turns his scorn on any number of social types. The choice between damnation and salvation, however, is not totally clear as the song unfolds. For one thing, the title phrase, "Gotta Serve Some-body," is never mentioned in the song, which states, "you're *gonna have to* serve somebody / Yes indeed, you're gonna have to serve somebody" (my emphasis). The title to the song, "gotta" suggests an obligation, the idea that our very being is in servitude; that we are all marked by sin. The lyric use of "gonna have to" implies a future that is known, but that is deferred. It turns the song into a song about time. "Grant me chastity and continency, but not yet," prays Saint Augustine before his conversion.[9] In Dylan's song we are not yet in service, at least for the five minutes and twenty-five seconds that the track runs. And in fact, it is while the song is unfolding that we learn what is implied in the "gonna" of "gonna have to serve somebody." In this regard, the song is a prophecy. The spooky organ blasts that punctuate the rhythm track harbinger bad news for the characters named. But the bad news is itself attenuated by Dylan's own pronunciation of the sentence he is delivering on those he targets: "Gonna have to serve some . . . body," he sings. The split between "some" and "body" opens up a space for variation. Dylan's pronunciation of "body" (sounded as "buddy") moves around, from a nasal bleat to a sarcastic sneer delivered out of the side of the mouth, to a full-throated condemnation. The distance between "some" and "body" places the rhythmic emphasis on "body." Yet what we will have to serve is not, after all, a "body," but a supernatural presence — either good or bad. Thus our own listening experience, through "some" to "body" and beyond, sets us up, preparing us, through the delay, for the powerful message. The doctrinaire logic of this revelation, which unreels at the level of the musical line and the rhythm of Dylan's diction, is then disclosed for all to see in the resolution: "It may be the Devil, or it may be the Lord." However this is not what "some...body" suggests. "Some...body" suggests that we could serve any number of entities—the law, the Mafia, the Texas Rangers, the Girl Scouts. This evocation of commitment is then narrowed to two options, "the Devil" or "the Lord." In other words, our moral choices are suddenly reduced when the harmony moves, in good blues fashion, to the fifth chord, and the form opens away from the obsessive rocking on A minor that structures the verses. As the melody and harmony move, the ideology gets more rigid.

The point here is that as the song unfolds, its form works to capture the attention of the listener. It seems to open possibilities for action, then it closes them down. It seems to stage the exposure of the author, but then it turns on the listener, catching us, as it were, in a kind of trap. "You may call me Bobby," it says. "Oh, yes," says the listener in a moment of recognition. "There he is. We know that name. It's on the cover of the album that we just purchased." But then we are informed that calling out Dylan's name is not what is important. In fact, it may precisely be the problem, since it smacks of rock star idolatry that distracts from what *is* important, which is our own situation. Rhetorically, we have been boxed in. In this regard, "Gotta Serve Somebody" offers an aesthetic response to the failure of authority that I pointed to above. At the center of that response is a reaffirmation of the power of the singer as artist, as shaper of language and decider of (our) destinies. The ultimate choice may be between God and the Devil, but Dylan claims the power to define the very language of the choice—"gotta" or "gonna." At another level, "Gotta Serve Somebody" presents in conversionary terms a phenomenon we have seen elsewhere in Dylan's work. This is the double register whereby Dylan assumes both the role of the character and the commentator on the song. Here he is both the (weak) protagonist, unmasked in name, and the (strong) prophet who puts us in our place.

Psalm
One of the clichés about the history of the blues is that often blues singers sang the "Devil's music" on Saturday night, only to sing God's music on Sunday morning. Dylan expresses this juxtaposition of

theological reformation and sexual hijinks in one of his earliest lyr-
ics, "Quit Your Low Down Ways" (1962). It is a blues (of course) that
offers as its refrain, "If you can't quit your sinnin' please, quit your
low down ways" (p. 46). In his Christian songs at the end of the 1970s
he returns to these paradoxes. However, he does not reactivate the
conventions of rural black "folk music," or of "spirituals." To be sure,
the Christian songs are very simple in structure. With a few notable
exceptions, they do not feature bridges, working instead on the verse-
chorus-verse model of much traditional gospel and folk music. Some,
like "Gotta Serve Somebody" are deeply dependent on riffs.[10] But they
also construct a new idiom, one attuned less to rural gospel tradi-
tions in one-room churches than to Dylan's new status as a rock star.
For suddenly Dylan begins to mimic the formulations of urban Black
English, or what linguists call African American Vernacular Eng-
lish. He changes his language. Two years earlier Dylan was offering
such baroque lines as, "You turn around for one real / Last glimpse of
Camille / 'Neath the moon shining bloody and pink" (from "No Time
to Think" [p. 550]), or "'Gentlemen,' he said, / 'I don't need your orga-
nization / I've shined your shoes / I've moved your mountains and
marked your cards'" (from "Changing of the Guards" [p. 548]). Now,
seemingly to break with his past work, he takes on the linguistic hab-
its of a specific ethnic group. So, "I Believe in You," from 1979, gives
us, "'Cause I don't be like they'd like me to" (p. 572) (instead of the
more standard, "I won't be"), and "when white turn to black" (instead
of "turns"). "Saving Grace" gives us "the death of life, then come the
resurrection" (p. 606); "Slow Train" says "it costs more to store the
food than it do to give it" (p. 574), and so on. These shifts in grammar
signify a new social location for the singing persona. They set him
apart. They make it possible for Dylan both to turn *away* from the
earthly domain and to turn *against* the material world of his largely
Caucasian record-buying audience. The affectation of Black English
becomes an allegory for his marginalization as a Christian rock star.[11]

As the convert both turns toward a new source of strength and
against what he once was he opens himself to scorn or calumny. But
social marginalization in a religious context maps as well onto a cli-
ché of popular music. Any number of traditional pop and rock songs
have chronicled the tension between the special world of a couple in
love and "them." "I think we're alone now," observed Tommy James
and the Shondells in their hit by that name in 1967. John Lennon's

intense 1971 song "God" had covered this same territory, calling out a number of perceived phonies (including someone named "Zimmerman") before concluding that only John and Yoko matter: "Yoko and me / And that's reality."[12] A bit later, in 1975 and on less exalted musical territory, Helen Reddy had a pop hit with a song called "You and Me against the World." Like Jesus, like any new religious convert, the heroes of many of Dylan's songs present themselves as victims, not only of the Arab oil embargo, but of incomprehension by friends and family. If "Gotta Serve Somebody" turns on the listener, disarming any claim we might have to judge the singer at the moment he is most vulnerable, elsewhere Dylan takes the cliché of the exclusive couple, rejected by everyone in town, and turns it to devotional ends. He does this by melding the trope of exclusivity with the language of the Psalms, where the beleaguered poet sings to God for help. This emerges most powerfully in the beautiful song "I Believe in You," the third cut on *Slow Train Coming*. The message of the song is directly related to the intricately woven form of the lyric, which we can understand only by looking at it in full:

They ask me how I feel
And if my love is real
And how I know I'll make it through
And they, they look at me and frown
They'd like to drive me from this town
They don't want me around
'Cause I believe in You

They, they show me to the door
They say, "Don't come back no more"
'Cause I don't be like they'd like me to
And I, I walk out on my own
A thousand miles from home
But I don't feel alone
'Cause I believe in You

I believe in You even through the tears and the laughter
I believe in You even though we be apart
I believe in You even on the morning after
Oh, when the dawn is nearing
Oh, when the night is disappearing
Oh, this feeling is still here in my heart

Don't let me drift too far
Keep me where You are
Where I will always be renewed
And that which You've given me today
Is worth more than I could pay
And no matter what they say
I believe in You

I believe in You when wintertime turns to summer
I believe in You when white turn to black
I believe in You even though I be outnumbered
Oh, though the earth may shake me
Oh, though my friends forsake me
Oh, even that couldn't make me go back

Don't let me change my heart
Keep me set apart
From all the plans they do pursue
And I, I don't mind the pain
Don't mind the driving rain
I know I will sustain
'Cause I believe in You (p. 572)

While "sincerity" is a word I have avoided applying to Dylan's vocals, on this song the term is apt. It is a deeply heartfelt performance, with the singer's voice modulating between yawps of intensity, where his voice breaks with urgency, and moments of actual dynamic diminuendo or softening. It may be the most dynamically nuanced of all of his vocal performances. His first mention of himself, in the second verse, "And I, I walk out on my own," has him pushing the pronoun beyond recognition, until it sounds in the throat like a cry, "aaahhhiii," as he reclaims his space from "they" who persecute him.[13]

The melody is built on a play between the third note of an E major chord, and the suspended fourth (back and forth between $G\sharp$ and A) in the first few notes.[14] This melodic figure is repeated in various forms until the fifth line in each verse, where a shift down to a major chord based on the flatted seventh corresponds to the climax of the verse that sums up the torment: "They'd like to *drive* me from this town" (my emphasis). This D major is the slightly discordant "surprise" chord that we saw appear at key moments on *Blood on the*

Tracks. Here it does its dramatic work, driving us out of key as the protagonist is driven out of town. The repetition of "they" at the beginning of each line creates an effect of intensification that is then overturned by the final expression of faith. Like the reversal seen in "Gotta Serve Somebody," where a lyric pointing to the humiliation of the singer turns into an accusation aimed at the listener, the voices of the crowd are silenced here by the final affirmation of faith.[15]

"I Believe in You" is a song about the relationship between permanence and change. Change is represented as both natural, through time (wintertime gives way to summer, night to day), and ontological (white turns to black). Yet it aims toward affirmations of constancy. "Don't let me drift too far / Keep me where You are," sings Dylan, in a gesture toward the old Bill Monroe gospel tune, "Driftin' Too Far from the Shore."[16] Moreover, the double register — both weak character and strong prophet — that I pointed to in "Gotta Serve Somebody" is reflected in the tension between the electric piano spelling out the melody and the steady jangle of the acoustic guitar in the background.

The formal elegance of this song is essential to its message. The seven lines of each verse unfold in an AABCCCB pattern. The first three lines suggest the basic situation. A and A ask a question, and B expands it. Lines four through six both break and continue this train of thought: "And" continues the string of events, while "they" takes us back to the first word. These lines fill us in on the opening question to the hero with an account of how he is being rejected. The opening challenges, first described through AA, are now expanded, as we get three rhyming lines, CCC. The final line resolves the situation with its affirmation of faith, even as the concluding B rhyme in "I believe in You" takes us back to "make it through" in line 3. This rhyme buckles the stanza together, creating the last five lines (BCCCB) as a kind of unit. Not surprisingly, the concluding phrase, "I believe in You," provides the answer to the question with which it rhymes: "How I know I'll make it through." The existential question and its answer come into clear focus only when seen within the formal structure of the stanza and its rhyme words.

The editors of Dylan's lyrics have capitalized the Y in "You," suggesting the devotional theme. However, it is crucial to point out that the evocation of the divine in the performance does not come all at once. It comes *as* the lyric unfolds, in a manner analogous to the play with delay and reversal we saw in "Gotta Serve Somebody." It is as the song moves ahead that it takes us from the vocabulary of erotic love to the vocabulary of spiritual devotion, from the "quit your low down ways" side of Dylan's music, to the "quit your sinnin'" side. This modulation is rendered perfectly in the bridges. The language of the first bridge suggests some type of erotic encounter. "Even though we be apart" is not the language of someone with Jesus in his heart, since the entire point of conversion in evangelical traditions is that God now lives within. Moreover, the phrase "even on the morning after" is not conventionally a phrase applied to religious conversion. We know what "the morning after" refers to. It refers to sex. Here the expression connotes the world of the hookup as a way of reinforcing the mutability of appetite and casual connection in a song that is ultimately about immutability and commitment. However the second bridge shifts the terms of the argument and penetrates to the mystery of conversion. For there the talk is no longer of "the morning after," but of miracles and prodigies, earthquakes and war. This is the language of the Psalms. The completely natural image of winter turning to summer gives way to the miraculous notion of "when white turn to black." Is this a moral commentary or a racial one? It is striking that it comes as one of several lines where Dylan is deploying the locutions of Black English, using "turn" instead of the more conventional "turns," and the slightly archaic and dialectical "be" instead of "may be." In other words, Dylan is "turning" to black speech patterns at the moment he evokes the miracle of the change of color. He is performing the miraculous transformation that he is narrating, which becomes a metaphor for the turn from this world to God. By the end of the bridge, we are assured that he will never "go back." Given what precedes it, this phrase points to the notion that religious conversion may involve either a process of surrender, or an act of the will, or both.

Thus, as the song unfolds it changes or turns its devotional focus from love ("the morning after") to God ("though the earth may shake me"). That is, within a song that asserts constancy, *not* changing, Dylan changes topics as we listen. The bridge dramatizes this dynamic through the elegance of its form. At first glance the bridges seem to work differently from the verses, since they seem only to have six lines, equally divided between "I believe" and "Oh." However, the last line of each of the bridges contains two rhymes. In the first bridge "still here in" builds on "disappearing" and "nearing," which precede it directly. But it ends with "in my heart" which takes us all the way back to "apart," in line two. This makes each of the bridges *both* a six-line stanza and a seven-line stanza — or, rather, a six-line stanza that behaves as if it were a seven-line stanza, like the verses. And, as in the verse, the last line, "in my heart," is the precise solution to the problem raised by "even though we be apart," from line two, with which it rhymes. The same technique applies in the second of the two bridges, where the final lines ("Oh, though my friends forsake me / Oh, even that couldn't make me") end with "make me go back," which takes back to the second line's "I believe in you when white turn to black." The dialogue across the stanza between "white to black" and "make me go back" suggests the further complexity of the song, which explores the relationship between a miracle and an act of will. Moreover, each of the bridges features Dylan repeating, in a kind of howl, the exclamation "Oh!" in a crescendo of intensity. This gesture perfectly encapsulates the force lines that structure the story. As the most expressive and least semantically specific of all utterances (and perhaps the very beginning of song and poetry) the exclamation "Oh!" suggests sexual ecstasy, spiritual surrender, and moral determination all at once. Dylan's final cry leads up to the moment at which his very voice wobbles in pitch and seems to give out for lack of breath, "Even that couldn't make me go baaaacck!"

Yet, if the song is about change within a vow of constancy — as both passive miracle and willful transformation — the final verse offers, here as in "Gotta Serve Somebody," a reversal or flipping over of the opening scenario. The scenes of ostracism and rejection by "they" in the first verse are recalled and redeemed by the request, in the last verse, to be "set apart / From all the plans they do pursue." It now turns out that the plans "they" pursue, which include putting the hero out of doors in verse one, are in fact part of a bigger design. We now learn that he *wants* to be ostracized because that means he is elect. What was a curse is now a blessing. The link back to the earlier scene is reinforced by the reappearance, in the concluding verse, of the rhyme between "though we be apart" and "still in my heart" from the first bridge. Now we get: "Don't let me change my heart / Keep me set apart / Where I will always be renewed." Suddenly, being "apart" is positive, something that the protagonist desires. This turns the song over on itself. The power of the protagonist's commitment to God (or to whomever is being addressed) transmutes the values that infuse the bleak atmosphere in the first lines. And the language of change that punctuates the song gives way to the final affirmation of a resistance to change: "I know I will sustain." "Sustain" is an interesting word. Here it seems primarily to mean "endure." Yet it is an idiosyncratic choice, since it is, in English, a transitive verb. You cannot, in fact, sustain. You have to sustain something. The only thing that can "sustain" intransitively, it turns out, is a musical note, which can be held through time. Thus the final phrase captures both the intensity of the believer and the persistence of the singer—and this in a song in which Dylan pushes notes to the limits of his own breath capacity. "I know I will sustain," means, at one level, "I know I will be heard."[17]

The finely modulated expression of faith set forth in "I Believe in You" works through two different linguistic codes, two levels of meaning, played out through the complex stanzaic scheme and rhyme patterns. It begins in a scene of social rejection and erotic encounter, before revealing itself to be about devotion and the blessing of being "set apart" through election. The only thing that can link these is the idea of constancy, the concept of a moral commitment to someone or something. Here the object of desire is no longer the elusive red-haired lady of "Tangled Up in Blue." He/she/it/they is the anchoring force to which the character is drawn and from which it can only move tentatively. And it is also the thematic element that powers the reversal in the lyric, whereby what was once a source of pain becomes the proof of commitment. This is why the form of the song is so tightly wound. The rhyme scheme itself suggests that when we seem to be wandering, we are called back by sonorous echo.

Penitential Psalm

Dylan's trilogy of Christian-influenced albums begins with "Gotta Serve Somebody," a song which, as we have seen, dramatizes the presence of the "author" as both exposed personality and master of form. The final song on the third of the three albums, the hymn-like "Every Grain of Sand," features analogous moments of reversal and suspension. In a sense, it is the answer and counterpart to "Gotta Serve Somebody." The stately song is powered by arpeggiated figures on the electric guitar, punctuated by piano chords and a pair of harmonica solos played, exceptionally, on what sounds like a double-reeded instrument (in contrast to Dylan's usual blues harp) that echoes the reverb-drenched guitar sound. The last verse fades in a horn accompaniment. The lyric consists of three verses of eight lines each. Each verse divides into two parts, built on major chords, like many Protestant hymns. The singing is controlled. The voice never breaks, as it does on some of Dylan's more energetic performances during this period. The voice modulates between a straightforward presentation and an occasional shift into a more nasally inflected tone ("the memory of decay"), which becomes the default in lines five through eight, as Dylan harmonizes with a backup singer. Especially striking is the use of the *tacet*, where the band suddenly stops—often on key words, such as following the phrase "this chain of events that I must break" (pause, *break*)—before taking up the forward movement, thereby mimicking the stop-and-start, hesitation-determination theme of the lyric.

"Every Grain of Sand" offers a detailed confessional moment at which Dylan's persona seems to be taking stock of the position of the sinful self in a universe controlled by a divine plan. The self recognizes that plan, but it cannot completely turn away from the weaknesses that have distracted it in the past. This is the moment where Augustine turns back to describe his own horrible sins, just before he takes up the Bible and reads. For Dylan, the self remains mired in the past, caught between the desire to change and the guilty inability to forget what has come before. He begins with a set of statements about voice and language. "In the time of my confession" (p. 646) is the first line. The confession is not what we are listening to, however; the song is a commentary on the practice and problems of confession, and on how confession necessarily involves the "turning back" to what is being left behind. Inside of confession, we learn, a "dying voice" speaks up, which recalls all that the confession is trying to reject. Thus we get a verbal artifact (a song) about a verbal sacrament (confession) that acknowledges a verbal remnant (the "dying voice"). Indeed, what is striking about the lyric is the tangled density of the figures of speech through which it puts across its message. The conceit of the grain of sand comes from William Blake's poem, "Auguries of Innocence," which longs "To see a World in a Grain of Sand / And a Heaven in a Wild Flower / Hold Infinity in the palm of your hand / And Eternity in an hour." The poem goes on to offer a catalogue of instances in which the tiniest movement in the universe affects broader forces.[18] In addition, as Michael Gray's discussion of the sources of this song has shown, it is deeply woven with phrases from the Bible.[19] Dylan sets the grain of sand next to Jesus's statement in Matthew 10:29–30, where he reassures His disciples that God watches over everything: "Are not two sparrows sold for a penny? And not one of them will fall to the ground without your Father's will. But even the hairs of your head are all numbered."[20] Shakespeare's Hamlet recalls this last phrase when speaking to his friend Horatio, as he prepares to take on his destiny by fighting Laertes: "We defy augury. There is a special providence in the fall of a sparrow. If it be now, 'tis not to come; if it be not to come, it will be now; if it be not now, yet it will come. The readiness is all."[21] Hamlet's reflection turns the problem of the sparrow's fall into a problem of time, which helps illuminate Dylan's interest in the herky-jerky structure of conversion, and the multiplicity of voices that echo through his journey. Thus the Bible, Blake, and Shakespeare here come together to offer vocabulary for a meditation on the relationship between the individual and the cosmos, between past and present. At one level, the song recalls Dylan's interest in the moment, discussed in such songs as "Mr. Tambourine Man," in Chapter 3. However here the emphasis is not on exploring the moment, or exploding it, but rather on acknowledging the forces that make each instant possible.

For our purposes, what stands out are the striking metaphors that describe less the hero's emotional state than the landscape of his adventures and missteps:

> In the time of my confession, in the hour of my deepest need
> When the pool of tears beneath my feet flood every newborn seed
> There's a dyin' voice within me reaching out somewhere
> Toiling in the danger and in the morals of despair (p. 646)

The "voice" that calls out in the moment of despair is ambivalent, since it implies both a cry for help and the voice of the past. This is why it is toiling in "danger." The dangerous idea of being "called" is repeated, in different figures, across the song. In the third stanza the hero will walk past the doorway of "temptation's angry flame" and hear his name called. And yet again, in the final lines, he will hear "the ancient footsteps like the motion of the sea" and will turn around (there's that gesture of turning again) to see who is behind him: "Sometimes I turn, there's someone there, other times it's only me." These are the counterparts to the "You can call me Bobby" moment in "Gotta Serve Somebody," moments where the self is named, in all of its vulnerability.

The song presents us with the classic image of the human being as pilgrim, what the Middle Ages called *homo viator*, man the traveler. Yet at every step, there is both the possibility of turning back and the necessity of turning back, if an account of the past is to be written:

> Don't have the inclination to look back on any mistake
> Like Cain, I now behold this chain of events that I must break
> In the fury of the moment, I can see the Master's hand
> On every leaf that trembles, on every grain of sand

The biblical reference is a bit wobbly, since Cain's murder of his brother Abel was not a "chain of events" but a single crime. But the image cuts to the center of the song. For the protagonist longs to escape the weaknesses of the past. In order to do this, he must break with what has come before. His historical prototype is Cain, who, as we remember, was marked by God, set apart, not for excellence, but for his sin.[22] Thus the reference to Cain "frees" the hero from the past (he will "break" "this chain of events") even as it condemns him to be called to again and again. We seem to be at the exact opposite pole from the world of "Like a Rolling Stone," where humiliation was also emancipation. Here the emancipated self is haunted by memory and temptation. This paradox is central to the song, which is both about a singular moment of awareness and repentance, and a sense of the ongoing, recursive and repetitive power of temptation and "danger."

We can see the work done by the lyric if we turn to the beginning of the second verse, where Dylan's language becomes densely metaphorical:

> Oh, the flowers of indulgence and the weeds of yesteryear
> Like criminals, they have choked the breath of conscience and good cheer
> The sun beat down upon the steps of time to light the way
> To ease the pain of idleness and the memory of decay

The language here is stately and draws on what I called, in Chapter 1, Dylan's "archaic" voice, with words such as "indulgence," "idleness," and, especially, "yesteryear." But more striking are the metaphors. Students of rhetoric have traditionally called figures of speech the "flowers" of rhetoric. You don't need to know this cliché — or to know whether Dylan knows it or cares about it — to see that we are off in the tall grass here. Following on the "newborn seed" image in the first verse, we now have "flowers" and "weeds." One involves a sin, "indulgence," the other simply the past more generally, "yesteryear." These two metaphors are then redefined through the use of simile, "like criminals." What have these "criminals" done? They have "choked" the breath of conscience. Now, it is true that criminals can often choke living creatures. But so can weeds. So, the simile "like criminals" is not really needed. It doubles down, describing the weeds as doing what they already do. But its purpose is different. It is included to add a moral inflection to the vegetal imagery. It is one thing to say that the "weeds" of the past keep you from breaking free into the future. It is something else to say that this tangled web is itself criminal because it keeps you from coming to terms with your spiritual state. Such overdetermined use of figures of speech suggests the ways in which the song is wavering between an image of the self as simply weak, on the one hand, and an image of the self as corrupt, on the other. Is this lack of will or original sin? Yesteryear can't merely be a weed that needs to be left behind. It must now be a criminal weed. A similar rhetorical layering occurs in the very next lines, where "the sun beat down upon the steps of time to light the way." The negative, oppressive connotation of "the sun beat down" turns into something else when the "steps" which it strikes, morph right before our eyes and ears, from an architectural feature to a unit of space covered and then to a slice of time ("step" as building/step as my step in walking/step as moment or hour) becoming, in the process a positive force, as we learn that the sun is not heat, but light, helping the hero move ahead.

Dylan is in full rhetorical mode here, manipulating figures of speech like a card sharp. Of special importance are the similes, which he inserts into a thick forest of metaphors. The similes ("like criminals") modify those metaphors, becoming in the process rhetorical figures about rhetorical figures. When we recall that rhetorical tropes are, etymologically, a "turning" of language away from its conventional meaning, we have here a turning on turning. But more is going on. The two similes we have looked at, "like Cain" in the first verse, and "like criminals" in the second, are the figures that make a cosmic fable out of a fairly conventional song about trying to move on from the past ("me, I'm still on the road," sang Dylan in "Tangled

Up in Blue" (p. 480); "I feel like I gotta travel on," he recalled in an old Eddy Arnold/Kingston Trio standard from *Self Portrait*). A song that starts out with the hero trying to turn away from a depressing situation and start anew takes on quite different colorations with the introduction of the similes "like Cain" and "like criminals." This figural excess reappears in the third great simile in the song, in the final quatrain: "I hear the ancient footsteps like the motion of the sea." It is not clear what "ancient footsteps" would be, except that they come from the past (more "archaic" language to describe the archaic). Yet one should be able to leave them behind — until it is revealed they are eternal, always returning and always in your ears, "like the motion of the sea." The simile suggests that being haunted is a natural phenomenon, one you cannot escape, and that you must turn back constantly to confront yourself in an endless process of self-castigation and regret. This is not the conversion from the torment of sin to the peace of salvation that Saint Augustine mentioned in his *Confessions*. It is a much more vexing form of turning, a turning back on a past that one must — but cannot — leave behind.

The dense metaphorical language that characterizes "Every Grain of Sand" is part of the point of the song. The song is about the desire to break with the past, even as it acknowledges the impossibility of escape from the past because one is inextricably bound up with it: "Every time I pass that way, I always hear my name." This means that the language one uses to free oneself is inevitably a metaphorical language. Only metaphor can give a name to the past so as to set it aside and apart, turning away at last from "temptation's angry flame," the "dark wood" (Dante) or the "dark night of the soul" (Saint John of the Cross). Yet the point of the song is that one cannot escape metaphors and similes. They are what give meaning to experience. This paradox is caught nicely by the image of "the broken mirror of innocence on each forgotten face." I look back at what is forgotten — the people I have betrayed or deceived whom I cannot even remember — and I see myself. But I see myself in a broken mirror, distorted and splintered. Not the "through a glass, darkly" that the Bible uses to describe our vision of the future in I Corinthians, 13.12; instead, the past seen through a broken mirror. And since the metaphor figures both the gesture of looking back at someone else and the process of self-reflection, it is unclear whether the "innocence" that has been lost is my own or that of the people I have betrayed. This existential paradox can only be captured in metaphor, in the figure of the "broken mirror of innocence."

In other words, the rhetorical excesses of the song, which some critics see as a weakness, are precisely what it is about. We cannot confront our past without slipping into metaphors and similes, but in order to break with the past we also need to break with the fictions and illusions (metaphors and similes) that bewitched us in those foolish days. Now we see through a glass darkly — but in fact we never escape the glass so long as we are in this world. This is why the punch lines to the verses are themselves figures of speech that increase in their figural intensity until we reach the climax in the final lines, with two similes in a row, "like every sparrow falling, like every grain of sand." The nuance of difference between these figures — the sparrow is still in the process of "falling," and thus hangs in "the balance," the grain of sand is simply numbered — suggests the difficulty of bringing an absolute break with the past, where everything is now numbered and in its place, into line with the sense of disequilibrium, of being in flux. This is what "in the time of my confession" (which is both now and not now) means. In the generic register of the penitential psalm, the metaphors and similes express the relationship between a present that, for theological reasons, must break with the past, and a past that, psychologically and emotionally, will never quite go away.

"I am hanging in the balance of the reality of man / Like every sparrow falling, like every grain of sand," comes the final insight. Dylan's performance underscores the importance of this instant, as he breaks with the quavers and nasality of the rest of the performance to pronounce "the reality of man" with an exaggerated clarity, as if the message were set off from all other instants in this song. Yet, it is remarkable that it should be, of all things, the clarity of Dylan's diction (from a singer famous for slurring lyrics), rather than lyric or cadence, that sets that key phrase, "the reality of man," apart from the rest. For it suggests the difficulty of articulating the balance of the instant in song. This may be why Dylan has offered two different versions of the punch line to the song. "I am hanging in the balance of the reality of man," took the alternate form, in a later-released outtake, of "I am hanging in the balance of a perfect, finished plan" (p. 635). Whether the human condition is a balancing act of misery or part of a perfect plan is one of the unresolved problems raised by "Every Grain of Sand."

No less than his youthful investment in the folk music scene of Greenwich Village, Dylan's embracing of the tenets of evangelical Christianity in his songs from the end of the 1970s locates him in a minority community. The Christian songs, as we have seen, reflect the ambiguities inherent in that self-positioning. "Gotta Serve Somebody" presents the distancing of the self from his community. "I Believe in You" gives us a reflection on the combination of willfulness and surrender that is involved in a conversion from one system of belief to another. And "Every Grain of Sand" explores the hesitations and temporal uncertainties that inform the relationship between a "new" self and the self that has been left behind. The contrast between the guitar accompaniment and the dramatic piano chords in the last song points to the different levels on which the lyric is working, as both the account of a steady forward progress ("onward in my journey") and the record of moments of crisis or reversal. What "Gotta Serve Somebody" achieves at the level of rhetorical drama (with the narrator turning against his listeners) and "I Believe in You" does through its elegant deployment of stanzaic form, "Every Grain of Sand" works out through the manipulation of figural language, metaphor, and simile. All of these songs, as my section headings have suggested, activate different generic or literary registers. And all work through process of overturning or reversal, in which moments of hesitation and recursion end up moving the story from one set of values to another.

Ode
One of the characteristics of the recordings of the songs I have been discussing is that at key moments all three required a turn to a particular gesture of intensification that was written not into the lyric or the structure but into the performance. Dylan's hesitations on "serve some . . . body," his ecstatic and tormented exclamations of "Oh!," in "I Believe in You," and his clipped enunciation of "the reality of man," just discussed, all point to the ways in which the vignettes of the songs, often about weakness and humiliation, are offset by an intensification of the authority of the singer or rock star to push the message across through sheer performative energy. This points to the problematic situation of Dylan's own work at the end of the 1970s. He was more famous and accomplished than ever, but what he was selling didn't seem, for all of its brilliance, to be getting through. The

solution was not more intensity in performance, or more perfec-
tion in composition ("I Believe in You" set the bar about as high as
it could be set, in that regard). At a more general level, the corrup-
tion and failures he had lamented in his lines about Mideast oil and
American weakness had mutated, by the early 1980s, into the rise of
Reaganism, with its greed disguised as patriotism and its rejection
of basic decency toward the poor masquerading as "tough love." In
this context we can look at Dylan's 1983 release called *Infidels*. It takes
us out of his "Christian period," but it draws on the imagery and
rhetoric of the religious songs to denounce false belief — including,
as we will see, belief in the illusions of art. These songs tell stories of
charlatans and phony prophets, of hubris and deceit, but without the
condemnatory counter claims that there was a clear metaphysical
alternative — namely, Jesus — to the vanities of this world.

Setting the tone of *Infidels* is the strong opening track, "Joker-
man," which signals, both harmonically and rhythmically, that we
are now out of the world of gospel. The lyric seems, metrically, as if
it could be sung over something closer to Dylan's earlier work, say,
a rocking shuffle of the type we hear on "Highway 61 Revisited,"
ultimately derived from something like Chuck Berry's "Johnny B.
Goode." So: "Standin' on the water, casting your bread" (p. 654),
can stand next to Berry's "Deep down in Louisiana, close to New
Orleans" or Dylan's own "God said to Abraham, 'Kill me a son'" (p.
216). Yet this template is driven in a different direction from classic
three-chord rock and roll by the nervous plucking of eighth notes on
the tonic chord from the great Jamaican bassist Sly Dunbar. It is his
resonant energy, along with the drumming of his partner Robbie
Shakespeare, that drive the musical machinery of the album.

Harmonically, "Jokerman" is tugged between monotony and sub-
tle modulations. It drives through a repeated B♭ tonic chord, shifting
to a minor on the second scale degree, then to a dominant on the
fifth, and back to the tonic. This is the classic II–V–I movement that
is at the heart of many jazz standards and Tin Pan alley songs. It is
used often by Leonard Cohen, but not often by Dylan. The harmonic
movement, punctuated by Mark Knopfler's compelling guitar riffs,
enables the composer to give the impression that something is chang-
ing, musically, when in fact it is not. In this case a simple harmonic
movement acts almost as a drone, over which Dylan recounts his tale.

Against this push-and-pull backing, the lyric opens a mystery.

Who, in fact, will the "Jokerman" turn out to be? Is this some reference to a playing card—in which case it would seem to be another version of the "Jack of Hearts," from "Lily, Rosemary and the Jack of Hearts," on *Blood on the Tracks*? Are we in the world of Batman, whose rival the Joker causes havoc? Or is this some Shakespearean tragedy with a fool-figure at center stage? "Jokerman dance to the nightingale tune / Bird fly high by the light of the moon / Oh, Oh, Oh, Jokerman!" comes the refrain at the end of each verse.

The verses paint the portrait of a figure of power who is set in an ominous landscape. "Standin' on the water casting your bread / While the eyes of the idol with the iron head are glowing," runs the opening, with the repetition of the long *i* across the second line (eye, idol, iron) presenting a powerful internal rhyme, each long *i* falling on an accented beat. This sonic richness then modulates in the third line, as the i-sound is shortened and run almost to excess: "D*i*stant sh*i*ps sail*i*n' *i*nto the m*i*st, / You were born w*i*th a snake *i*n both of your f*i*sts, / While a hurricane was blow*i*n" (my emphasis). The prototypes are clear; the figure on the water suggests Christ, whereas it was Hercules who strangled snakes in his cradle. The "folksinger" in "A Hard Rain's a-Gonna Fall" vowed to "stand on the ocean until I start sinkin'" (p. 76). Now he is able to keep his balance.

The key qualities here are power and energy, as internal rhyme and rhythm work to propel the song forward. And we are given the image of a figure of domination who can "walk on the clouds" and "manipulate crowds," rising above challenges, "a friend to the martyr, a friend to the woman of shame." This is Jokerman as rock star—or rock star as Jokerman. We can think back to the marauding Joker of "All Along the Watchtower." He cuts a romantic figure: "In the mist of the twilight on a milk white steed / Michelangelo indeed could have carved out your features." However, these last images, which suggest mastery and elegance, also push the song toward a kind of cheesy romanticism, like something out of a TV commercial. And this overblown image of romance and power, which is, as Aidan Day has noted, problematically ambivalent, is brought definitively to earth by the penultimate stanza:[23]

Well, the rifleman's seeking the sick and the lame
Preacherman seeks the same
Who'll get there first is uncertain
Nightsticks and water cannon, tear gas, padlocks,

Molotov cocktails and rocks
Behind every curtain
Falsehearted judges dying in the webs that they spin
Only a matter of time till night comes stepping in (p. 654)

With or without the hero on hand, the slightly menacing decor
of the opening lines is now expanded, and we find ourselves in a
world of violence and murder. The evocation of — and parallel
between — pure violence and religion (rifleman/preacherman) sug-
gest that both characters threaten the powerless in this fallen world.
As if that were not bad enough, the "falsehearted" judges — like the
corrupt judiciary throughout Dylan's work — will finish the job. The
description of these figures of violence as "rifleman" and "preacher-
man" echoes the name of the song's hero, Jokerman. The echo sets all
three in competition. Who can save us from the "rifleman"? Only, it
would seem, the "Jokerman."

From this point, the catastrophe of the song moves quickly into
view. The incessant pulse of the bass, punctuated here and there by
the piano, drives the song to its climax, which is the appearance of a
figure who seems to be the Antichrist. "It's a shadowy world skies are
slippery gray," sings Dylan, before revealing that trouble is coming:

A woman just gave birth to a prince today and dressed him in scarlet
He'll put the priest in his pocket, put the blade to the heat
Take the motherless children off the street
And place them at the feet of a harlot

Here we meet the first of the "infidels" evoked across the album. We
might well think of ourselves in the world of William Butler Yeats's
famous poem "The Second Coming," with its image of the "rough
beast, its hour come round at last" that "slouches toward Bethlehem
to be born."[24] Yet the key — where Dylan adds something to Yeats's
apocalyptic vision — comes in the concluding lines. Here the Joker-
man is called out in an apostrophe:

Oh, Jokerman, you know what he wants
Oh, Jokerman, you don't show any response

And with this the action ends. The final apostrophes echo the refrain
following every verse: "Oh, Oh, Oh, Jokerman!" In the process, they
indicate the impotence and failure of the power that the song seems

so interested in both describing and performing. Evil is here; the Jokerman has power, but he does nothing.

What is striking, however, is that the crisis in the song is written into its form, as well as its theme. The conclusion to the song works, retroactively and dialectically, to undo the entire first half. Everything we have been led to admire about the Jokerman, his beauty, his vibrancy, his mythical strength, is revealed by the last lines to have been an illusion. The song itself, with its pulsating drive, has led us along to a point at which it reveals itself to have been a kind of trap. If we admired the Jokerman, on his "milk-white steed," we were fools, because he is impotent. The album may be full of infidels and idolaters, but we may be the biggest infidels of them all, if we believed Jokerman could fix things. This self-consuming dimension of the work extends to the imagery, as the overwrought romanticism is shown to have been a dream. Indeed, we might even expand this critical perspective to the chorus itself, which, as Michael Gray has noted, is never sung the same way twice. What does "Oh, Oh, Oh, Jokerman!" mean? Is it a lament, a celebration, a gesture of praise? By the end it sounds like an accusation.[25]

This progressive undoing of the power of the Jokerman is paralleled in the setting. The refrain tells us that the Jokerman dances to the tune of the nightingale — perhaps *the* cliché bird in the Romantic tradition, at least since Keats — and by the light of the moon. When it first appears this beautiful figure of harmony and beauty seems to set up a link between nature and art. As the song unfolds, however, the wavering between nature and moral allegory ("standing on the water...") comes down on the side of allegory. This is made clear when evil appears: "Only a matter of time till night comes steppin' in." It is always a "matter of time" when night comes, since all we have to do is wait for it. Here that seemingly natural fact of nocturnal arrival becomes allegory (as it "steps in"). It tells us that this particular night is a moral or ethical night, not a natural one. It announces the arrival of the "shadowy world" of evil. The dark ending reveals that the idealized vision of the Jokerman dancing to the song of a bird is simply a bad cliché. The whole romantic setting turns out, in retrospect, to have been a setup, a gesture of musical prestidigitation to lure in the listener. As we saw in "Gotta Serve Somebody," the form turns around on itself to reveal that it has placed us, as listeners, in the position of weakness. "Oh, Oh, Oh," indeed.

At a larger level, of course — and this is my main point — the song is about the limits of art. Dylan's picture of the Jokerman is also a picture of the maker of illusions, the magician who can dazzle the crowd, the rock star. It partakes of the discourse of the ode, the poetry of celebration, addressed to the object of its praise. However, as I am suggesting, it is, like many odes, deeply ironic. Like many of Dylan's protagonists, the Jokerman is alone ("you rise up and say goodbye to no one"), and like the figures in many of the recent songs he is split against himself: "Shedding off, one more layer of skin / Keeping one step ahead of the persecutor within," runs the second verse. But here is the artist figure, able, it would seem, to do anything — except, that is, act when evil appears. This is not an indictment of a sinful self, as one would have seen in Dylan's Christian songs, but a questioning of the power of the artist in the face of anarchy and chaos. It speaks to the situation of Dylan's own work after the Christian digression, as a new class of grifters comes stepping in to take over the country.

The post-1960s cliché that the personal is the political had become newly problematic in the Reagan years, when the self-expansions of the 1970s that Dylan had touched on with such albums as *Desire* and *Street Legal* had given way to a politics of violence (principally in Central America and in the inner cities) and a culture of ostentatious greed and self-indulgence. The problem for popular art then became linking the intimate world of the self and its desires to the larger world of capitalist market expansion. *Infidels* offers a set of indictments of capitalism, greed, and power. Because of its allegorical nature, "Jokerman" works to mediate between private experience and the public experience that was being retooled for the full onset of neoliberalism. Everything is for sale in the world of *Infidels*. Yet one cannot always write allegory, and Dylan's songs on this album turn often to dramatic shifts of scale and context to link private and public. Thus, for example, "License to Kill" describes the rapacious exploitation of natural resources ("Oh, man has invented his doom / First step was touching the moon" [p. 659]) while presenting a woman witness, who sits "in a cold chill" and asks who will stop the madness, "Who's gonna take away his license to kill?" The image of the paid assassin or James Bond figure is generalized to the larger species, which thinks it can destroy the earth. And just as the Jokerman cannot act, the woman can only ask.

This tension between public and private reappears with startling power in the second song on the album, "Sweetheart Like You," in which the narrator turns to yet another of Dylan's fallen female figures with the refrain, "What's a sweetheart like you doin' in a dump like this?" (p. 656). We learn that things are tense in the crime world, as "the boss" has gone north, leaving a beautiful woman behind to save herself or sink into oblivion. Here, again, a powerful figure of authority has quit the scene, leaving everyone else to pick up the pieces. In the final lines Dylan goes literary. He alludes to a famous quip by the Enlightenment essayist Samuel Johnson: "They say that patriotism is the last refuge to which a scoundrel clings." Then Dylan adds his own observation about what "they say": "Steal a little and they throw you in jail, steal a lot and they make you king" (p. 656). Johnson was speaking about fake patriotism (probably alluding to his rival William Pitt) under a monarchy. Dylan updates the phrase by reversing the politics. In America you don't need royal blood to be a king. All you need to do is steal bigtime—like the "boss" in the song, who has "gone north for a while," "they say that vanity got the best of him / But he sure left here in style." In the early years of Reagan (whose campaign slogan was "It's Morning in America!"), false patriots and thieves were everywhere, taking over the government, celebrating the greed of Wall Street. Who remains to protect the innocent? The placement of the moralistic political proverb at the end of the song acts retroactively on the rest of the lyric, in a manner analogous to what we saw in "Jokerman." The song initially seems to be an elegy to another one of Dylan's ladies who has seen better days (Queen Jane, Miss Lonely), but it turns into a commentary on greed and violence. By the song's end we are not even sure if the "sweetheart" is a woman or an ideal. Is she the "thief," or is the thief the "boss" who has left her behind? Either way, as he says in "Jokerman," "it's a shadowy world," and all the artist can do, like the woman in "License to Kill," is ask what we are doing "in a dump like this."

Epic

As powerful as "Jokerman" is, it pales in comparison to another song recorded at the same sessions and not released until a number of years later. This song is "Blind Willie McTell." McTell was a Piedmont-based blues singer active in the first half of the twentieth century. He is probably best known today as the composer of

"Statesboro Blues," a standard performed by many rock musicians. Dylan's song, however, is not a blues. It is an epic. It draws on the conventions of visionary epic spectacle, the kind of spectacle depicted in the journeys to the underworld by Odysseus or Aeneas — not to mention Dante. It recounts the experience of a narrator on a trip through both the geography of the Old South and the tragic events of southern history. It opens by pointing us on our way: "Seen the arrow on the doorpost," it begins, "saying 'This land is condemned / All the way from New Orleans to Jerusalem'" (p. 670). The idea of the South as a kind of crime scene — linking the modern newscast to the Civil War — is expanded as the narrator gives us a series of vignettes from southern history. The descriptive details enable us to trace, loosely, the journey. "I've traveled through east Texas," begins Dylan. From there we move to the deep South, presumably Georgia ("Seen them big plantations burning"), Florida (the displaced Seminoles "a-moanin'"), Charleston ("seen the ghosts of slavery ships"), and on to the banks of the Mississippi, where we meet a woman and a "fine young handsome man" drinking bootlegged whiskey in the days of Reconstruction. Each verse features an evocation of some type of musiclike sound: the hoot of an owl, the ringing of a bell, the cry of the rebel soldiers. But all of those noises are dwarfed by the achievement of McTell. For each verse ends with some variation on the phrase, "I know no one can sing the blues like Blind Willie McTell."

This visionary mode is unlike the Rimbaud-influenced "vision music" Dylan put forth in the 1960s. Its deeply ethical focus and condemnatory tone link it to some of the Christian songs, with their cosmic and geographical visions ("West of the Jordan / East of the Rock of Gibraltar," from "The Groom's Still Waiting at the Altar" [p. 628]). Here the vision is carefully turned into a narrative that blends the referential register of southern history with the literary conventions of epic. As in an epic vision of history, characters and types parade before the singer. And when we recall that Homer was supposed to be blind, we can see the connections between Homer as blind bard and McTell, the blind blues singer. McTell is the one who can "tell" the story of American history. "Tell me, Muse, of the man of many ways," begins the *Odyssey*.[26] But will Willie tell? we might ask, punning on McTell's first name, as Will Shakespeare punned on his. Only he can, it would seem, even if Dylan here tries.

Dylan's appropriation of the conventions of epic for the matter of American history suggests that, here, as in "Jokerman," we are getting a comment on art. Specifically what seems to be at issue is the relationship between different literary forms and the catastrophe of American history. Dylan takes the European epic tradition and twists it to his American theme, giving shape to visionary experience and replacing Homer with the figure of the blind blues singer. But his point is that it is not epic that can keep faith with American history. Epic is *narrative* history, a form that chronicles events after they have happened. Epic is the traditional genre of war and conquest. The history of the American South certainly provides the subject matter for an epic treatment — however we understand "epic" (from *Gone with the Wind* on down). Dylan provides one such treatment here, in brilliantly condensed detail, complete with blind singer, evocations of divinity, battles, and parades of heroes and villains. Yet the entire song is about the fact that it cannot, itself, do what is needed. What is needed is the blues — the blues of Blind Willie McTell. The blues is *lyric*, a form that registers the effect of violence on the bodies and spirits of its victims. Dylan's exploration of the genre of epic becomes, by the end, commentary on a quite different literary form. Thus, like "Jokerman," the song confronts the limits of art.

The song ends in the present, with the narrator evoking God, who, like Zeus in the *Odyssey*, is "in his heaven." All that remains in this world, says Dylan, are "power and greed and corruptible seed," terms that stake out the moral universe of *Infidels*. And we close with a last scene of vision: "I'm gazing out the window of the St. James Hotel / And I know no one can sing the blues like Blind Willie McTell." The St. James Hotel evokes what is probably the first canonical blues song, "St. James Infirmary," recorded by Louis Armstrong in 1928. It is this tune that Dylan has, in fact, adapted for his own melody. Dylan's emphasis on the details of history has led some students of this song to focus on the question of where, specifically, the "St. James Hotel" might be, as if a literal identification were called for. (There seems to have been one in New Orleans, another in New York, one in St. Louis, and so on.) This, however, misses the point. The point is that Dylan is staying in the hotel because he is a latecomer in history. The famous "Infirmary" is long gone and all that remains is a place for, well, tourists. (It helps, and deepens the power of the song, that St. James was a patron saint of pilgrims.)[27] The sense that Dylan's own narrative is somehow "outside" the events narrated, after the fact, too late, is strengthened by his adaptation of the traditional tune. He expands it for the refrain ("I know no one," etc.) by introducing a powerful sequence of major chords that transform the minor key of the main melody. Perhaps not surprisingly, when he asserts McTell's authority to "sing the blues," that phrase is supported by a major chord on the piano that breaks up the harmony of the rest of the song, as if it, like the lyric itself, were commenting musically on its own marginality to the events described.

Whereas "Jokerman" stressed the distance between the artist figure and the evil that threatens his world, here the limits of art are evoked through the play of genre. This epic is indeed epic, but what is needed is the blues, which this song is not. Nor can the white singer approach the power of the black singer to whom his song sends us for illumination. Instead of taking on the affectation of the black singer ("I believe in you when white turn to black") Dylan tells us to look elsewhere for truth. Epic can tell history, but the real truth of this condemned land must be sought in the blues. It is perhaps only fitting, given the song's acknowledgment of its own limits, that Dylan decided not to release it with the rest of *Infidels*. He was, in this sense, trusting his own art.

Dylan's work as the 1970s turned into the 1980s is marked by swings between a rhetoric of accusation and willfulness, on the one hand, and a rhetoric of surrender, on the other. The paradoxes of personal or religious transformation offer a window into the consequences for selfhood and identity of a moment at which the middle-class fantasies of personal liberation (underwritten by economic expansion) that had fostered Dylan's rise to stardom were beginning to pale. As the hesitations of Carter's foreign policy and the end of cheap oil give way to the vicious reaction of Reaganism and a world controlled by private equity, Dylan depicts musical scenarios of repentance, guilt, and uncertainty — even when he is preaching certainty. His claims to personal stability are belied by the nuances of the songs themselves, which repeatedly turn back to depict dramas of perplexity. These fables of surrender and hesitation are counterbalanced by demonstrations of formal elegance and rhetorical dazzle that showcase Dylan's own mastery of his craft. However, as "Jokerman" and "Blind Willie McTell" suggest, the artist's increasingly expansive demonstrations of technical mastery are counterbalanced by a sense of art's limitations. Dylan's final gesture in "Blind Willie McTell" is to point beyond his own art to another's work. The fact that such a gesture implies both a generous embrace of tradition and an awareness of the limits of his own power to change history tells us something about the position of Dylan's art — or, for that matter, of any art — as the ethical promises of the 1970s begin to fade.

CHAPTER SIX

"A Wisp of Startled Air":

Late Style and the Politics of Citation

After having struggled through the later years of the 1980s on a variety of uneven projects — films, albums, even a collaboration with the Grateful Dead — Dylan records Good as I Been to You *(1992) and* World Gone Wrong *(1993), two collections of unaccompanied traditional songs taken from several centuries and countries. These recordings, which seem to reground him in tradition, prepare a return to eminence. Dylan records a sequence of four records (*Time Out of Mind, *1997;* Love and Theft, *2001;* Modern Times, *2006; and* Together through Life, *2009) that carry him back to the top of the charts and garner praise and awards. These records dig deep into early twentieth-century American music, from the blues to the Tex-Mex* conjunto. *He recalibrates his image as well, appearing as a riverboat gambler with a broad-brimmed hat and a pencil mustache, performing, often on keyboards, in front of a small string band. He then turns, in the second decade of the new century, to a set of albums that draw on the so-called Great American Songbook — Cole Porter, Gershwin, Jimmy Van Heusen, Harold Alden, et al. He absorbs and updates the lonely pose of Frank Sinatra, now aging and stoic, his voice cracked, suffering yet again the torments of love. In 2016 he is awarded the Nobel Prize in Literature.*

Bob Dylan's recording production in the early 1990s, *Good as I Been to You* (1992) and *World Gone Wrong* (1993), featured him, as he was on his very first records, on guitar and harmonica. Included were blues tunes, murder ballads, seafaring songs, a Stephen Foster number, even a children's song. The second song on the first of these two records was called "Jim Jones." An Australian folk song from the nineteenth century, it opens, like Dylan's "The Times They Are a-Changin'" with an invocation: "Come and listen for a moment, lads, and hear me tell my tale." It goes on to feature a character who has been sent from England to New South Wales to live out his life in misery on a chain gang. His crime is to have engaged in poaching — the classic transgression, since the time of Henry VIII, of the starving peasant. The song ends with Jones defiantly vowing to escape his chains and kill those who have tormented him: "They'll yet regret they sent Jim Jones in chains to Botany Bay."

We can imagine that one of the things that drew Dylan to this song was the beautiful internal rhymes in the lyric. "They'll yet regret" is the best of them, coming at the climax of the song, but earlier we also get "take a tip before you ship," "don't get too gay in Botany Bay," and "I'll give the lot a little shot," as well as a number of wonderful near-rhymes ("hear me tell my tale") and alliterations ("with the storms a-ragin' round us," "full five hundred strong"). The sonic richness pushes the lyric forward, powering the combination of doom and defiance that shapes the story.[1] The plight of Jim Jones is the plight of a person cut off from his past. He did something — "poaching" is conveniently vague — that he *had* to do to survive, but that thrust him out of his familiar world, into exile. The sea between England and Australia offers a geographical metaphor for a crisis of the self in history.

Regrets

The focus of this chapter will be the string of Dylan records that closes out the millennium and rings in the 2000s, after the two "acoustic" albums just mentioned. No less than the trio of 1960s-era "electric" albums I discussed in Chapter 3, or the pairing of *Blood on the Tracks* and *Desire* studied in Chapter 4, these recordings, beginning with *Time Out of Mind* (1997), share certain characteristics, in theme, cultural resonance, and sound. Though perhaps less well known than those earlier collections, they offer, in their quite different way, an extraordinary body of work that ranks with Dylan's best.

Cultural critics often use the label "late style" to refer to a particular approach to making art that involves a deliberate fragmentation or looseness, as if the masterful writer or composer had moved beyond the exigencies of formal coherence and expression. The phrase was most famously used by the philosopher Theodor Adorno, who evoked it to describe the "irascible" nature of the last Beethoven compositions — disjointed, exorbitant, lacking a clear logic of expression, marked by ornaments and figures that are never integrated into a neatly digestible whole. For Adorno, what was at issue was the need to focus on Beethoven's actual approach to composition, what he called the "laws of form," against a tradition of criticism that attributed Beethoven's late pieces to some type of existential crisis, his deafness and impending death.[2] Thus, paradoxically, even though the focus is on Beethoven's last works, "late style" has little to do with the time in the author's life at which art is produced, and everything to do with a kind of stylistic or structural relationship to more conventional kinds of art.

Though it might seem a good distance from Adorno's gnarly account of Beethoven to Dylan's swampy blues style in his recordings around the millennium, the concept of "late style" can help us frame an approach to these dense, atmospheric albums. Dylan is certainly older here, and he sounds older. But it is important not to stress the biography of the author, to which we have limited access anyway. What matters is how this work illustrates a kind of loose composition and ambiguity of design. This is an *aesthetic* problem more than a biographical problem because, at some level, "late style" is available in every moment of artistic creation — even if it presupposes a kind of ironic mastery of craft and convention. At certain historical moments, in certain social formations, "late style" emerges as the most effective tool for making legible the social and moral climate.

The intense blending of regret and dark destiny that we saw in "Jim Jones" lays the groundwork for much of Dylan's work from the mid-1990s onward. The same narrative scenario — a broken past, a hopeless future, futile gestures of defiance — will reappear in many of the songs included on these albums. We can find it in the very opening lines of "Love Sick," the first song on *Time Out of Mind*: "I'm walking through streets that are dead" (p. 794), begins the protagonist. The song emerges inside a postapocalyptic landscape defined, not by bombs or hurricanes, but by a love affair so catastrophic as to make return impossible: "You destroyed me with a smile / While I was sleeping." The protagonist is both love sick and "sick of love." He cannot continue, but he cannot stop.

Throughout these songs Dylan repeatedly presents us with characters who, like Jim Jones, cannot understand or control their situations, whose world seems to exist in fragments or shards of some earlier wholeness. Disaster has struck. They have been thrown back on their own resources with no help. Explicitly, given the conventions of popular song, amorous disappointment or betrayal is often near the center of this desolation. But beyond the cliché of lost love (which by this time in his career Dylan uses as a kind of scaffold to talk about any number of other topics), the crisis of cultural form is palpable, both in the themes of the songs and in their use of formal elements. In such songs as "Mississippi," "Love Sick," "Highlands," "Not Dark Yet," "High Water," and "Workingman's Blues #2," to name only the most obvious candidates from this period, we are plunged into crises of community, of history, of climate, of friendship. Just as Dylan's mid-1960s work simultaneously criticized and exploited the expanding mediasphere that shaped middle-class identity, so here does he explore what we might call, a bit grandly, the crisis of the neoliberal self. By this I mean the situation of the individual in the postindustrial West after the collapse of the Berlin Wall and the dark viciousness of the Reagan/Thatcher years. This is the world of public "austerity" and privatized risk, of defunded schools, gated communities, abandoned mill towns, *maquiladoras*, and credit card debt. In Dylan's post-1989 song world, characters are precipitously flung into a maelstrom of risk and confusion, deprived of any resources save personal ingenuity and emotional intensity, grasping for support from communities that are no more. "I'm twenty miles out of town / In cold irons bound" (p. 801), sings another of Dylan's anxious, immobilized characters on *Time Out of Mind*. "When I was in Missouri / They would not let me be / Had to leave there in a hurry / I only saw what they let me see" (p. 798), says the hero of "Tryin' to Get to Heaven," from the same album. "You can't turn back — you can't come back" (p. 830), he sings on "Sugar Baby," from *Love and Theft*. "Got not future / Got no past," says "Mississippi" on the same record. "Had to go to Florida dodging them Georgia laws" (p. 828), adds "Po' Boy," a couple of songs later. This last lament explicitly reverses Dylan's earlier, grand celebration of movement and art on 1975's "Shelter from the Storm," from *Blood on the Tracks*. There he sang, "I'm living in a foreign country now / But I'm bound to cross the line / Beauty walks a razor's edge / Someday I'll make it mine" (p. 194). In a different context, at the height of the Reagan years, the fast-talking narrator of the 1986 picaresque tale "Brownsville Girl" (cowritten with Sam Shepard) would add that "I've always been the kind of person that doesn't like to trespass but sometimes you just find yourself over the line" (p. 709). In Dylan's post-1989 work the "line" spells disaster. You can't or shouldn't cross it, if you can avoid it. If you do, as he says in "Mississippi" (1996), "You can always come back, but you can't come back all the way" (p. 814). The protagonist of "Shelter from the Storm" is a wounded warrior who turns lost love into an artistic quest; ten years later, the narrator of "Brownsville Girl" is a con man and a coward. By contrast, "Mississippi" tells the story of a bounded figure, brave and resolute, but hemmed in by forces that cannot be overcome. Generically, it is a move from romance to the picaresque and then to tragedy.

These scenes of immobility are the obverse of the focus on the "moment" that we saw in Dylan's work from the 1960s. The infinite possibility in the exploration of the sensorium, the absorption of the self into a single instant, chronicled in such songs as "Mr. Tambourine Man" and "Chimes of Freedom," has given way to a disjointed vision of barren life. Here the "moment" is a disconnected slice of vacant time, emptied of possibility. The crisis in the relationship between self and community, between present and past, between public and private, can be seen in powerful terms on *Time Out of Mind*'s third song, "Standing in the Doorway." And here we can see that the crises depicted in the stories of the songs also weigh upon their style of presentation:

I'm walking through the summer nights
Jukebox playing low
Yesterday everything was going too fast
Today it's moving too slow
I got no place left to turn
I got nothing left to burn
Don't know if I saw you, if I would kiss you or kill you
It probably wouldn't matter to you anyhow
You left me standing in the doorway crying
I got nothing to go back to now (p. 796)

The event of heartbreak here provokes a vision of time as split into distinct phases. There is no return, as is signaled by the fifth and sixth lines, a rhyming couplet ("turn / burn") that centers the ten-line stanza.[3] The "time" that is "out of mind" on the album title is also, as Hamlet might say, "out of joint," as events move at a rhythm that

confounds the protagonist — "too fast," "too slow." Yet what is strik-
ing in this bleak vision are the seventh and eighth lines, where, after
the acknowledgment of no return, the character can't decide whether
to kiss or kill his old lover, adding, "It probably wouldn't matter to
you anyhow." He seems to be wiser from his loss, but he claims the
authority to presume that the woman wouldn't mind dying. This is,
of course, a completely outrageous claim, especially since the lady in
this story seems to have moved on and be doing well. But the entire
point of these songs is that exorbitant and exaggerated assertions such
as this one cannot be recuperated or explained away through any kind
of psychological logic or plot coherence. Rather, they appear as flash-
ing images, blips of intensity designed to signal that we are in a land-
scape of desperation. So, in "Till I Fell in Love With You," from the
same record, the narrator has "come to the end of [his] way" (p. 799),
before announcing that he will go on to win wealth and fame and then
conclude that he'll be Dixie-bound tomorrow "if I'm still among the
living." He is stopped, but he isn't stopped, just as the hero of "Stand-
ing in the Doorway" is both resigned and restless. The hero of "Tryin'
to Get to Heaven" reminds us that "I was born here and I'll die here,
against my will" (p. 800), even as he points out that he's also been all
around the world ("I've been to London / Been to gay Paree"). Which
is it, enclosure or rootlessness? The narrator of "Can't Wait" can't
wait for his love, even as he points out that they were together "some-
where back there along the line" (p. 803). And the hero of "Not Dark
Yet" simply claims, "There's not even room enough to be anywhere"
(p. 800). "A worried man with a worried mind / No one in front of me
and nothing behind" (p. 890) states "Things Have Changed," another
song from the same period, written for a film.

The point here is that across *Time Out of Mind* and its partner
albums, Dylan drives the language of emotion and selfhood to exor-
bitant extremes, to points at which historical catastrophe can take
form as a failure of resolution — in both the psychological and aes-
thetic senses of that term. As he says on *Together through Life*, "Beyond
here lies nothin'" (p. 896). We can see here a kind of style of disjunc-
tion, in which traditional approaches to plot and scenario seem to
be under pressure. The lines just cited might be seen less as parts
of stories or dramas than as a repertoire of late-style ornaments,
the detritus of broken ideas or old images, like the trills in a late
Beethoven quartet.

The larger implications of Dylan's quickly allusive style can be seen if we move a bit further on in the same song. The third verse shifts away from the broken love affair:

Maybe they'll get me and maybe they won't
But not tonight and it won't be here
There are things I could say but I don't
I know the mercy of God must be near (p. 796)

A moment ago, we were told that the hero had "nothing to go back to now" because his heart was broken. Now, we learn, all of a sudden, that he is on the lam, running from an unidentified "them." Is there any relationship between his lost love and his outlaw status, between private disaster and public shame? Is lost love a metaphor for lost legitimacy, or vice versa? We are never told. The outlaw plot only lasts a few lines; then it vanishes. Moreover, the reference to God (and there are many like this in these songs) feels like filler or ornament, since it, too, is never integrated into the rest of the scene. When jammed into the same song, these disparate (and desperate) details resist logical coherence as story or dramatic scenario. They create an atmosphere of dread.

This a new approach. Even in Dylan's most mysterious works from the mid-1960s, long songs such as "Sad-Eyed Lady of the Lowlands," for example, it was possible to integrate the exotic imagery into a unified vision. The gentle rhythm of that song invited the listener in. In these later songs Dylan seems to be working with fragments. He offers up sketches of stories but leaves it to the listener to try to piece together some type of action. This atmosphere of fragmentation or imperfect resolution extends to the sound of the albums. *Time Out of Mind*, which was coproduced by Daniel Lanois, is a sonic wonder. It presents ensemble performances that do not, however, feel like ensembles. For example, "Standing in the Doorway" features at least three guitars, plus a pedal steel guitar and an organ. None of them plays a solo, but all play bits of lines, little squiggles of music that start and stop, coming out of nowhere. There is no sense that the different instruments are "trading" lines or trying to echo each other, as is frequent in, for example, jazz, or on some recordings by The Beatles. On some songs, such as "Till I Fell in Love With You," we are treated simply to blasts of sound, like punches or swipes, coming from the guitars. When the vocal stops, the band continues, without solos, working its way through the form of the verse. This creates the impression of a self-contained sonic space devoid of human presence — just as the lyrics tell stories of characters disconnected from their hostile environments, "in cold irons bound" or "with the heat rising in my eyes." Some songs seem not to have enough lyrics (ironically enough, "Can't Wait"), so that Dylan's vocal meanders against the background. His vocal is high in his nose and he pushes the *r* sound ("waterrrrr," "parlorrrrr") as if driving his timbre into the range of the twanging guitars. When he plays the harmonica, it is minimal, limited, on *Time Out of Mind*, to one surprising solo, on "Tryin' to Get to Heaven," where Dylan simply plays sequences of sixteenth notes on the same tone, as if marking out the passage of time through this world of tears.

Lamentations

The pervasive sense of an error, a mistake, a catastrophe, a break in time, is clearest and most developed on perhaps the best-known song from 2001's *Love and Theft*. This is the song called "Mississippi," which has been recorded by several other artists besides Dylan. Whereas Jimmie Rodgers's 1932 "Miss the Mississippi and You" had trafficked in sentiment and nostalgia, Dylan's song paints desolation. "Only one thing I did wrong / Stayed in Mississippi a day too long" (p. 814), runs the refrain. Why did the protagonist stay in Mississippi too long? And what happened that ruined his life? Was he a poacher too? We are never told. Possibly, he made the mistake of leaving home in search of the lover whom he praises throughout the song. But they are both suffering from the consequences of catastrophe. "So many things we never can undo / I know you're sorry, I'm sorry too," he intones at one point. The mystery of the fateful error in judgment haunts the song, which is filled with images of disaster and doom. We get a picture of a protagonist who has "struggled and scraped" to get along, living in the city, where he doesn't belong, caught up in schemes. The protagonist evokes the sacrifices he has made for love when he says, "I crossed that river just to be where you are," but it is never clear if this was his great error, or whether the mistake lay elsewhere and the river was his attempt at redemption. Is he Washington crossing the Delaware to victory or Santa Ana crossing the San Jacinto to disaster?

The disjointed poetics of Dylan's late songs come into focus if we note that "Mississippi" offers the gloomy counterversion of a famous Dylan song from much earlier in his career, "Stuck Inside of Mobile with the Memphis Blues Again," from 1966's *Blonde on Blonde*. The narrator of that song finds himself caught in a city in Alabama noted for its racial disharmony. He longs to get to Memphis, the home of the blues. In fact, he has the blues because he can't get to the home of the blues. He is in a curious situation. He seems to be well treated; he's surrounded by beautiful women: "The ladies treat me kindly / They furnish me with tape." He dallies with a lovely called "Ruthie," who "says come see her, in her honky-tonk lagoon / Where I can watch her waltz for free / 'Neath her Panamanian moon" (p. 246). It sounds ideal. But he's in the wrong place. "Deep inside my heart, I know I can't escape," he admits before turning, in the first verse, to the famous chorus, "Oh, Mama, can this really be the end / To be stuck inside of Mobile with the Memphis blues again?" It is very clear that this is not "the end," especially since the punch line to the song has the protagonist asking if he'll have to go "through all these things twice." The hero of "Mississippi," also stuck in a southern space, echoes the earlier song when he cries that "we struggle and we scrape / All blocked in, nowhere to escape." The difference between the two situations goes to the heart of Dylan's late-style poetics. The protagonist of the earlier song can confront the hypocrites and swindlers around him and set them right ("You see, you're just like me / I hope you're satisfied," as he says to one of them). The narrator of "Mississippi" lives in a world in which morally inflected human relationships have given way to the soulless mechanisms of economic exchange: "There's nothing you can sell me / I'll see you around." The hero of "Stuck Inside of Mobile" longs to get out of good society (he's pursued by "debutantes") and hit the road. The hero of "Mississippi," huddled with his lover, can only grimly assert that, in the end, it might all turn out okay after all. It's hard to believe him.

The stylistic peculiarities of Dylan's work in this period are apparent in the scenography of "Mississippi." Whereas Memphis and Mobile are real places, here we waver between an actual geographical entity, the great state of Mississippi, and an allegorical setting. "Sky full of fire, and the pain is pouring down," sings Dylan, where we would expect "rain is pouring down." The shift of one letter, from *r* to *p*, turns the landscape into a spiritual allegory, suggesting, retrospectively, that "sky full of fire" is not just the description of a sunset. As with the abrupt juxtaposition of a love plot and an out-law plot in "Standing in the Doorway," mentioned a moment ago, here, at the level of setting, we have a clashing of linguistic regis-ters, between geography and allegory. And we waver between these striking images and claims about the limits of the singer's capacity to describe his world: "All my powers of expression and thoughts so sublime / Could never do you justice in reason or rhyme," he sings just before delivering the first iteration of the refrain and his lament that he stayed too long in Mississippi.

The interweaving, in "Mississippi," of an allegorical narrative of doom with repeated expressions of love comes to a climax in the final verse where we move into yet more allegory:

> My ship's been split to splinters and it's sinking fast
> I'm drownin' in the poison, got no future, got no past
> But my heart is not weary; it's light and it's free
> I've got nothin' but affection for all them who've sailed with me

The sea of poison takes us back to the "sky full of fire" earlier in the song. Yet now the allegory begins to wear a bit thin. The image of the self as mariner is a cliché — going at least back to the poetry of Horace — which unfolds into an image of camaraderie and accep-tance. This may be stoic cheer, or it may be self-delusion. He then turns to his beloved one last time, asking her to stick with him, asserting, against all possible evidence, that "I know that Fortune is waiting to be kind," and asking her for a pledge of fidelity. Whether Fortune's kindness involves an improvement in the weather forecast or whether it is the pledge of love itself, is, again, left unclear. But the ambiguity created by affirmations of true love mixed with descrip-tions of disaster is part of the point of the song. The allegory then takes a turn of its own: "My clothes are wet, tight on my skin / Not as tight as the corner that I painted myself in." Dead metaphors are pil-ing up. The moribund allegory of the self as sinking ship is qualified through the (very dead) metaphor of painting oneself into a corner. The painting metaphor illustrates the ship metaphor, which illus-trates the metaphor of destiny as crossing a river. This slippage from one metaphor to another links back to the hero's earlier claims that, no matter how eloquent he may be, he can never do justice to his beloved. Here the movement of the lyric enacts his confusion, as he grasps for a language to describe his situation by stacking one tired figure of speech on another. When faced with catastrophe, some poets fall silent. Here, in the midst of disaster, the limited eloquence of Dylan's unexceptional hero can generate only clichés. This continues in the final phrases, where another cliché tells us that "the emptiness is endless, cold as the clay." "Cold as the clay" should suggest death; but here we get a death that is merely an empty future, more of the same, as suggested by the repeated s-sounds and hard c-sounds. The punch line to the final verse sets the situation in relief: "You can always come back, but you can't come back all the way." So, there it is. There has been an error, a misstep, a mistake. Any attempt to redeem the situation will inevitably leave one somewhere other than where one was before the mistake, and where one would want to be. Contingency oppresses the hero, but none of the tricks he uses to outwit it — allegory, prophecy, solidarity — seems to work.

The song's musical structure enacts a similar dynamic of endlessness and catastrophe. "Mississippi" consists of three verses, each sixteen lines long, ending with the refrain. Within this large structure there are other structures. Each sixteen-line verse is divided by the harmony of the tune into four four-line units. The opening eight lines play the same melody twice. Then Dylan opens the structure, moving to a V chord for four lines (9–12). The phrases on the dominant ("Don't even have anything for myself anymore" and "Nothing you can sell me, I'll see you around") are accentuated by a rare ascending bass line. This creates a dramatic climax at the center of each verse. Then we come back, in the final four lines, to the opening cadence (lines 13–16) repeated again, ending on the refrain.

The classic structure of American popular song is often denoted as AABA, two verses, a bridge, and a third verse. Two statements, a comment or change of viewpoint, then a third statement. "Mississippi" displays this song structure *within* each of the verses. Structurally, each verse is a song in itself; the song is a sequence of mini-songs. No wonder the hero can never resolve his problems; the same pattern keeps coming back, no matter what he does. It may not be coincidental that Dylan released two different versions of this song, one on *Love and Theft* and an outtake on 2008's "bootleg" *Tell Tale Signs*. The outtake has a bluesy feel to it, with instrumentation dominated by two guitars, one electric, one acoustic, in dialogue. The "official" version is anthemic, featuring interludes in which the band marches in unison up the diatonic scale and back down. The two versions illuminate two different sides of the song, as both a single voice crying, blueslike, from the wilderness, and a meditation on history and destiny that speaks to larger, collective experience. The narrator's own wavering between personal lament and allegory works to bridge these two aspects of the lyric.

Rhythms

It might be tempting to see this cognitive and existential chaos, as some commentators have, in biographical or psychological terms, as if the aging Dylan himself were simply overwhelmed by too many phrases, too many song paradigms, too many scenes. Yet these songs are marked by lucid meditations on the power of circumstance to swallow the will, and by a deep empathy with the losers and scoundrels whose struggles we witness. Nowhere are the larger cultural stakes of this situation better explored than in "Summer Days," also from *Love and Theft*. It is an electric blues, a form Dylan had explored with great results in the middle years of the 1960s and that he returns to frequently on the albums under discussion here. The usefulness of the blues form may come from the fact that it requires no set or limited number of verses ("Leopard-Skin Pillbox Hat," from 1966 has five verses; "Thunder on the Mountain," from 2006, has twelve, "Highlands," from 1997, has *twenty*). Moreover, there is a long tradition in the blues of jamming together bits of different stories. Narrative coherence is not assumed the way it is, say, in the ballad tradition. Thus, the structural looseness of late style dovetails with the conventions of the most archaic of forms, which lends itself perfectly to the disjointed postmodern world being painted.

"Summer Days" explores this territory. It evokes the situation of an aging hero who, like the protagonist of "Mississippi," continually asserts, contrary to evidence, that everything is going well:

> Summer days, summer nights are gone
> Summer days, summer nights are gone
> I know a place where there's still something going on (p. 816)

And he goes on to describe life as a kind of endless party. He's got a fancy car ("eight carburetors"!) and a bevy of lovely women to follow him. They warn him that he's just a "worn out star," but they stick with him nonetheless, as he spends his remaining cash like a sailor. Perhaps there really is no tomorrow; but there is clearly a yesterday:

She's lookin' into my eyes, she's a-holdin' my hands
She's lookin' into my eyes, she's a-holdin' my hands
She says, "You can't repeat the past," I say, "what do you
mean you can't; of course you can"

In contrast to the conclusions of the narrator in "Mississippi," the optimistic narrator of "Summer Days" seems to claim that you can, in fact, "come back all the way." Yet history has crept in through the side door. For the last lines point us to a passage from F. Scott Fitzgerald's 1925 novel *The Great Gatsby*. At the emotional core of the tragedy, as Gatsby reveals the story of his lost love for Daisy Buchanan to his friend Nick Carraway, Nick warns him, "'I wouldn't ask too much of her. You can't repeat the past.' 'Can't repeat the past,' he cried incredulously. 'Why of course you can!' He looked around him wildly, as if the past were lurking here in the shadow of his house, just out of reach of his hand." And Nick goes on to comment a few lines later:

> Through all he said, even his appalling sentimentality, I was reminded of something, an elusive rhythm, a fragment of lost words, that I had heard somewhere a long time ago. For a moment a phrase tried to take shape in my mouth and my lips parted like a dumb man's, as though there was more struggling upon them than a wisp of startled air. But they made no sound, and what I had almost remembered was uncommunicable forever.[4]

Gatsby's grasping for the past becomes Nick's grasping for the past. Gatsby's search for lost love becomes Nick's search for lost language, for some magic formula, some phrase always just out of reach. At this powerful moment in the novel Gatsby's emotional catastrophe becomes a figure for contingency itself, for the weight of time and circumstance that grips us all, as we emit "a wisp of startled air" that can never quite take form. Gatsby's lover's tragedy is also the tragedy of the witness, who can never find adequate language to testify to what he has seen and felt.

At one level, this ironic reminder suggests that it may be useful to read Dylan's persona in these late songs less as a version of the rambler Woody Guthrie, the rebel Arthur Rimbaud, or the wounded lover Petrarch, than as the bootlegger Jay Gatsby, who rose, like Dylan, from humble origins in the Midwest, changed his name, and made a fortune among the glitterati in New York. Like Gatsby, "Bob Dylan" is a fiction. But that is only part of the story. For Dylan figures in here as *both* Gatsby, the shape changer, and Nick, the witness who, Proust-like, gropes for a language to recapture the past. Dylan has always wanted it both ways: to be famous but to retain his privacy; to be taken seriously, but not examined too closely; to be popular, but not mainstream. Fitzgerald's narrative, with its double structure of tragic hero and conflicted witness, makes this possible. It resonates across Dylan's late songs, where characters often say more than they know. In this case, the larger cultural and moral implications of *Gatsby* for our understanding of American identity pour through "Summer Days." Melancholy is everywhere in this scene; the "summer days" of the partying hero of the song now become the gorgeous parties at Gatsby's Long Island estate — as well as the increasingly tawdry surfaces of the Clinton-era 1990s. The bigger the parties, the more luxurious the fundraisers, the greater the sense of emptiness.

But even more is at work in this ambiguous moment of recollection. The memory is a memory, not only of Fitzgerald, but of Dylan's own earlier wisps of startled air. For if "Mississippi" returns us to "Stuck Inside of Mobile," the literary reference in "Summer Days" takes us back to one of the most powerful of all of Dylan's mid-1960s rejections of orthodoxy, the 1965 piano-based melodrama "Ballad of a Thin Man." There Dylan evokes a type of the establishment man, "Mister Jones," a combination of reporter and detective (think of William Powell in the Thin Man movies) who struggles to understand the world of strange objects and characters that swirls around him. Mister Jones is ridiculed because he doesn't know "what is happening." Dylan isn't saying what is "happening," but he makes it clear that if you don't know what it is already, you are in trouble. And college won't help:

> You've been with the professors and they've all liked your looks
> With great lawyers you have discussed lepers and crooks
> You've been through all of F. Scott Fitzgerald's books
> You're very well read, it's well known
> But something is happening here, and you don't know what it is
> Do you, Mister Jones? (p. 175)

The aging, pathetic narrator of "Summer Days" contemplates the past by sending us, unwittingly, to the great modern novelist F. Scott Fitzgerald. The citation evokes Dylan's earlier dismissal of Fitzgerald as irrelevant, thereby proving that Fitzgerald *is* relevant, after all — that the classics *are* the classics. And in a brilliant move, Dylan has his character remember "a fragment of lost words" from an author who contemplates our inability to repeat or even recall the past. Dylan, who, it turns out, is *very* well read, recalls his past contempt for canonical high culture with an exhortation to remember placed in the mouth of a pathetic narrator who is clearly deluded. The reference — the mark of Dylan's hand on the song as he, in good Nick Carraway fashion, tells a sad story of lost love — also tells us that Fitzgerald is now the explainer of the past. He is the skeleton key who lends ironic literary authority to a hollow affirmation of experiential rebirth, the eternal American optimism of "why, of course you can!" This ironic link makes it possible for Dylan's character to remember by alluding to Fitzgerald, even as the allusion gestures toward an earlier moment of revolutionary modernist fervor, now long gone. In the bleak world of "Summer Days," we are left with "a fragment of lost words that I had heard somewhere, a long time ago." Yet this citation of a citation works precisely because no one who has listened deeply to "Ballad of a Thin Man" can ever forget it. We are left with the memory of an elusive rhythm, etched on the mind because once, long ago, etched on vinyl.[5]

The Fitzgerald reference takes us to one of the central features of Dylan's late work, the ubiquity of citation. As early as the songs on *Time Out of Mind*, Dylan's lyrics increasingly repurpose and circulate bits of other works, from traditional songs to novels. Of course, this is what all folk songs do, as they draw upon a deep well of commonplaces and phrases that float around from song to song. Michael Gray has pointed out that one of the best songs on *Time Out of Mind*, "Tryin' to Get to Heaven," includes a set of lines in songs taken from a single published folk song anthology that Dylan must have consulted. This is an old technique, what literary historians call a *cento*, when a poet builds poems out of lines from other poems. Dylan's literary companion Petrarch included one such poem in his fourteenth-century *Canzoniere*, where he cites a line from each of the great poets who precede him — Dante, the troubadour Arnaut Daniel, the Italian philosopher/poet Guinizelli. But the citation of other works and songs becomes an almost obsessive feature throughout Dylan's late work.[6]

This process is particularly complicated on *Love and Theft*, which takes its title (rendered in quotation marks on the album cover) from Eric Lott's 1993 book of the same title on the history of the minstrel show in American culture. Lott's dense exploration of the dynamics of imitation, desire, and mimicry underpinning minstrelsy offers the framework for Dylan's songs on this album, which are built on types from southern American society in what would seem to be the early years of the twentieth century. I noted in Chapter 1 that Dylan's combinatorial approach to songwriting often makes it difficult to find him "inside" his songs. He is in them, but not completely of them. That usual strategy changes here. Now he begins to ventriloquize in very explicit ways. He takes on the voices of various typical characters from southern society — the poor white ("Po' Boy"), the violent nativist ("Floater"), the unhappy city-dweller ("Mississippi"), the traveling-salesman seducer ("Moonlight"), the dangerous lovesick kid ("Bye and Bye"). This means that the narrative "I" does not provide a reliable interpretive window onto the events around him. As a contrast, we might think of the narrator of 1965's "Tombstone Blues," where a violent and corrupt society is filtered through a persona who can only conclude, "I'm in trouble with the Tombstone blues" (p. 208). There, what the narrator is telling us is, explicitly, the truth about our own social moment. Here the events *are* the narrator. We cannot separate storyteller from actor. To the extent that we can judge these characters, we are able to do so, as in "Summer Days," through the allusions and citations that Dylan weaves into their stories.

Dylan's evocation of past cultural moments is integrated into the setting and vibe of the songs on *Love and Theft* and *Time Out of Mind*. The overlaying of multiple guitars, tinged with reverb, working out blues riffs in the background, creates the slightly creepy or gothic feel of *Time Out of Mind*. This sound is punctuated, for good measure, by occasional geographical references ("Going down the river / Down to New Orleans"). By contrast, on *Love and Theft* the regionalism becomes explicit, through references to place names and, especially, through Dylan's often gorgeous lyrical renderings of the natural settings of his stories: "The trailing moss and mystic glow / The purple blossoms soft as snow," from "Moonlight" (p. 824); "I got here following the southern star / I crossed that river just to be where you are" from "Mississippi" (p. 814); "Down over the window / Come the dazzling / Sunlit rays / Through the back alleys, through the blinds / Another one of them endless days" from "Floater" (p. 820). The musical ambiance is much more subdued, as a number of tunes feature carefully arranged ensemble playing. The guitar sounds are muffled, compared to the earlier album, with a fuller, less twangy, more mellow "jazz"-like tone on the solos and acoustic backgrounds. There is little piano. We are neither in the world of Dylan's beloved Chicago blues, nor in the deep whine of the Delta sound, but somewhere closer to an imagined genteel prewar South. The world in which Gatsby first met Daisy Buchanan.

The vividly sensual natural setting connects as well to the theme I noted at the outset of this chapter, the problem of a kind of break in history, of an error that set everything awry. For if anything defines the history of the American South, it is the presence of a wound that can never be healed, of a sin that can never be forgotten, no matter what one's politics. As Dylan put it in the passage from *Chronicles: Volume One* that I cited back in Chapter 1: "I was beginning to feel that maybe the language had something to do with the causes and ideals of the circumstances and blood of what happened over a hundred years ago over secession from the Union" (p. 76). Here Dylan sets us, geographically, in the aftermath of those "circumstances," and in the space where their memory haunts life and love. A number of the protagonists who walk through the lovely fragrant landscapes of these songs have violence in their hearts: "If you ever try to interfere with me or cross my path again / You do so at the peril of your own life," says the protagonist of "Floater." "I'm gonna establish my rule through civil war / Gonna make you see / Just how loyal and true a man can be" (p. 818), vows the character of "Bye and Bye," a kind of Confederate skinhead, trying to impress his girlfriend. "I'm here to create the new imperial empire" (p. 826), concludes "Honest with Me" with a pleonasm.[7]

These themes of Southern politics and history, of a broken world haunted by violence barely disguised as amorous desire, reveal the historical content at the center of Dylan's late work. The whiff of nostalgia is both the atmosphere that permeates the songs and the danger that they constantly point to. No longer interested in making "straight" society more "hip," as he was in the 1960s, and having given up on the redemption of the generation evoked in the mid-1970s albums, Dylan turns here to a single region whose music is central to his own development yet haunted by loss and violence. Within this wounded landscape — a landscape, as I have suggested, that reflects our own wasteland moment of philandering presidents and oligarchs, of climate change and ATM fees — the role of citation takes on its significance. For if we cannot move beyond the sins of slavery, Reconstruction, and Jim Crow, neither dare we forget them, any more than we dare forget the wisdom of the folk songs on *Good as I Been to You*, the commonplace citations in "Tryin' to Get to Heaven," or the language of *Gatsby*. In an economic and social system that thrives on amnesia, the only possible aesthetic and political response must be to offer fragments of the past: here an "elusive rhythm," there a "wisp of startled air." And the task of the artist becomes, not to reintegrate these shards into some new representational totality or semblance that would paper over the destruction, but to hold them up, in their disjointedness, for all to see or hear. In a sense, we are back to the situation of Jim Jones, in the song with which I began this chapter. Whereas Jim Jones was sent to Australia for poaching, Dylan shows us here that poaching—cultural poaching—may be the only possible solution to life in a world of ruins. Dylan's interest in "love and theft" runs through his later work at a number of levels, in both the thematic references to fragmentation and loss, and the formal reassemblage of the past through a kind of mosaic effect. In this account, we may all be some version of Jim Jones.

It is this nonredemptive return to the cultural material of the past that helps explain Dylan's explicit turn to citation and repetition on 2006's album *Modern Times*. Here the practice of citation becomes generalized and flagrantly interesting. The title recalls Charlie Chaplin's 1936 film about the destruction of the worker's dignity by modern capitalism—a theme that runs throughout Dylan's songs on this album. Dylan draws deeply on cultural material from a variety of places, possibly including the autobiography of a Japanese Mafioso and the plays of Shakespeare. At the time of the release of the album, many fans and critics found these copious references puzzling, and there were claims that Dylan was somehow lacking in originality because the songs pointed beyond themselves. This, of course, completely misses the point. Dylan's music has always drawn from a wide group of contexts and mobilized commonplaces from folk song and poetry. Indeed, the very opening lines of "Spirit on the Water" ("Spirit on the water / Darkness on the edge of the deep" [p. 845]) cite the Bible and may also echo Milton echoing the Bible—before we even get to the Japanese Mafioso.

Yet even more striking than the lyrical citations are the musical references, if that is what we should call them. For several of the melodies to the songs on *Modern Times* send us to other songs. The most impressive ones remind us of hits performed first by Bing Crosby in the 1930s. "Beyond the Horizon" points to "Red Sails in the Sunset," "When the Deal Goes Down" calls to mind Crosby's signature song, "Where the Blue of the Night Meets the Gold of the Day," right down to the introductory guitar riff. For good measure Dylan throws in an adaptation and rewriting of Hambone Willie Newbern's 1929 blues "Rollin' and Tumblin'," a song often associated with Muddy Waters.

We may be forgiven for wondering what is going on here. A closer look at "When the Deal Goes Down" might yield some insights.[8] It is a song that breaks with the bleak mood of many of Dylan's millennial songs, as it celebrates the beauty of each moment and affirms the value of commitment. The title cites an old commonplace phrase in blues and folk music. The first great star of what is now called bluegrass music, Charlie Poole, had a 1925 hit with "Don't Let Your Deal Go Down." (A kind of backwoods version of the bootlegger Gatsby, Poole was also a noted moonshiner.) A decade later, in 1936, Dylan's early hero Robert Johnson recorded a tune called "My Last Fair Deal Gone Down," and one of Dylan's favorite 1930s string bands, The Mississippi Sheiks, offered "Honey Babe Let the Deal Go Down."[9] Dylan himself had used the phrase "my last deal gone down" in "Changing of the Guards," from 1977's *Street Legal*. Here, however, the classic commonplace expression of bad luck, of being up against adversity, takes on a deep existential sense, as "when the deal goes down" refers to destiny, the moment of truth, possibly the moment of death. "I'll be with you, when the deal goes down," is the refrain at the end of each verse. Like Dante or Aeneas, Dylan's protagonist sits awake in worry. "My bewildered brain toils in vain / Through the darkness on the pathways of life" (p. 847), he begins. But he is redeemed by commitment through love. The body of the song evokes, with powerful lyricism, the importance of grasping each precious moment of life. The hero is cheerful, despite the pain of existence, and celebrates the value of love and community:

> We eat and we drink, we feel and we think
> Far down the street we stray
> I laugh and I cry, and am haunted by
> Things I never meant nor wished to say

The midnight rain follows the train
We all wear the same thorny crown
Soul to soul our shadows roll
And I'll be with you when the deal goes down (p. 847)

The sensuality of love is blended with the abstraction of spiritual union and the sense of the common destiny for each human. Like the snow that covers Ireland at the end of James Joyce's story "The Dead," destiny, in the form of rain, follows the train that would outrun it. Indeed, the relationship between the spiritual and the physical is explored with beautiful complexity here, as the "rolling" of shadows at midnight suggests the silhouettes of two lovers in embrace, even as they are simultaneously emptied of physical presence and recast as "souls" in a spiritual union. Or, as he puts it elsewhere in the song, "More frailer than the flowers / These precious hours / That keep us so tightly bound." The frail, precious hours evoked here recall the language of the nineteenth-century American poet Henry Timrod's "Rhapsody of a Southern Winter Night." Timrod's poet looks back to an earlier sensuous summer moment when he took refuge from worry and fatigue ("shielding with both hands my throbbing brows") to lie down amid the flowers and daydream, "and strove, with logic frailer than the flowers / To justify a life of sensuous rest."[10] As he lies back in a moment of southern reverie ("Hush, sweetest South! I love thy delicate breath"), he calls forth the "Fairy Shadows" that play in the glen.

Timrod was known as the "Poet Laureate of the Confederacy." An unreconstructed secessionist, his long lyric "Ethnogenesis" celebrates the birth, from nothing, of the great new country based on slavery to which he dedicated his career. Yet Timrod's presence in the song is not restricted to his historical destiny, as interesting as this is. What is at issue is not whether it is "good" or "bad" to hear his voice, or whether this tells us something about Dylan's "politics." Such a reading would be reductive, to say the least. For Timrod's presence in the song can be felt at the level of form, in the way a knowledge of his work helps frame the story. The "Rhapsody" is in large measure a meditation on literary genre. The poet elegiacally recalls, in winter, a summer afternoon in which he was engaged in reading a book about war: "Which, in good sooth, was but the long-drawn sigh / Of some one who had quarreled with his kind." This is the genre of epic. He casts aside this epic text in order to spend the afternoon dreaming, lying among the flowers by the water, a different kind of "sigh." This is the moment of literary pastoral, which from the time of Virgil's first eclogue has been set in opposition to the poetry of war. Thus, Timrod's poem is about carving out a space for poetry, and about his fantasy of the South as the space of pastoral reverie. Here is poetry generating the very conditions of its own emergence; a logic "frailer than the flowers" means that the setting of pastoral, among the flowers, is used to offer the justification for a poem about lying among the flowers. Yet Dylan sends us to Timrod's self-reflexive meditation on dreams and pastoral solitude in order to overturn it, affirming, in contrast, the value of love and commitment. Dylan begins the song with the misery of solitude: "In the still of the night / In the world's ancient light / Where wisdom grows up in strife." This is Timrod's sense of epic, "someone who had quarreled with his kind." Yet for Dylan strife becomes a source of wisdom, not a book to be set aside. And he goes on to depict a figure who transcends strife through love: "We live and we die and we know not why / But I'll be with you when the deal goes down." That is, Dylan's lyric points toward the great secessionist at the very moment Dylan asserts that solidarity and comfort, not solitude or nostalgia, are what give life meaning in the face of our common destiny.[11]

So now we have a Dylan song in which the title evokes a commonplace phrase that was also used by the great black singer Robert Johnson and The Mississippi Sheiks, as well as the white North Carolinian banjo player Charlie Poole. The lyrics in part send us to the work of the white supremacist Henry Timrod. The melody, however, brings us to Bing Crosby, the major American singing star of the Great Depression. His signature tune, "Where the Blue of the Night Meets the Gold of the Day," is a sentimental love song. It begins with a patter-like introduction, sung over rapidly picked guitars, and pointing out that the past is gone. Then he launches into the brief, repeated chorus:

> Where the blue of the night meets the gold of the day,
> Someone waits for me.
> And the gold of her hair, crowns the blue of her eyes
> Like a halo, tenderly.
> If only I could see her, oh how happy I would be!
> Where the blue of the night meets the gold of the day
> Someone waits for me.[12]

From here Crosby offers a lively demonstration of his whistling technique.

Dylan's hymn to devotion updates this situation, turning a song about the past into a song about the future, offering a more philosophically dense and wiser account of the importance of commitment. He breaks up the harmony and form of Crosby's song, adding minor chords here and there to lend a more melancholy feel. Most striking is that here, as in "Mississippi," Dylan's composition swallows the entire song form, as each of his verses offers a repetition of Crosby's entire verse-bridge-verse lyric. Especially powerful is his transformation of that fifth line: "If only I could see her, oh how happy I would be!" Dylan uses internal rhyme to break the line into three different semantic units: "The midnight rain follows the train / We all wear the same thorny crown." This reinvents the stanza as a three-part structure. The internally rhyming fifth line seems key, as that is where Dylan offers some of his most delicate images: "Each invisible prayer is like a cloud in the air tomorrow keeps turning around"; "More frailer than the flowers these precious hours that keep us so tightly bound"; "In this earthly domain full of disappointment and pain you'll never see me frown," and so on. The tool of rhyme, which links separate bits of semantic information through the play of similarity and difference, plays out the logic of these comments about the unity or disunity of our lives on earth.

Dylan's harmonic additions and performance underscore the seriousness of the lyric. "Oh, how happy I would be," sings Crosby, with a virtuoso trill on "be." Dylan hesitates and swallows the end of his line, "our shadows . . . roll"; "you'll never . . . see me . . . frown," with a near sob, so that we know that resolution and constancy are in the air. Crosby's performance is filled with vocal ornaments; Dylan's is eccentric, as notes are hit slightly ahead of or behind the beat. These anticipations and hesitations prepare us for the key phrase, "I'll be WITH YUH, when the DEAL GOES DOWN" (//-, //-,—). Crosby's romantic dream gives way to a colloquial expression of solidarity and love.

Crosby's song was partly written by the singer himself, and during the recording process he changed the line "When the blue of the night meets the gold of the day" to "Where the blue of the night," a phrase that turns time into space and makes a story about a tryst into the evocation of an impossible dream. The meeting place of the "Blue" and the "Gold," of night and day, offers an allegory of the very process that Dylan is deploying here, juxtaposing commonplaces used by several black blues musicians with the echo of the white poet Timrod. Certainly, at one level, the song is about what Dylan is doing, about finding the point where opposites touch in a fragile unity. Race and identity are never far below the surface. Crosby's version was first performed in a 1931 short film, *Blue of the Night*, in which he plays himself and falls for a girl on a train who, while flirting, pretends to be engaged to "Bing Crosby, the crooner." Crosby plays along, not revealing who he is. Then, later, when he tries to identify himself, he is disbelieved. To prove that he is who he says he is — and to get the girl — Crosby ends up crooning the famous song over the closing credits, thereby claiming his identity as a performer through a performance inside a filmed performance.[13]

This game of identity seizure takes on extra resonance in the context of Dylan's song, since Crosby is widely recognized as the first major modern white appropriator of African American culture. As Elvis Presley would do with black rhythm and blues two decades later, Crosby adapted Louis Armstrong's innovative, laid-back vocal approach and turned it into his signature style, thereby displacing the more operatic style of earlier white singers such as Rudy Vallee. Crosby became the first great male vocal star of the age of radio by making Armstrong's style available to white audiences. His professional generosity to Armstrong was noteworthy, as he cast him in several of his films, beginning with 1936's *Pennies From Heaven*. But, curiously, Crosby also seems to have been obsessed with the traditions of the American minstrel show and the spectacles of blackface. From his earliest days as a performer, back in Washington State, Crosby participated in blackface shows. He later injected blackface into many of his films, often in contexts where it seemed gratuitous beyond any possible narrative explanation (in 1942's *Holiday Inn*, for example). No less than Jim Jones, Crosby was a poacher, both at the level of performance — the "style" of another — and at the level of "content," in his staging of earlier white poaching from black culture.

Thus, Dylan brings together phrases that circulate in black music (Johnson, the Sheiks) with lines that send us to white cultural figures (Poole, Timrod). He himself sings a tune that reminds us of a white crooner who introduced the melody by pretending to be "himself" in a film. That crooner turns out to be someone who ambiguously moved between racial traditions, who built his career on African

American performance and who was obsessed with a form of white mimicry of black identity. Dylan's own hesitating vocal opens up a space between his murmured message and the more dramatic longing of the Crosby tune — a space punctuated by the recording's warm, unadorned guitar solos. Dylan seems to be holding these conflicting traditions up to the light, asking us to think about them and, above all, to remember them as both our violent heritage and the raw material on which contemporary music is built. They are among the cards that "go down" in the deal of cultural history. All of these elements touch on the issues of race, history, and community, yet those themes are never mentioned. They are simply present, lending density to the fabric of the song, hiding in plain sight.

We have come a good way from Dylan's citations of Woody Guthrie on his first album. As we noted in Chapters 1 and 2, Dylan's early approach involved taking scenarios or melodies from other singers and turning them to new purposes. Here we witness an excavation carried out on the sites of past dramas, leading to a mosaic-like juxtaposition of fragments that call attention to themselves. We can gauge the work done by Dylan's citations in these late songs by comparing them to an earlier, iconic moment in his corpus. "Desolation Row" (1965), one of his most famous and ambitious songs, ends with a flurry of cultural references. Here is the second to the last verse:

> Praise be to Nero's Neptune
> The *Titanic* sails at dawn
> Everybody's shouting out
> "Which side are you on?"
> And Ezra Pound and T. S. Eliot
> Fighting in the captain's tower
> While Calypso singers laugh at them
> And fishermen hold flowers
> Between the windows of the sea
> Where lovely mermaids flow
> And nobody has to think too much
> About Desolation Row (p. 220)

The song paints a nightmarish vision of modern culture, plagued by corruption and vice, in which people and things parade before the narrator's eyes, like a giant freak show. Now we see that disaster is ahead. Nero's Neptune recalls Nemo's Neptune, the submarine

216

from the Jules Verne novel *Twenty Thousand Leagues under the Sea* (of which Dylan may have seen the 1954 cinematic adaptation). Captain Nemo, the commander, is here transformed into Nero, who fiddles while Desolation Row burns, an image glossed by the allegory of the Titanic. What are the people of energy doing all this time? Instead of helping out, they're shouting at each other, via the old coal miners' strike song "Which Side Are You On, Boys?" This image of dysfunction is then extended in the reference to the two "captains" of modern poetry, Pound and Eliot, who are fighting for control of a ship that, in any case, is about to founder. Not by accident were Pound and Eliot both masters of the fragmentary, poachers of earlier culture. "These fragments have I shored against my ruins," asserted Eliot gloomily.[14] Yet in this mid-1960s version of Dylan, there is an alternative to the mess of a culture in disarray, in the image of the calypso singers, who laugh, the fishermen who hold flowers, and the mermaids who flow. These images of beauty and fertility — basically, images connoting a different kind of art, popular art — offer the salutary answer to a high culture on the way down. The mention of the mermaids recalls the final lines of Eliot's "Love Song of J. Alfred Prufrock," where the neurotic speaker, who cannot name or speak his own desire, mentions the singing of mermaids with the lament, "I do not think that they will sing to me."[15] But they *will* sing to Dylan's persona, and to us, it would seem, if we listen to them. A final verse laments the narrator's misery and addresses a friend before asking for letters, as long as they come from Desolation Row — dispatches from the front, as it were. This leads to Dylan's extraordinary harmonica solo, which concludes the song — a song, if not of calypso, then at least of rock and roll.

Dylan's repertoire of cultural images — high modernist literature, protest songs, Hollywood — unrolls before us to depict a society at odds with itself, headed for an iceberg. By contrast, the late songs I have been studying here offer much less integrated, more fragmentary visions of suffering and frustration. The shattering of coherence located by Pound and Eliot in the realm of high culture now afflicts everyday life. And to respond to this ruination, Dylan's late songs work out a poetics unlike what we saw in the great 1960s compositions, or the Kerouackian/Petrarchan evasions of the mid-1970s. These diverse poetic approaches offer different ways of making meaning; they evolve and develop across the decades.

Sayings

Dylan's post-1989 work explores the processes of cultural memory and the isolation of the individual cut off from past and community — themes that unfold under the sign of Fitzgerald's tragedy of Gatsby. The answer to desolation seems to be self-conscious performance and the circulation of bits of cultural information. Dylan's songs from the 1960s envisioned the transmission of knowledge to the unwoke: "Twenty years of schooling and they put you on the day shift" (p. 172), notes 1965's "Subterranean Homesick Blues." These later songs signify in quite different ways, not through cultural name-dropping (*Highway 61 Revisited*, from 1965) or through self-dramatization (*Blood on the Tracks*, from 1975), but through elaborate and oblique processes of allusion. Yet, if, as I have been arguing, Dylan's "late style" involves a rhetoric of the fragment, who is it that speaks from within the jumble? And what is the situation of the audience, as witness and consumer of this dark matter? Early on in Dylan's career, we remember, his authority was linked to his ability to "ramble" or move about. By the mid-1960s, this had shifted; immobility replaces mobility ("we sit here stranded," as 1966's "Visions of Johanna" would have it), and the focus shifts to exploration of new types of sensory experience. In his late work, however, Dylan plays the ventriloquist, speaking through invented characters who are most definitely limited in understanding. In his early work, when he created a "character," the imagined listener was included in that persona, as he sang to it — we are all implicated in Miss Lonely, Queen Jane, or Mister Jones. Now he has flipped the equation, the contingent "characters" are the characters in the songs, the singing subjects. Even when a "you" is named, such as in "Nettie Moore," from *Modern Times* (the name also titles a late nineteenth-century sentimental song), that character is evoked as a kind of fulcrum around which the singer can spin his own experiences. Nothing is communicated about her.[16]

The moral and aesthetic possibilities of this ventriloquism become clear if we turn to one of Dylan's most moving late songs, "Workingman's Blues #2," from *Modern Times*. The title recalls a traditional Lonnie Johnson blues. But more pertinent is Merle Haggard's 1969 hit "Workin' Man Blues," about stopping off in the tavern on the way home from work to celebrate solidarity and the dignity of honest labor. Haggard seems to be the target here.[17] For whereas his song is a blues in form only and offers a celebration of men who have "never been on welfare," Dylan gives us a song that is not a formal blues — it's a stately lament — but that depicts the bleak situation or "blues" of the workingman who might like to cavort with Haggard's drinkers but who appears to have been laid off from his job:

There's an evening haze settling over town
Starlight at the edge of the creek
The buying power of the Proletariat's gone down
Money's getting shallow and weak
Now the place I love best is just a sweet memory
It's a new path that we trod
They say low wages are reality
If we want to compete abroad

After this account of things, nothing remains of Haggard's smug claim that self-respect is merely a matter of having the proper work ethic. Dylan grasps the essence of the postindustrial economy, which saps the dignity of even the most industrious. This working-man looks out on his mill town and sees only a version of Desolation Row. But what is striking here is the language that the narrator uses. "Proletariat" would be something the workingman has heard some-where, a word bandied about at the union hall. "You know, Capital-ism is above the law" (p. 661), Dylan had exclaimed with authority in 1983's "Union Sundown." Now his protagonist simply repeats a rumor, "They say low wages are reality." It is a secondhand thought, something picked up, perhaps, at a tavern like the one celebrated by Haggard's well-employed hero. This is not Bob Dylan speaking; it is his character. And the poetry that the narrator presents is marked by a poignant slippage of one metaphor into another, as the idea of money getting "shallow" seems to be motivated by the shallow water at the edge of the creek. The natural world has been bled by the language of politics and economics, as a walk down to the water turns into the "new path" that the country has taken in the age of global capital.

What consoles the narrator of "Workingman's Blues #2" is his beloved: "Come sit down on my knee," he sings. "You are dearer to me than myself / As you yourself can see." The internal rhyme of knee/me/see and the play with "myself" suggest the depth of this devotion. And we shouldn't be surprised that here, too, scholars have identified an allusion. This time it is to the *Tristia*, or *Book of Sorrows* by the exiled Roman poet Ovid, sent by Caesar Augustus to the Black Sea in the first century C.E. Ovid's poem, the last in his book—the last word, as it were—praises his wife for sticking with him through misery and notes that his fame as a poet will give her a good name forever, as consolation for everything they have been through. It is appropriate that it should be the *Tristia* that seems to speak here, since Ovid's book stresses his suffering in exile; he wants to get back to Rome. The entire point of Dylan's song, however, is that, in the world of globalized capital, *everyone* is an exile. Even if you are at home, you are not at home. Home is just a "sweet memory." Thus, the break in history that I have highlighted throughout Dylan's late work, the split between an empty present and some earlier moment of plenitude and meaning, is here intensified through the Ovid reference. Not even Ovid had it this bad.[18]

The slippages between metaphors that shape the setting of the song reappear in the hero's depiction of his life:

> I'm listening to the steel rails hum
> Got both eyes tight shut
> Sittin' here trying to keep the hunger from
> Creepin' its way into my gut
> In the dark I hear the night birds call
> I can feel the lover's breath
> I sleep in the kitchen with my feet in the hall
> Sleep is like a temporary death

These lines offer an unsettling juxtaposition of different worlds. The "hum" of the steel rails evokes the now defunct world of the railroad and the possibility of escape from a small town—something like the "mail train" that Dylan pretended to hop in his great 1965 song "It Takes a Lot to Laugh, It Takes a Train to Cry." But hunger takes over to break up the fantasy.[19] A second later, the imaginative leap that remembers love and erotic passion gives way to the jokey phrase, "I sleep in the kitchen with my feet in the hall." This is a blues commonplace. Among many others, Robert Johnson had used it in a "hokum" song called "Hot Tamales" ("I got a woman, she's long and tall, she sleeps in the kitchen with her feet in the hall"), which Dylan himself had gestured toward for a song on his second album, "Honey, Just Allow Me One More Chance." Here it punctures the moment of

erotic imagining. Sleeping in the kitchen is okay when it is the mea-
sure of how tall your good woman is. When you have to do it yourself,
it is a humiliation. And the bleakness of the situation is sealed with
the concluding line to the verse: "Sleep is like a temporary death."
It's another "overheard" phrase, to be sure, but here it brings heart-
breaking sadness. Not the "little death" or *petite mort* that the French
associate with erotic pleasure. Just a break from the depression.

The complexity of the situation is reflected in the modulations
between different types of information that are presented as each
verse unfolds, often with disarming quickness:

> I'm a-tryin' to feed my soul with thought
> Gonna sleep off the rest of the day
> Sometimes no one wants what you got
> Sometimes you can't give it away

With remarkable brevity, these four lines bring out three moments in
the consciousness of the narrator and convey three completely differ-
ent, though related, bits of information. The resolution to "feed" the
soul with thought is the speaker's self-consolation. For the worker
who has been laid off, the first thing on the agenda is to "do some
thinking," or to "get my priorities straightened out." However, this
immediately gives way to a description of what the unemployed *really*
do, which is to sleep a lot. But then there is the bitter, concise realiza-
tion of what thought and sleep have brought up: that what you have
to offer is no longer needed in this economy. These shifts between
self-consolation and clear-eyed acknowledgment of the harshness of
the situation structure the lyric.

Thus, the protagonist of "Workingman's Blues #2" is caught, at
the very level of the poetic line, between escape into the imagina-
tion and the brutal reality of life in a dying town. His own language
betrays him. Moments of dream or comfort disintegrate into humil-
iating self-descriptions. Whereas Dylan's early songs, as I showed
in Chapter 1, deploy a kind of linguistic patchwork—bits of "Okie"
speech, archaic phrases, Greenwich Village ideology-talk—here
linguistic variety of a very different kind works within the char-
acter himself, enacting his own confusion. His description of his
misery and his response to that misery unfold in dialogue within the
same voice as we listen. This character, like the characters in many
of Dylan's late songs, shuttles between commonplaces from other

songs, bits of reported speech, and resigned descriptions of misery. Yet his position, between the fragments of various discourses, also makes possible the moments at which Dylan pauses and allows these speakers baldly and forcefully to speak their own truths: "I give my heart to you / And that's sayin' it true," says the narrator of "When the Deal Goes Down," to conclude the last verse. Here is my truth, even though I may speak only from within and among the voices of others. And in "Workingman's Blues #2" we hear the narrator rail against his misery and against those who "never worked a day in their life / Don't know what work even means," as he urges his listener(s) to join him in fighting back: "You can stand back or fight your best on the front lines / Sing a little bit of these workingman's blues." He, too, speaks his truth: "All across the peaceful sacred fields / They will lay you low / They'll break your horns and slash you with steel / I say it so it must be so."

Perhaps it is not by coincidence that Chaplin's film *Modern Times*, which gives the album its title, is the first moment when Chaplin's own voice was ever heard on film, singing in a nonsense mixture of Italian, French, and a few other tongues, as the little tramp is forced to perform for a group in a bar.[20] At last, the worker speaks from the world of silent cinema, speaking, like Dylan's characters, bits of remembered language. And in "Ain't Talkin'," the final song on *Modern Times*, the message the worker offers is not a happy one. "Ain't talkin'," says the narrator, "just walkin'" (p. 853). "Heart burnin'... still yearnin'," are the answering lines in the chorus of the song. But the "yearnin'" is not for love. It is for justice and vengeance. And each verse offers a contrast between two lines of reflection on the ways of the world ("They say prayer has the power to heal"; "Well, the whole world is filled with speculation"), followed by two lines of menace ("If I catch my opponents ever sleeping / I'll just slaughter 'em where they lie"; "There'll be no mercy for you once you've lost"). Here is the voice of the workingman who at last has had enough. We have come a long way from the revolutionary fervor of the Greenwich Village crowd stirred up by Dylan's early 1960s work. This is the barely contained rage of the rural laborer, who has had his fill of fancy talk and excuses from "the ladies in Washington" (p. 844), as Dylan calls them elsewhere on the album. "Ain't Talkin'" supplements the anger of "Workingman's Blues #2," which says, "You can stand back or fight your best on the front lines." In these songs Dylan chronicles the struggle of life, of "modern times," as the everyday grappling for dignity and a living wage. It is a less romantic vision than the "revolution in the air" that Dylan remembered in "Tangled Up in Blue." But it is the struggle of this moment, our moment, absolutely modern.

The space to "say it so it must be so," however fragile and temporary that statement may be, is what Dylan leaves for his characters. They speak from within the shards of culture that pile up in his late songs. Their voices come through the rattling of other discourses, evanescent but clear. Their possibilities for action are few, and when they think they have mastered a situation, their statements — often clumsy, often blindly optimistic, often uttered through clenched teeth — make us wonder if they are merely deluding themselves. "Some people still sleepin', some people are wide awake" (p. 852), runs the last line of "The Levee's Gonna Break," from *Modern Times*. Through these voices — direct, unselfconscious, grounded in the past of Robert Johnson, Nettie Moore, Bing Crosby, and even Henry Timrod — Dylan's late art reclaims cultural heritage in all of its ambiguity. It suggests that, however problematic the past may be, we cannot find our way without it. He places us among the ruins of a culture where — in contrast to the kaleidoscopic modernism of many of his 1960s songs — the voices we hear are not called up to confuse or enchant us. They merely clamor to be heard, as traces of working women and men, faded beauties and lost heroes, actors in histories that need reclaiming, without nostalgia or sentimentality. They gather the past around us, but in fragments, like some forgotten rhythm or wisp of startled air.

Frankness: Voice and History

The voice I hear this passing night was heard
In ancient days by emperor and clown.
—Keats, "Ode to a Nightingale"

I began this book by asking us to think about voice, about the voices that echo through Bob Dylan's songs. We have seen that his work is crisscrossed in powerful ways by an extraordinary variety of elements, by lyrics, dramatic scenarios, genres, and traditions. The volume and expansiveness of Dylan's work have long been recognized. Our discussion has shown, however, that in the details of their structures, as well as in their dynamic unfolding, Dylan's songs derive their extraordinary vitality from the interplay of different registers and forms of utterance. The mingling of voices shapes the form and impact of the work. These include everything from citations of the classics to invented dialects of American speech. This means that listening deeply to Dylan is much less a matter of tracing Dylan's "influences" or unearthing "sources" than remaining open to the interplay of forms, conventions, and expressions within each song — and, in some cases, between songs.

Because of the composite nature of Dylan's lyrics and the constant interplay between lyric expression and musical form, Dylan's songs generate meaning beyond the sum of their parts. Thus, for example, we have seen that the complex melding of disparate elements — citations, made-up proverbs, cultural references, and the like — both presents intricate "plots" or "vignettes" through the songs and calls attention to the ways in which they are "made" by the hand that has composed them. This enables Dylan to be present, as we noted, both as protagonist and as maker — to take the literary paradigm we discussed in the last chapter, both as Jay Gatsby, the tragic hero, and as Nick Carraway, the chronicler. It is a double game that unfolds from some of Dylan's earliest songs and takes different shapes as his work develops. This ironic, dialectical model of writing extends to Dylan's famous performing style, where the songs are rarely sung in a way that could be captured through the blunt tools of musical transcription. Dylan manhandles the songs, pushing the words this way and that, delaying and anticipating in such a way that a distance opens up between the "song" and the "performance." The effect of this touches on the social role of art itself. For Dylan's energetic manipulation of song calls attention to the ways in which all of the elements that make up his career — aesthetic breakthroughs, performing personas, sheet music collections, rock stardom, suede jackets, song lengths, publishing rights, sing-along refrains, and communities of listeners — are in their own ways constructs, historical artifacts, shaped by labor, power, and desire. Moreover, Dylan's manipulation of form generates perspectives on the material that he sets into his songs: citations undercut other citations; sonic effects clash with ideological pronouncements; metaphors transform characters before our eyes; harmonic modulations illustrate dramatic transitions; and so on. This is why it is best to understand Dylan's work, as I have suggested, poetically, in the history of forms, rather than through the filters of biography, national history, or myth. Dylan's willingness to question and push beyond the building blocks that make up comfortable careers, comfortable politics, comfortable identities, and comfortable songs accounts for much of the power and difficulty of his work.

My own concern across these chapters has been to let the songs speak as clearly as possible, in all of their nuanced complexity and power. This has meant close attention to language and diction and to the construction of verse, chorus, harmony, and, in some cases, performance. I have sought to put different songs in dialogue with themselves, to show their inner workings, and in dialogue with other songs, from both inside Dylan's work and elsewhere. We have seen that the songs certainly talk to other songs, by Memphis Slim and Bing Crosby, by Woody Guthrie and Chuck Berry, and to other forms of imaginative expression, from Petrarch to Rimbaud. But they often talk to each other as well; "Mississippi" offers a later version of the scenario of "Stuck Inside of Mobile," and we hear that song differently after having spent time with "Mississippi." In its epic journey through past and present, "Blind Willie McTell" might be seen as a companion to "A Hard Rain's a-Gonna Fall," almost like a piece of historical research that explains the conditions that made the earlier song possible. In this way, as I pointed out in my introduction, we can think of Dylan's songs as a kind of galaxy, as a set of points that are related yet distinct, radiating outward. My focus on the workings of the songs has tended to downplay biographical or journalistic background, leaving Dylan's many interviews and adventures for another day. For today, the important thing is to grasp the constellation of the songs and to articulate the ways in which their aesthetic dynamics reflect and generate different kinds of social experience. To recall again the phrase from Robert Pinsky that I cited in my introduction, "Poetry penetrates to where the body recognizes the stirring of meaning." Music penetrates beyond meaning. This book has explored how Dylan's work offers a set of diverse and changing meditations on the relationship between the social world and the individual.

Dylan's songs offer examples of what Pinsky has called the "social actions of meaning." Those actions are given voice through aesthetic form at different moments. Poetic models modulate from album to album, from song to song. Thus, for example, the seriousness of "Blowin' in the Wind," is built, as we saw, through the interplay of the energetic questioning of the lyric and the stabilizing role of alliteration and rhyme. A bit later, "Visions of Johanna" unfolds as visionary experience places pressure on the fragile song form. The historical meditation of "Tangled Up in Blue" is inseparable from the form of the sonnet and the harmonic modulation that gives it voice. The stately elegance of "Every Grain of Sand" is built from a dense, impasto-like layering of rhetorical figures — metaphors and similes — on the thematic scenario of confession and regret. And the solidarity of "When the Deal Goes Down" cannot be separated from the diverse voices — poetic and musical, black and white — that echo through the song world. These aesthetic effects — at the meeting point of music and lyric — help us grasp some of the ways that Dylan's art works. They unfold outside the details of Dylan's biography, or the clichés of pop music history. Indeed, the melding of form and rhyme, harmony and genre, helps generate the aesthetic — what I have called the "poetic" — dimension of the songs. This dimension should be especially important when we stop to acknowledge that, for all of his rootedness in American musical history, Dylan's work now and henceforth lives in a global musical culture, as a kind of toolkit to be used by other writers and composers.

This is not, however, to advocate for a kind of evolutionary or "narrative" model of Dylan's work. The point here has not been to write a disguised biography or portrait of the composer via the songs. Rather, the goal has been to explore the diversity of forms that make up the larger body of work, to show how they speak the experience of modernity, from JFK to Enron. To be sure, certain techniques seem to answer problems raised by earlier songs. Certain forms and vocabularies emerge at particular times; for example, Dylan embraces gospel in a central way at one moment in his career, the end of the 1970s, despite what is obviously a long-term interest in that tradition.

By elaborating different styles of writing and composing, Dylan creates a variety of tools to which he and others can return and from which they can draw. Thus, for example, I stressed the ways in which Dylan's mid-1960s "visionary" work explored the technique of name-dropping, of throwing in imagined or real personalities who populate the world of the songs, as a kind of shorthand for social types. As Dylan develops new approaches to writing, toward the end of the 1960s, he tends to ditch this technique. However, it can reappear at any time, as a kind of resource, such as in 1999's "Things Have Changed," where we hear, from out of nowhere, that "Mr. Jinx and Miss Lucy, they jumped in the lake / I'm not that eager to make a mistake" (p. 890). This kind of gesture, like the "visionary style," or the "late style" (to recall a few of the labels I have used), provides a resource for writing that Dylan has introduced into popular song and that can be accessed when needed. Techniques like this are a toolkit. Part of the project of this book has been to discern how those tools work and why they are useful at certain times.

I have been considering "voice" in a fairly abstract sense — as when we speak in literature or history writing of a "poetic voice" or a "narrative voice." I have skirted until now the question of Dylan's vocal style, the actual voice of "Bob Dylan," whoever he may be. "I'm just as good a singer as Caruso," Dylan joked in D. A. Pennebaker's 1967 documentary *Don't Look Back*. If Robert Pinsky says that poetry functions as a "somatic ghost," a phantom version of the social dimension of meaning in language, we could note as well that a singular singer such as Bob Dylan leaves his own imprint on certain words, expressions, and cadences. Many people find it difficult to listen to Bob Dylan's singing voice. From the time of his beginnings in the music business his singing has been criticized, first by listeners interested in a more "polished" sound (say, Doris Day or Perry Como), then by folk fans who wanted Dylan to color inside the lines so that everyone could join in, then by lovers of a kind of vocal consistency, who couldn't understand why he was droning one moment and shouting the next, and more recently, by advocates of youth culture, who couldn't grasp why a singer whose voice wavers and cracks would still want to sing. What could he possibly have to say? Toward the end of his life, Dylan's friend Leonard Cohen bolstered his performances with backup from female voices, often singing in unison. Everyone's voice grows deeper with age. But Cohen's developed a powerful presence that lent it an authority and, in a sense, a normalcy that was absent from the uncertain tone on his earliest records. Joni Mitchell's voice deepened markedly as well, supposedly urged on by years of tobacco use. To my ears, this gave it an experiential seriousness that it often lacked earlier on. In Dylan's case, the one thing I think we can always say about his voice is that it moves us the way it does (for better or worse) because it is the voice of someone who is not "supposed" to be singing. He is either too young, too rough, too old, too stoned, or too angry.

Dylan's 1969 recording *Nashville Skyline* is one of his most sonically beautiful albums. Part of the beauty comes from Dylan's own voice, which appeared to have changed from his earlier recordings, and now took on a trumpetlike brightness. In such romantic ballads as "Lay, Lady, Lay" and "Tonight I'll Be Staying Here with You," he hits the notes on time, offers simple, clear melodies, and even does a brief parody of Elvis (on "Peggy Day"). We might say that, for once, he colored inside the lines. But the larger significance of this sonic shift was to reveal the arbitrary, willed character of Dylan's "normal" singing voice, or of any "normal" singing voice. After *Nashville Skyline*, listeners realized that Dylan sings the way he does not because he can't sing any other way (he just did), but because he *wants* to sing this way. When he yowls, it is because he wants to yowl, and he is yowling for a reason. And throughout his work in the 1970s and 1980s, Dylan seemed bent on exploring all of the different qualities of his vocal range, singing often at the very top of his register, or growling sarcastically out of the side of his mouth. (The exception to this is the falsetto, which Dylan seems, wisely, I think, to have abandoned after about his fourth album.) Only at the end of the 1980s did it begin to become clear that the voice itself, not surprisingly, was showing signs of natural aging. A raspy whisper began to find its way into some of the performances. But Dylan seemed to counter this inevitable "decline," or physical limitation, by recalibrating the use of the vehicle. Thus, on the first track from the 1993 folk song collection *World Gone Wrong*, he opens the title song, an old blues, high up in his nose, pushing the harshness of his nasal tone, particularly when he addresses the woman as "Baby." On some words he seems to be fighting saliva or phlegm in the back of his throat — a detail that he manipulates by setting it in the middle of key words — as in "Ain't got no hoooommme." Yet the resolution in each verse comes in the chorus, "I can't be good Baby / Honey because the world gone wrong." "Baby" is held out and gets extra harsh nasal treatment, before the final cadence, starting on "Honey," which takes the melody back to its starting point and lets us down easy. As he sings this resolution, the timbre of Dylan's voice changes. It draws back from the nasality of "Baby" to settle in the back of his throat and the chest on "the world gone wrong." The last line offers a release from the anger in the rest of the song. "Honey," as it were, sweetens the message. The harshness of "Baby" reflects his frustration with his unfaithful lover. But then the voice migrates from one part of the body to another, as the lyric shifts from whining excuse to resigned acknowledgment of the ways of life: "The world gone wrong." The movement toward the deeper and softer conclusion is the vocal equivalent of Dylan's earlier trick, on "A Hard Rain's a-Gonna Fall," of alternately strumming his guitar on the lower strings and the higher strings, depending on where he is in the conversation of the verse. Here, as the lyric unfolds, Dylan's voice slides, as it were, from one timbre and body site to another, generating its own rambling "somatic ghost."[1]

The experimentation continues. On Dylan's recordings from the 1990s he often draws on the breaks in the voice itself as a tool, so that sobs in the lyric and scrapes in the voice correspond, as if he were bent on turning vocal debility into an expressive strength. On 2006's *Modern Times*, as we saw, he channeled Bing Crosby, if not in terms of tone quality or timbre, certainly with occasional scoops or trills on some of the long notes. On 2012's brilliant "Duquesne Whistle" (written with the former Grateful Dead lyricist Robert Hunter) from

Tempest, he goes back even further in the history of song, as his vocal sounds uncannily like something we would hear from Louis Armstrong. He pushes the song around, bending it to the needs of the performing personality. He privileges song-as-sung over song-as-ideal. He puts over a personality as much as a text, and much more than an image.

In 1997 Dylan appeared in a television special to wish Frank Sinatra a happy 80th birthday. He sang a song from 1964 called "Restless Farewell," which ends with a most appropriate line for the swinging Sinatra: "I'll bid farewell and not give a damn" (p. 120). When he was done, he added a few words over the applause: "Happy Birthday, Mr. Frank." Fifteen years later he began releasing a series of recordings of classic American standards, many of which had been recorded by Sinatra. These albums, *Shadows in the Night* (2015), *Fallen Angels* (2016), and *Triplicate* (2017), range across a wide swath of Tin Pan Alley music. The effect was richly evocative and the implications of Dylan's turn to this particular body of music were several. For one thing, we could remember the contempt with which music critics and industry people had spoken of Dylan's singing voice when he first came on the scene. Sinatra was held up as the gold standard. Dylan, it was said, sounded like a frog. But now Ol' Blue Eyes was gone, and a slightly younger blue-eyed singer — the "voice" of a slightly younger generation — was reshaping these songs in his own sonic image. But perhaps more important, he was reclaiming these songs as American folk songs, as songs that don't need a full orchestra or a slick arrangement to be sung. They could stand up as country-inflected tunes played by a small string band. In this regard, Dylan acted as a musicologist, as a devotee and advocate for great songwriting. The effect was to reshape tradition; Dylan suddenly became a "folksinger" who turned songs that were initially thought to be the very opposite of "folk songs" into folk songs.

Fallen Angels opens with the Caroline Leigh and Johnny Richards tune "Young at Heart," from 1953. It is difficult to hear the recording without hearing Sinatra's version echoing in the background, like a ghost. Dylan follows Sinatra's arrangement almost exactly, singing in the same key, beginning in slow time before hitting full tempo, stressing the word "young," and sitting out while the band plays the first half of the verse on the second go-round before coming in for the final cadences. But of course there are the inevitable differences.

Sinatra's version swings with the optimism of the postwar genera-
tion, looking at a bright future of station wagons and dry martinis.
Dylan's version is stately and serious. His voice has changed since
his late 1990s voice, where, as noted, he often seemed to be singing
in the back of the throat, fighting phlegm. Here it has a consistent
but coarse surface that integrates well with the bowed sound of the
viola on several of the cuts from the album. On "Young at Heart," it
turns a lyric about the power of mind over matter into a thoughtful
commentary on the passage of time. The final lines are particularly
revealing. The published melody ends by zigzagging over a minor
third interval — a passage that Sinatra takes with jaunty reassurance,
bouncing up and down and up again: "If you are among the very
young at heart!" Dylan's version eliminates the melodic intervals. He
sings the concluding affirmation on a single pitch. This turns the last
cadence from a happy musical affirmation into a bit of sober advice,
almost spoken, about the secret to a well-lived life. Sinatra inhabits
the line. Dylan comments on it.[2]

No less striking is the climax of the song, where the melody goes
high: "And if you should survive / To a hundred and five / Think of
all you'll derive / Out of being alive."[3] Sinatra skates through this
with a smile, hitting the climactic word "a-l-i-v-e" with ease. Dylan's
recording captures the sound of him inhaling deeply to prepare
for the final push. And, indeed, his voice wavers on the high note,
"alive." But he recovers and pushes through by breaking the word
up phonetically. He hits the preceding rhyme words with conven-
tional Midwestern pronunciation ("survahve," "hundred and fahve,"
"derahve"). However, he breaks the climactic word "alive" into a
delicate whine, "alaiieeeve." Here he is doing what the song says,
making "alive" come alive. At one level, it seems like a technical trick,
a way of jerking his voice up, to loop it around the target note, like
the flex in a dancer's knee before she leaps, or the hitch in a batter's
swing before he swats the ball to left field.[4] But it is also where the
past speaks, where history resonates through the performance. For
this "alaiieeeve" recalls distantly the times where Dylan has turned
to the same sound throughout his career. It takes us back to the
very first appearance of this improvised diphthong: "Ain't it just
like the nigheeet" (p. 242), at the very opening of the third song on
Blonde on Blonde, "Visions of Johanna" (1966). There the strangeness of
"nigheeet" initiated us into the disturbing modernist soundscape of

that album, with its droning, half-chanted vocal style and mannered pronunciation. But it evokes as well the live version of "Don't Think Twice" that emerged from Dylan's return to concertizing (captured on 1974's *Before the Flood*), where he shouts out the moral of the tale: "Don't think twieeece. It's alrigheeet!" Another live performance (on 1976's *Hard Rain*) finds him springing it on the song like a revelation, as midway through "Idiot Wind" it erupts out of nowhere: "They say I shot a man named Gray and took his wife to Italy / She inherited a million bucks, and when she *dieeed* it came to me." On "Young at Heart" he doesn't push the sound; he adds just enough seasoning to open the word up. This is the mark of the Dylanesque. This is where Dylan turns language against itself, opening it up to a new message, a message in which word and music are bound together into a form of communication that is both and neither. On the highest note, when the breath falters for an instant and the voice wavers, he remakes the word, cracking it open to reveal the life inside of "alive." He summons his vocal imagination to leave a mark on the language, on rhythm, on sound itself. And so, at last, he delivers the song, sending it out toward the stars. Young at heart.

Acknowledgments

Two sections of this work have previously appeared in print. Part of Chapter 3 appeared in *Representations* 132 (Fall 2015), and part of Chapter 4 appeared in *Critical Inquiry* 39.4 (2013). I am grateful to both publications for the permission to reuse this material and to Jean Day, Richard Neer, W. J. T. Mitchell, and the editorial boards of these journals for good comments on drafts. Lyrics are cited by permission; thanks to Jeff Rosen and David Beal for their help.

I would especially like to thank Ramona Naddaff, Meighan Gale, Gregory McNamee, Jeremy Wang-Iverson, and the staff of Zone Books for their patience, professionalism, wisdom, and help with revision and publication. And thanks to Eric Kotila.

I am deeply indebted to a group of friends and colleagues who have encouraged this critical expedition, and who have provided insightful, generous, and expert responses to various parts of my work. First, thanks go to Rob Kaufman and Alan Tansman, whose ideas, suggestions, and criticisms have been a constant source of help. They read most of the work as it unfolded and offered dozens of useful suggestions, corrections, and counterarguments. I am truly grateful for their time and friendship. Charles O. Hartman read the completed manuscript and offered very helpful suggestions, both in general and in specific. I am also indebted to Martin Harries, Seth Lerer, Ira Marlowe, Kate van Orden, and Nigel Smith as well as an anonymous commentator, who read key parts of my writing, helped me with articulation, and saved me from mistakes. All errors or imprecisions are, of course, on me. Thanks as well for encouragement and more to François Bon, Kathryn Crim, Virginia Jackson, Tom McEnaney, Hassan Melehy, Jane Newman, Peter Sahlins, Debarati Sanyal, Mary Ann Smart, and Diana Thow. Sarah Coduto and Hailey Johnson have been exemplary research apprentices through the UC Berkeley URAP program. Fellow conspirators in the Doreen B. Townsend Center for the Humanities at Berkeley listened patiently to earlier versions of some of these arguments and offered their insights. Thanks to Rebecca Egger and John Paulas for hosting. Thanks go as well to colleagues and students in the Poetics/History/Theory group at the University of California, Irvine, at Tulane University, and at the Dahlem Center of the Free University in Berlin, who responded thoughtfully to bits of my work as it developed. The Institut d'Etudes Avançées in Paris hosted me while I began thinking about this book inside the margins of another project. Students in my Freshman Seminars on Dylan and Rimbaud at Berkeley helped me clarify some of my ideas about these two artists. I would also like to acknowledge the Transcribe! musical transcription software program and Eyolf Østrem's former dylanchords website. And from a time now long gone, my thanks to Malcolm, Bob, Larry, Bill, Gail, Will, Annette, and Rachel.

My greatest debt, as always, is to my family, Jessica, Emily, and Sophia. Their love, humor, and creativity are a constant source of inspiration and strength. They make every day a song.

Notes

INTRODUCTION: A MAKER

The epigraph is my translation from the French text of Rimbaud's *Illuminations*, included in John Ashbery's version (New York: Norton, 2011), p. 55.

1. Ever quick on the draw, Dylan soon saw through the illusions of stardom and, during his period of greatest popularity, in the mid-1960s, his occasional interviews became exercises in evasion or playfulness. The most famous of the early interviews was done with Nat Hentoff for a 1966 *Playboy* issue. Some of the other interview material can be found scattered across *Bob Dylan: In His Own Words*, ed. Chris Charlesworth (London: Omnibus Press, 1993).

2. Thus we might think, not only of the critical writing that treats the songs intertwined with accounts of Dylan's life adventures — for example, biographies such as Anthony Scaduto's *Bob Dylan: An Intimate Biography* (New York: Grosset & Dunlap, 1972), Clinton Heylin's *Bob Dylan behind the Shades: A Biography* (New York: Simon & Schuster, 1991), or Michael Gray's massive and fascinating critical study *Song and Dance Man III: The Art of Bob Dylan* (London: Continuum, 2000) — but also a document such as Todd Haynes's filmic account of Dylan's multiple "identities," *I'm Not There*, from 2007.

3. See, especially, Christopher Ricks, *Dylan's Visions of Sin* (New York: HarperCollins, 2003), as well as, more recently, Richard Thomas, *Why Bob Dylan Matters* (New York: Dey Street Press, 2017). One could mention as well the earlier study by Jonathan Cott, which often places Dylan's work in a frame taken from Jungian psychology. See his *Dylan* (New York: Doubleday, 1984).

4. On Dylan's role in American culture, see the distinguished work of Greil Marcus, especially *The Old, Weird America: The World of Bob Dylan's Basement Tapes* (New York: Picador, 2011) originally published as *Invisible Republic*. Sean Wilentz's *Bob Dylan in America* (New York: Vintage, 2011), offers important historical framing, and Wilfrid Mellers's *A Darker Shade of Pale: A Backdrop to Bob Dylan* (New York: Oxford University Press, 1985) sets Dylan's musical prehistory. Mellers's later book, *Music in a New Found Land: Themes and Developments in the History of American Music* (New York: Oxford University Press, 1987),

provides a capacious vision of American musical traditions, from "classical" to blues. For Dylan's presence as a disruptive political artist, see Mike Marqusee's *Wicked Messenger: Bob Dylan and the 1960s* (New York: Seven Stories Press, 2005).

5. For a good account of the early history and emergence of "world music" often in dialogue with "American music," see Michael Denning, *Noise Uprising: The Audiopolitics of a World Musical Revolution* (London: Verso, 2015), esp. chs. 6 and 7.

6. Robert Pinsky, *Democracy, Culture and the Voice of Poetry* (Princeton: Princeton University Press, 2002), p. 22. For a theoretically informed meditation on the importance of "lyric" (in all its forms) for contemporary culture, see the introduction and subsequent commentaries by Virginia Jackson and Yopie Prins to *The Lyric Theory Reader: A Critical Anthology* (Baltimore: Johns Hopkins University Press, 2014). On the role of poetic form in structuring poetic meaning see, Robert Hass, *A Little Book on Form: An Exploration into the Formal Imagination of Poetry* (New York: HarperCollins, 2017). Hass turns to a sonic vocabulary when he stresses the importance of "the resonances we experience in a well-made thing, a passionately made thing, a thing made from a full commitment to the art it instances." He goes on to quote the poet Lyn Hejinian, who notes that "writing's forms are not merely shapes, but forces." See Hass's discussion of form as articulation on pp. 5–7 of his book.

7. Pinsky, *Democracy, Culture and the Voice of Poetry*, pp. 46–47. For a related but different take on lyric's role in collective life, see the remarks on "Lyric Poetry and Society," in Theodor Adorno's *Notes to Literature*, trans. Shierry Weber Nicholsen (New York: Columbia University Press, 1991), vol. 1, pp. 37–54. Here is Adorno: "The highest lyric works are those in which the subject, with no remaining trace of mere matter, sounds forth in language until language itself acquires a voice" (p. 43). On the power of poetry to generate knowledge that lies beyond conceptual thought, see Robert Kaufman, "Lyric's Constellation, Poetry's Radical Privilege," *Modernist Culture* 1.2 (2005), pp. 209–34.

8. On style as the mediation between individual subjectivity and social hierarchy see the discussion in Theodor W. Adorno and Max Horkheimer, *Dialectic of Enlightenment*, trans. John Cumming (New York: Seabury Press, 1972), pp. 130ff.

9. The key Bakhtin texts here are the long essays found in *The Dialogic Imagination*, ed. Michael Holquist, trans. Michael Holquist and Caryl Emerson (Austin: University of Texas Press, 1981). Also of interest are *Speech Genres and Other Late Essays*, trans. Vern W. McGee, ed. Emerson and Holquist (Austin: University of Texas Press, 1986), and M. M. Bakhtin and P. N. Medvedev, *The Formal Method in Literary Scholarship*, trans. Albert J. Wehrle (Cambridge, MA: Harvard University Press, 1985).

10. For some of the theoretical problems involving "voice" and "many-voicedness" in musicology, see the colloquy of brief essays "Why Voice Now?," ed. Martha Feldman in the *Journal of the American Musicological Society* 68.3 (2015).

11. Ezra Pound, *The ABC of Reading* (New York: New Directions, 2013), ch. 4.

12. The impact on the senses of the forces of industrial capitalism was first identified

and conceptualized by the French poet Charles Baudelaire. For a study of Baudelaire's reflections, see Walter Benjamin, *The Arcades Project*, trans. Howard Eiland and Kevin McLaughlin (Cambridge, MA: Harvard University Press, 1999).

13. In Martin Scorsese's 2005 documentary *No Direction Home*, Dylan refers to himself as a "musical expeditionary." On the archaic impulse in Dylan's work, see Greil Marcus's *Old, Weird America*. On the self-presentation of the poet and its link to the gathering of lyric material, see Jonathan Culler, *Theory of the Lyric* (Cambridge, MA: Harvard University Press, 2015), ch. 5.

14. On the problem of dating modernism and on modernism as a cosmopolitan force, see Raymond Williams, "When Was Modernism?" in his *The Politics of Modernism: Against the New Conformists* (London: Verso, 1989), pp. 48–52. My own thinking about the aesthetic problems and solutions raised by modernism has benefited from Fredric Jameson's book *A Singular Modernity* (London: Verso, 2012), as well as T. J. Clark's *Farewell to an Idea: Episodes from a History of Modernism* (New Haven: Yale University Press, 1999). Jameson's Part II, "Modernism as Ideology," and Clark's essays on Jackson Pollock and on abstract impressionism are useful for thinking about the question of a "late modernist" aesthetic. Just as modernism is the art of the city, of the disorientation of modern urban experience, so might one trace, in a different register, a pop music modernism that emerges in its own right at the end of the 1950s, to replace first the urbane, aristocratic fantasies of, say, Cole Porter, and then the limited experience of the small town or high school neighborhood microcosm that had provided the content of 1950s rock and roll. The local struggle for love or justice, chronicled by Chuck Berry and Buddy Holly, is exploded. This happens first through the ethical vocabulary on which the newly popular "protest song" or "folk song" movement relied, as well as through the topicality and, indeed, internationalism of that movement (songs from the Spanish Civil War, from Cuba, etc.). The expansion becomes generalized in the years of John F. Kennedy through an increasing internationalization of popular art (French New Wave Cinema, existentialist literary themes in popular writing, abstraction, and so on) that informs a newly complex landscape.

15. The key text on disenchantment is Max Weber's 1920 *Sociology of Religion*. The Dylan quote is from Bob Dylan, *The Lyrics: Since 1962*, eds. Christopher Ricks, Lisa Nemrow, and Julie Nemrow (New York: Simon & Schuster, 2014), p. 188. All subsequent citations of Dylan's lyrics will refer to this edition and feature page numbers in the text.

16. On Mitchell's work, see the fine study by Lloyd Whitesell, *The Music of Joni Mitchell* (Oxford: Oxford University Press, 2008), which systematically breaks her recordings down into their constituent elements. But all is not harmony. Greil Marcus quotes Mitchell in an interview, discussing Dylan: "Bob is not authentic at all. He's a plagiarist, and his name and his voice are fake. Everything about Bob is a deception." The first phrase in this comment seems to be a reproach. The last sentence may be a compliment. Quoted in Greil Marcus, *Bob Dylan, Writings 1968–2010* (New York: PublicAffairs, 2010), p. 427.

17. We should note that an alternate version of the lyric, released on the 2008 compilation *Tell Tale Signs*, casts Dignity as a woman. This both sharpens the focus and limits the scope of the song.

18. Raymond Chandler, *Later Novels and Other Writings*, ed. Frank MacShane (New York: Library of America, 1995), p. 714.

19. For example, "I Shall Be Released," one of the major songs from the *Basement Tapes*, could easily fit among the songs on *John Wesley Harding*, recorded during the same period (1967). Similarly, "You Ain't Goin' Nowhere" coheres with the songs on *Nashville Skyline*, recorded a year later.

20. This is probably a convenient place to acknowledge that the subtitle to this book, "How the Songs Work," may elicit readerly impatience ("Yes, but . . ."). Obviously, *everything* in a song or a recording contributes to how it "works." My goal is to describe as clearly and simply as I can the interplay of language and music, and to stress features of the work that can be marshaled into broader arguments about how Dylan's art unfolds. The point is precisely not to account for everything. Do not mistake this book for an encyclopedia.

CHAPTER ONE: CONTAINING MULTITUDES

1. Bob Dylan, *Chronicles: Volume One* (New York: Simon & Schuster, 2004), p. 70. Further references to this work will indicate page numbers in the text.

2. T. S. Eliot, "Tradition and the Individual Talent," in *Selected Essays of T. S. Eliot* (New York: Harcourt, Brace and World, 1964), pp. 3–11. The "essentialist" or innate nature of Seeger's talent—as depicted by Dylan—resonates in a number of ways with Eliot's famous essay, which makes it clear that "tradition" is to be understood as Caucasian and principally Northern European.

3. On the dynamics of the "field" as a spatial figure through which professions are managed see Pierre Bourdieu, *The Field of Cultural Production*, ed. Randal Johnson (New York: Columbia University Press, 1993), part 1. Bourdieu's discussion of the subculture of late nineteenth-century aestheticism is useful for thinking about the folk music movement.

4. For portraits of the folk music community during this period, see Robert Cantwell, *When We Were Good: The Folk Revival* (Cambridge, MA: Harvard University Press, 1996), and Laura Archibald's 2012 documentary film *Greenwich Village: Music That Defined a Generation*. Ethan and Joel Coen's film *Inside Llewyn Davis* (2013) offers a fictional version of the same scene. With specific reference to Dylan, see Sean Wilentz, *Bob Dylan in America* (New York: Vintage, 2011), chs. 1–2; Clinton Heylin, *Bob Dylan behind the Shades: A Biography* (New York: Simon & Schuster, 1991), chs. 3–6; and Daniel J. Wolff, *Grown-Up Anger: The Connected Mysteries of Bob Dylan, Woody Guthrie, and the Calumet Massacre of 1913* (New York: HarperCollins, 2017). On the links between this context and the larger emergence of a "New Left" political movement, see Todd Gitlin, *The Sixties: Years of Hope, Days of Rage* (New York: Bantam, 1987), chs. 2 and 3.

5. These confines of the folk music project have been traced in Joel Dienerstein's book *The Origins of Cool in Postwar America* (Chicago: University of Chicago Press, 2017), esp. ch. 6, as well as in David Hajdu's account of Dylan's early career in *Positively 4th Street* (New York: Farrar, Straus and Giroux, 2001). The uneasy relationship to conventional culture and the forces of commercialization is explored in Thomas Frank's *The Conquest of Cool: Business Culture, Counterculture, and the Rise of Hip Consumerism* (Chicago: University of Chicago Press, 1997). It is important, in discussing the contours of the "folk" moment, not to confuse its sophisticated and urban-based focus with the later, hippie-inspired "back to nature" moment of the early 1970s, which deployed much of the same music as that circulated by the folkies (now called "old-timey" music) for a much less modernist project.

6. Gilles Deleuze and Félix Guattari, *Kafka: Toward a Minor Literature*, trans. Dana Polan (Minneapolis: University of Minnesota Press, 1986), p. 17. Deleuze and Guattari use the case of Franz Kafka, a Jew living in Prague, writing in German, to consider the role of subcultures inside of larger cultural spaces. In their marginality, writes Kafka, the Jews are like "gypsies who have stolen a German child from its crib." We can place the complex dynamics of borrowing, urbanization, and the "return" to traditional song embodied in the folk music movement in this context—not to mention, of course, Dylan's own famous interest in what it means to be "without a home."

7. See María Rosa Menocal, *Shards of Love: Exile and the Origins of the Lyric* (Durham, NC: Duke University Press, 1993).

8. On the complex dialectic between authenticity and standardization at work in the process of commodification, see Gary Tomlinson, *Metaphysical Song: An Essay on Opera* (Princeton: Princeton University Press, 1999), p. 130: "Just as the social forces of labor are outshone by the unlimited exchangeability of the commodity they produce, so the alluring sheen of the authentic, self-sufficient subject obscures the secret of its social creation." Tomlinson is glossing the section called "Gold Assay" from Theodor Adorno's *Minima Moralia*. I am grateful to Alan Tansman for pointing me toward Tomlinson's book, which, especially in its account of Nietzsche's thinking about Wagner, resonates in interesting ways with Dylan's post-folkie folk music.

9. M. M. Bakhtin, "Discourse in the Novel," in *The Dialogic Imagination*, trans. Caryl Emerson and Michael Holquist (Austin: University of Texas Press, 1981), p. 276.

10. For a somewhat different approach to Dylan's "collage" technique, focused less on stylistic details and more on imagery, see Rona Cran, *Collage in Twentieth-Century Art, Literature, and Culture* (Burlington, VT: Ashgate, 2014), ch. 4. The idea of the poetic text as "constellation" that can both engage with philosophical concepts and stretch them beyond their own rigid definitions comes from the work of Walter Benjamin and Theodor Adorno, two thinkers associated with the so-called Frankfurt School of critical theory—though the use of the term seems to reach back through Nietzsche to Emerson. For a full account of this concept and its importance for modern poetry and the heritage

of Romanticism, see Robert Kaufman, "Lyric's Constellation, Poetry's Radical Privilege," *Modernist Culture* 1.2 (2005), pp. 209–34.

11. All citations of Dylan's lyrics refer to *The Lyrics: Since 1962*, ed. Christopher Ricks, Lisa Nemrow, and Julie Nemrow (New York: Simon & Schuster, 2014). Page numbers will be indicated in the text.

12. Cited from www.woodyguthrie.org/lyrics.

13. Of course, one could add other voice models—the literary name-dropper, the beatnik who still speaks hip jive ("the sweetest gone mama," from 1970's "One More Weekend" [370]), the sarcastic hipster, the preacher, the doggerelist. It is worth noting that the play with "abide" / "obey" is one of the first instances of a technique that Dylan uses throughout his career whereby he presents phrases with unusual words that can only be fully grasped through their relationship to other words not spoken. We might think of a song such as 1967's "Too Much of Nothing," which became a radio hit for Peter, Paul and Mary. It begins as follows: "Too much of nothing, can make a man ill at ease / One man's temper might rise / Where another man's temper might freeze" (p. 402). The striking feature here is the word "temper," which puts us with the disenfranchised, denied the riches of the world. It is true, in conversational English, that tempers can "rise"; we say that particular person has a "hot temper." And deprivation makes one angry. However, tempers do not freeze. What freezes are *temperatures*. Yet, Dylan cannot sing "another man's temperature might freeze," since the song is not about temperature. In order to make the point about deprived people being "ill at ease" Dylan has to use the less specific word "temper." That is, the phrase only works if we "know" that "temperature" is lurking beneath the surface of "temper" (poor people freeze), but that it cannot emerge as a principal meaning, since the line would make no sense. Dylan is writing between words to suggest an outrage that is more physical than "temper" but more ethical than "temperature." For an insightful account of the dynamism of "American English" that makes reference to a number of Dylan's lyrics, see Christopher Ricks, "American English and the Inherently Transitory," in *The Force of Poetry* (Oxford: Clarendon Press, 1984), esp. pp. 428–34.

14. Theodor Adorno, *Notes to Literature*, trans. Shierry Weber Nicholson (New York: Columbia University Press, 1991), vol. 2, p. 86.

15. See Walt Whitman, "Song of Myself," in *Leaves of Grass*, ed. Justin Kaplan (New York: Library of America, 1992), p. 87.

16. See www.woodyguthrie.org/lyrics.

17. We might note, as a measure of this archaic flavor, the state song of New Mexico, "O Fair New Mexico," from 1917, written by Elizabeth Garrett, the daughter of the famed Lincoln Country sheriff Pat Garrett.

18. The countermelody and lyric in Simon and Garfunkel's version were composed mostly, it would appear, by Art Garfunkel, who thereby made the "traditional" song radioworthy. Indeed, the key to "folk music" success on the radio seems to have been through

modern "composed" folk songs. Peter, Paul and Mary's massive radio hits were never "traditional" songs, despite their reputation as "folksingers." Only the much-maligned Kingston Trio, it would seem, could actually hit postwar pay dirt with "folk" songs. We can point out, finally, that Dylan's first professional musical gig was playing the piano, for a short time, in the band of teen idol Bobby Vee. On one level, "Girl from the North Country" offers a reworking of the story of Vee's 1961 pop hit "Take Good Care of My Baby."

CHAPTER TWO: RAMBLIN' BOY

1. At one level, the rambling singer is the heir to the nineteenth-century *flâneur*, or stroller, who, as depicted by Charles Baudelaire and theorized by Walter Benjamin, haunts the crowded boulevards of the modern city. For Benjamin, the *flâneur* is both participant and observer, a kind of artist of daily life. He stands as a type of the intellectual or the artist in nineteenth-century Paris, just as the city is beginning to be modernized. Yet he quickly becomes associated, in Benjamin's account of modernity, with the prostitute and the sandwichman. Whereas the idle *flâneur* strolls and observes, the prostitute and the sandwich man carry the new world of commodity capitalism on their very bodies. And in both of these cases, economic survival is linked to mobility. See Walter Benjamin, "The Paris of the Second Empire in Baudelaire," trans. Rodney Livingstone, in *The Writer of Modern Life*, ed. Michael Jennings (Cambridge, MA: Belknap Press, 2006), pp. 66–72. For a useful commentary on this work see Susan Buck-Morss, "The Flaneur, the Sandwichman and the Whore: The Politics of Loitering," *New German Critique* 39 (1986), pp. 99–140. On the importance of Jimmie Rodgers in the invention of the modern rambler/cowboy/bard see Peter Doyle's fascinating book *Echo and Reverb: Fabricating Space in Popular Music Recording, 1900–1960* (Middletown, CT: Wesleyan University Press, 2005), ch. 3.

2. Woody Guthrie, *Bound for Glory* (New York: Penguin, 1983), p. 20.

3. Jack Kerouac, *On the Road* (New York: Signet, 1985), p. 26.

4. Jack Kerouac, *The Dharma Bums* (New York: Penguin, 1976), p. 7. We can note that *On the Road* was published in September 1957. Thus, *The Dharma Bums* opens two years exactly before the publication of Kerouac's blockbuster.

5. Guthrie, *Bound for Glory*, p. 36.

6. Kerouac, *On the Road*, p. 25.

7. This aura is reinforced by Dylan's recording, on his inaugural album, of a series of old blues tunes on the theme of death. The voice sounds old in part because it sings about oblivion.

8. See the excellent discussion of this song in Christopher Ricks's *Dylan's Visions of Sin* (New York: HarperCollins, 2003), p. 44, as well as Michael Gray, *Song and Dance Man III: The Art of Bob Dylan* (London: Continuum, 2000), p. 141.

9. Quoted from www.woodyguthrie.org/lyrics.

10. Here, again, and for all Guthrie lyrics, see www.woodyguthrie.org/lyrics.

11. Daniel Wolff's book *Grown-Up Anger* brilliantly reconstructs the links between Dylan and Guthrie, tracing the history of the Calumet massacre and Guthrie's song about it. My own reading of Dylan's song to Guthrie, however, differs from his. Ricks (*Visions*, p. 53) notes the self-referential ambiguity marking the "last thing" phrase. On the importance of canon creation for second-generation postwar modernist writers, see Fredric Jameson, *A Singular Modernity* (London: Verso, 2012), pp. 185–88. The question of the folksinger as proletarian was raised in a 2011 interview with Ian Tyson and Sylvia Fricker, of the Canadian folk duo Ian and Sylvia, who crossed paths with Dylan in the Village. Tyson, who was raised in ranch country (and returned there to become a successful rancher), recalls being struck, upon his arrival in Greenwich Village, by how much the American folksingers sang about working men and women, and by how little actual physical labor any of them ever seemed to have done. See the "Studio Q" interview: www.youtube.com/watch?v=UsLNZEt5d44.

12. Both of these songs take us back to Robert Johnson's "Hot Tamales" (1936), of which I will say more in Chapter 6.

13. Quoted from www.woodyguthrie.org/lyrics.

14. Quoted from the Genius.com website under Paul Clayton's lyrics.

15. The question of how Dylan indicates the "you" in his songs is a complicated one. For insights and guidance, see Charles O. Hartman's essay "Dylan's Deixis," in *Polyvocal Dylan*, ed. Joshua Toth and Nduka Otiono (London: Palgrave Macmillan, forthcoming).

16. This is in contrast to more ironic uses of "my friend" in such songs as the contemporaneous satire "I Shall Be Free," where Dylan imagines himself in dialogue with President Kennedy. "He said, 'My friend Bob what do we need to make the country grow,' I said, 'My friend John, Bridget Bardot, Anita Ekberg, Sophia Loren'" (p. 86). This is more than a racy joke or a comment on the wonders of immigration. When set next to the more intimate scenario of "Blowin' in the Wind," it points to the recalibration of public and private that Dylan's music was trying to work out. Friendship is not a major theme of Dylan's writing, but we can note that the outtakes for his first album include the traditional song, "He Was a Friend of Mine," which he appears to have learned from Eric von Schmidt. See Elijah Wald's interesting June 2016 blog post about this song at elijahwald.com.

17. See *The Irving Berlin Anthology* (Milwaukee: Hal Leonard Music, 1994), p. 108. For a different reading of the Dylan song and its questions, see Ricks, *Dylan's Visions of Sin*, p. 323.

18. In order to compare the structures of the two songs, one might consult the recording of Dylan himself doing "No More Auction Block" on the 1985 *Biograph* collection.

19. We can recall here Guthrie's "This Land Is Your Land," where alliteration is also present ("I've roamed and rambled . . . followed my footsteps"). Alliteration, it would seem, underpins the anthemic register. For an insightful account of Dylan's different vocal mannerisms in his early work, see Michael Cherlin and Sumanth Gopinath, "'Somewhere down in the United States': The Art of Bob Dylan's Ventriloquism," in *Highway 61*

Revisited: Bob Dylan's Journey from Minnesota to the World (Minneapolis: University of Minnesota Press, 2009), pp. 225–36. Especially interesting is their discussion of Dylan's voice as "public bard" versus his voice as "private person." See pp. 223–24. For a broader exploration of Dylan as singing persona, see Daniel Karlin, *The Figure of the Singer* (Oxford: Oxford University Press, 2013), ch. 9.

20. See the discussion in Van Ronk, *The Mayor of MacDougal Street: A Memoir*, written with Elijah Wald (New York: Da Capo Press, 2006), p. 206. Van Ronk calls the song "folk music" fused with "modernist poetry."

21. Transcribed from YouTube: www.youtube.com/watch?v=acWQMs6BXX8. Christopher Ricks claims that the song "declines to be an allegory" (*Dylan's Visions of Sin*, p. 329). I don't quite understand this, since much of it is obviously allegory. Dylan (*Chronicles: Volume One*, pp. 68–69) writes beautifully about his admiration for Belafonte as both a singer and an ethical presence. This is the Dylan song that Patti Smith performed at the ceremony for Dylan's reception of the Nobel Prize in Literature. For a good discussion of the jumbled, collage-like juxtaposition of the various "vignettes" in the song, see Rona Cran, *Collage in Twentieth-Century Art, Literature, and Culture* (Burlington, VT: Ashgate, 2014), p. 190. The topos of the conversation between parents and children alienated from each other would spawn a collection of songs by "singer-songwriters" a few years after this. See, for example, "Sit Down Young Stranger" by Dylan's friend Gordon Lightfoot and "Father and Son" by Cat Stevens.

22. Dylan, *Chronicles*, pp. 274–76. In Martin Scorsese's documentary about Dylan, *No Direction Home*, Joan Baez recounts that the song came out of an incident in which Dylan, accompanying Baez on tour, was denied lodging in a hotel. The personal turned out to be the political.

23. In point of fact, Ms. Carroll died of a heart attack, not from the blow delivered by the racist Zanzinger.

24. *Brecht on Theater*, ed. and trans. John Willett (New York: Hill & Wang, 1992), p. 42. This is from the discussion of songs in the section called "The Literarization of the Theater." See as well the comments by Fredric Jameson in his *Brecht and Method* (London: Verso, 1999), pp. 180–84.

25. In his luminous reading of "Hattie Carroll," Ricks underscores the risk that the victim might be forgotten in the process of reperformance, as Dylan sings the song again and again. My focus here is on the double-leveled structure of the lyric form. See his analysis in *Dylan's Visions of Sin*, pp. 16–17 and 221–33.

26. For illuminating comments on Dylan's genius for "playing his timing against his rhyming" see *ibid.*, p. 19.

27. As Robert Cantwell writes of The Kingston Trio, the music "seemed essentially aural, amateur, and traditional — what would loosely be called 'folk' music — and hence independently reproducible, theoretically, by any untrained person." See *When We Were*

Good: The Folk Revival (Cambridge, MA: Harvard University Press, 1996), p. 316. He points out that the Kingstons studied professionally to achieve this effect of amateurism.

28. Cited in Jameson, *Brecht and Method*, p. 75.

CHAPTER THREE: ABSOLUTELY MODERN

1. The entire press conference may be seen online at www.youtube.com/watch? v=D cPoZZVm3Dk&list=PL463DE68A9789EC5A.

2. As will become clear, my use of the term "vision" involves specific stylistic features that may be identified at a particular moment in Dylan's work. I distinguish it from the more general use of the term in Christopher Ricks's well-known book *Dylan's Visions of Sin* (New York: HarperCollins, 2003).

3. It may not be irrelevant, in evoking this contrast between East Coast and West Coast popular culture, to note that between the time of Dylan's appearance at Newport and the San Francisco press conference the popular music charts were topped by a hit single from the Mamas and the Papas called "California Dreamin'," which reinvented California not as a place of surf and Hollywood (say, the Beach Boys and Doris Day) but as the "safe and warm" existential alternative to the gray skies and cold of New York. The song, after all, is a conversion parable, in which the singer takes refuge in a church to contemplate his destiny. Saint Augustine never sounded so good.

4. See, among many examples, Ginsberg's very early compositions "On Reading William Blake's 'The Sick Rose,'" "Vision 1948," "Psalm I," and "The Shrouded Stranger," in Allen Ginsberg, *Collected Poems: 1947–1997* (New York: Harper & Row, 1988).

5. My citations of Rimbaud will come from the versions of Louise Varèse. These were published as *A Season in Hell and the Drunken Boat* (New York: New Directions, 1961) and *Illuminations* (New York: New Directions, 1957). I have just cited *Illuminations*, p. xxx. Henceforth, I will indicate page references in my text. The *Illuminations* volume also contains, in its prefatory material, portions of Rimbaud's two great letters on poetics: the May 13, 1871, letter to his teacher Georges Izambard, and the letter to his friend Paul Demeny written two days later. I have also worked with Wallace Fowlie's excellent bilingual edition, *Rimbaud: Complete Works, Selected Letters*, ed. Seth Whidden (Chicago: University of Chicago Press, 2005). Fowlie's edition first appeared in 1966; I cite it, when necessary, to establish context, not to suggest that Dylan could have read it at the period I am studying here. It is the edition, however, that will be read by The Doors' Jim Morrison, a few years later.

6. Rimbaud, *Illuminations*, trans. John Ashbery, p. 16. This is from Ashbery's preface. Georges Poulet has linked this moment of singularity to the moment of waking up from sleep and has traced it back to some of Rimbaud's earliest poems. See his influential study *Exploding Poetry*, trans. Françoise Meltzer (Chicago: University of Chicago Press, 1980), pp. 75–87.

7. Anglophone critical writing on Dylan has tended to neglect the importance of Rimbaud. For even the most distinguished commentators, Rimbaud's influence seems

mostly to be centered on the phrase, "I is someone else." The historian Sean Wilentz notes that Ginsberg encouraged his teacher at Columbia, Lionel Trilling, to read Rimbaud as a prophet of a new morality. Trilling, not surprisingly, perhaps, was unimpressed. See Wilentz, *Bob Dylan in America* (New York: Vintage Books, 2011), pp. 54–57. However, in his own retelling of Dylan's listing of his canon at the 1965 news conference, Wilentz does not mention Rimbaud. Thus Rimbaud, fittingly perhaps, is both present and absent in the critical tradition. See Wilentz's discussion in "American Recordings: On 'Love and Theft' and the Minstrel Boy," in *Do You, Mr. Jones? Bob Dylan with the Poets and Professors*, ed. Neil Corcoran (London: Chatto and Windus, 2002), pp. 300–301. In his massive study of Dylan, *Song and Dance Man III: The Art of Bob Dylan* (New York: Continuum, 2000), Michael Gray devotes the second chapter to "Dylan and the Literary Tradition," in which he stresses Blake as an influence and dwells on Whitman.

8. See Miller's *The Time of the Assassins: A Study of Rimbaud* (New York: New Directions, 1946), which is not a "study" of Rimbaud but a collection of Miller's musings about himself. In Patti Smith's memoir *Just Kids* (New York: Ecco, 2010) the twin exemplarities of Rimbaud and Dylan are inscribed into the form of the narrative. The chapter depicting Smith's pilgrimage to Rimbaud's birthplace ends with an account of her first big show in a New York club, when she learns back stage that "Bob Dylan had entered the club" (p. 248). She takes "power" from his presence. Rimbaud and Dylan are the bookends to her scene of triumph.

9. Van Ronk writes in his memoirs, "Somewhere in my bookcases I probably still have a paperback collection of modern French poetry with Bobby's underlinings in it . . . he was reading that stuff very carefully." Dave Van Ronk, with Elijah Wald, *The Mayor of MacDougal Street: A Memoir* (New York: Da Capo Press, 2005), pp. 206–207. We assume that Dylan did not read this material in French.

10. The contrast between visionary experience and literary realism is visible as early as Victor Hugo's work. As Walter Benjamin writes of Hugo, "In the visionary strain that runs through Hugo's conception of the crowd, social reality gets its due more than it does in the 'realistic' treatment which he gave the crowd in politics." See "The Paris of the Second Empire in Baudelaire," in *The Writer of Modern Life*, ed. Michael Jennings and trans. Howard Eiland et al. (Cambridge, MA: Harvard University Press, 2006), p. 92. On the theme of work (in all of its senses) in Rimbaud's poetry, see Kristen Ross, *The Emergence of Social Space: Rimbaud and the Paris Commune* (London: Verso, 2008), ch. 1. Harold Bloom's *The Visionary Company: A Reading of English Romantic Poetry* (Ithaca, NY: Cornell University Press, 1961) remains a useful guide to one aspect of the visionary tradition, even as I am arguing that Rimbaud and Dylan exceed the bounds of that tradition.

11. See Jameson's essay "Rimbaud and the Spatial Text," in *The Modernist Papers* (London: Verso, 2007), p. 421.

12. For Theodor Adorno, who takes Rimbaud's admonition to be "absolutely modern" as the virtual motto for his own *Aesthetic Theory*, a turn to abstraction is characteristic of all modern art, which "abstracts" from tradition in order to reflect on it. It is both the sign of its power and of its limits: "The modern is abstract by virtue of its relation to what is past," writes Adorno. "Irreconcilable with magic, it is unable to speak what has yet to be, and yet must seek it, protesting against the ignominy of the ever-same." See Adorno, *Aesthetic Theory*, trans. Robert Hullot-Kentor (Minneapolis: University of Minnesota Press, 1997), p. 27.

13. We might think here—to expand the dialogue with Rimbaud—of the ways in which some of Rimbaud's most influential texts, for example "Alchemy of the Word," consist of mini-anthologies of earlier poems, bits of self-citation in which earlier impulses are now reinterpreted. In fact, the two letters on poetry were much longer in the original than in the Varèse translations. Other editions of Rimbaud in circulation included translations by Delmore Schwartz. For a listing of some of Dylan's "thefts" from Rimbaud, see Richard F. Thomas, *Why Bob Dylan Matters* (New York: Dey Street Press, 2017), ch. 5.

14. On the importance of the "moment" as a unit of aesthetic experience within modern art, see Karl Heinz Bohrer, *Suddenness: On the Moment of Aesthetic Appearance*, trans. Ruth Crowly (New York: Columbia University Press, 1994) ch. 9. See as well Fredric Jameson's appropriation of Bohrer's work in *A Singular Modernity* (London: Verso 2012), pp. 188–96.

15. On the changing figural language of Symbolist poetry, see Octavio Paz, *Children of the Mire*, trans. Rachel Philips (Cambridge, MA: Harvard University Press, 1974), ch. 4. On Rimbaud's move away from the analogical poetics of Baudelaire, see Tzvetan Todorov, "A Complication of Text; the *Illuminations*," in *French Literary Theory Today*, ed. Tzvetan Todorov (Cambridge: Cambridge University Press, 1982), pp. 223–37. "Chimes of Freedom" is one of the first examples of a subgenre of popular song that we might call the "1960s sublime." That is, in lieu of the classic themes of popular music—romantic love, teenage desire, nostalgia, ambition—these songs introduce the theme of experience itself. They are focused on a single moment, on exhausting the experience of a simple swatch of time that seems removed from past and future. This is a topos that would become a virtual cottage industry in the world of songwriting over the next five years or so, often under the influence of psychedelic drugs, most famously in The Beatles' "Lucy in the Sky with Diamonds" and "Tomorrow Never Knows." For an insightful study that reads Dylan's move into rock music as emblematic of the contradictions of the New Left, caught between an ethos of individual liberation and a quest for communal authenticity, see Barry Shank, "'That Wild Mercury Sound': Bob Dylan and the Illusion of American Culture," *boundary 2*, 29.1 (2002), pp. 97–123.

16. Here is Rimbaud on the associative power of language: "One has to be an academician, deader than a fossil, to complete a dictionary in any language whatsoever. Weak people would begin to think about the first letter of the alphabet, and they would soon rush into madness" (*Illuminations*, p. xxvii). Rimbaud's sonnet "Vowels" also explores this associative poetics by assigning colors to particular letters. One might think here as well

of the reflections on language in Mallarmé's "Crisis of Verse," of Kandinsky's treatise, "Concerning the Spiritual in Art," or of Proust's reflections on the hidden resonances of names in the final section of the first volume of *In Search of Lost Time*.

17. The connection is even clearer in French, where the reference to the "milky sea" is rendered as "infusé d'astres, et lactescent," with the notion of lactescence recalling the "Voie lactée" of the Milky Way. This confusion of distinct sensory zones is replayed in the very editing history of the poem, inasmuch as editors are uncertain whether to correct "les azurs verts" to become "azure verses" or leave them as "green azures," as the manuscript has it. The radiating power of this particular passage may be why it was translated by Ted Berrigan, one of Dylan's New York contemporaries, and included as a freestanding "sonnet" in his 1964 book *The Sonnets* (London: Penguin, 2000), p. 62.

18. Mike Marqusee is one of the few commentators to note the Rimbaldian provenance of Dylan's opening lines. He sees the song as a "sweeping vision of solidarity" with those marginalized by society (indeed, his own book was, in a first edition, named after this song). My concern is with the role of the stanzaic structure and with the imposition of personal vision on what are, in the end, fairly stock figures of suffering. See his insightful discussion in *Wicked Messenger: Bob Dylan and the 1960s* (New York: Seven Stories Press, 2005), pp. 98–102. For a discussion of the ideological work done by the modernist notion of the "autonomous" aesthetic object, see Fredric Jameson, *A Singular Modernity* (London: Verso: 2012), pp. 141–56.

19. The cosmic vision here calls to mind the extraordinary closing to Theodor Adorno's *Minima Moralia*, in which Adorno stresses that the task of the philosopher is to "attempt to contemplate all things as they would present themselves from the standpoint of redemption." "Perspectives must be fashioned," he goes on, "that displace and estrange the world, reveal it to be, with its rifts and crevices, as indigent and distorted as it will appear one day in the messianic light." See Adorno's *Minima Moralia: Reflections from a Damaged Life*, trans. E. F. N. Jephcott (London: Verso, 1974), p. 247.

20. For a critique of the uneven quality of the lyrics of "Hard Rain," as well as an account of the powerful effect it had on contemporaries, see Van Ronk's comments in *The Mayor of MacDougal Street*, p. 206.

21. The extreme instance of the idea of multiple images and multiple selves might be found in the work of the Portuguese poet Fernando Pessoa, who invented an entire series of "heteronyms," or poetic identities, each of which wrote a different type of verse.

22. See, for example, the clip in Martin Scorsese's 2005 documentary *No Direction Home* of Dylan improvising on the phrases printed in the window of an English pet shop, turning sentences inside out to generate new bits of nonsense language.

23. Indeed, in an early lyric, "What Is Said to the Poet Concerning Flowers," Rimbaud begins with the line, "Thus, always, toward the black azure." I quote Fowlie's translation, from *Rimbaud: Complete Works, Selected Letters*, p. 109.

24. For example, in 1969 the song was a major hit that helped spark the return to popularity of former teen idol Ricky Nelson. The major chord on the second step of the major scale, leading to a dominant on the fifth, is often used to create a dramatic climax effect, especially in ballad settings. See, for example, the bridge to the Beach Boys' "Surfer Girl," from 1963 or the bridge to Carole King's "Will You Still Love Me Tomorrow?" recorded by the Shirelles in 1960. The much less common shift from II to IV that Dylan uses here was used by The Beatles in "Eight Days a Week" and "You Won't See Me," from the same year as "She Belongs to Me." However, neither of these songs bears any relationship to the blues.

25. The power struggle at the heart of this drama of representation may be read in miniature in Dylan's play with pronouns. At one level, "you" who is addressed by the singer may be a placeholder for "I," the singer, as is current in conversational English. That is, I'm telling you what it's like for me now, by telling you what will happen to you if you mess with her. Dylan has been quite clear about his manipulation of pronouns to create poetic and psychological effects: "Sometimes the 'you' in my songs is me talking to me. Other times I can be talking to somebody else. . . . It's up to you to figure out who's who." This is from a 1985 interview with Scott Cohen, quoted in Barbara O'Dair's essay "Bob Dylan and Gender Politics," in *The Cambridge Companion to Bob Dylan*, ed. Kevin J. H. Dettmar (Cambridge: Cambridge University Press, 2009), p. 84. The question of how Dylan uses "deixis," the linguistic faculty of pointing, has been explored by Charles O. Hartman in "Dylan's Deixis," forthcoming in *Polyvocal Dylan*, eds. Joshua Toth and Nduka Otiono (London: Palgrave Macmillan). I am grateful to the author for having shared this work with me in manuscript.

26. Indeed, several of Dylan's unreleased compositions from this period ("She's Your Lover Now," "Tell Me Momma") simply ramble about, piling reproach upon reproach.

27. Charles O. Hartman speaks of Dylan's "ransacking of the possibilities of the refrain, a staple of popular song from the earliest times, but never more thoroughly investigated" than in these Dylan songs. See his essay "Dylan's Bridges," *New Literary History* 46.4 (2015), p. 746. For a more comprehensive discussion of the structure and performance of "Like a Rolling Stone," see Greil Marcus's excellent book *Like a Rolling Stone: Bob Dylan at the Crossroads* (New York: PublicAffairs Press, 2005). Christopher Ricks's account of the song in *Dylan's Visions of Sin*, pp. 179–92, notes the changes in the chorus from verse to verse.

28. During this period, Dylan seems to have begun trying to broaden his elemental, "folk song" three-chord harmonies by introducing more minor chords of the kind used to great effect by The Beatles (we remember, for example, "Here, There, and Everywhere," from 1965, or "If I Fell," from a year earlier). In some cases, they animate melody lines that speak across songs. Thus, the beautiful cadence of "Please don't let on that you knew me when," from "Just Like a Woman," is replayed in "My warehouse eyes, my Arabian drums" (p. 255), from the same album's "Sad-Eyed Lady of the Lowlands." Another "small

group" Dylan song from the *Blonde on Blonde* sessions, "She's Your Lover Now," mimics the chord sequences of "Like a Rolling Stone." "Queen Jane Approximately," from *Highway 61 Revisited*, reverses the progression, beginning with a chord on the fourth scale tone and moving down to the I. That is, it moves backward from the opening of "Like a Rolling Stone" and uses the sequence deployed in the middle of each verse of that song ("Now you don't talk so loud..."). This may be why "Queen Jane" feels like it begins in the middle of a line — because it does.

29. See Hartman's insightful discussion in "Dylan's Bridges," pp. 750–53.

30. For an account of the recording history and circumstances of this song, see Sean Wilentz, *Bob Dylan in America*, ch. 4.

31. In live performances from the same period Dylan often added an eighth line, "He examines the nightingale's code." See the live version included in the 1985 *Biograph* collection and *Lyrics*, p. 243. Though I am obviously not interested in reading Dylan biographically, I assume that the "Johanna" of the title is supposed to remind us of Dylan's former girlfriend and patroness Joan Baez, to whom he clearly owed a professional debt. On the visual dimension of the song, see Rona Cran, *Collage in Twentieth-Century Art, Literature, and Culture* (Burlington, VT: Ashgate, 2014), p. 209.

32. I stress that the low E is not a dissonant or "wrong" note, since it is not unusual for the bass to alternate between the tonic and dominant notes in a major chord. That is what bass players do. The point is that in this instance the low E follows a series of cadences that land on A as Dylan repeats the same line again and again. To suddenly hit an E breaks that pattern before the form of the song itself shifts.

33. For an insightful account of Dylan's creative gropings during his "retirement" following the *Blonde on Blonde* period, see François Bon, *Bob Dylan, une biographie* (Paris: Albin Michel, 2007), pp. 369–417.

CHAPTER FOUR: TANGLED GENERATION

1. Bob Dylan, *Chronicles: Volume One* (New York: Simon & Schuster, 2004), p. 118.

2. I quote from "Life and Death of Emile Ajar," in Romain Gary, *King Solomon*, trans. Barbara Wright (New York: Harper & Row, 1983), p. 243. The literary historical problem I am after here falls somewhere between the problem studied by Theodor Adorno, in "Bach Defended against His Devotees," where an audience distorts an artist's work after his death, on the one hand, and, on the other hand, the problem of a "late style," studied by Edward W. Said, where an artist tries to write against his own moment and own earlier work. I will have more to say about "late style" in Chapter 6. See Adorno's *Prisms*, trans. Samuel and Shierry Weber (Cambridge, MA: MIT Press, 1983), for the Bach essay, and Said's *On Late Style: Music and Literature against the Grain* (New York: Pantheon, 2006).

3. For a useful account of Dylan's various engagements with members of the "Beat Generation," especially Allen Ginsberg, see Sean Wilentz, *Bob Dylan in America* (New York:

Vintage, 2011), ch. 2. However, Wilentz does not discuss *Blood on the Tracks*. He notes that Dylan and Kerouac never met.

4. The quote is from Paul Maher Jr., *Kerouac: The Definitive Biography* (New York: Taylor, 2004), p. 414. Eight years later a broken, drunken Kerouac would appear on William F. Buckley's *Firing Line* television show, where he repudiated the hippie movement (and Ginsberg) that had partly been inspired by his own writing, asserting that the press had redefined as a "beat insurrection" a movement that was originally about "order, tenderness, and piety." "It was pure in my heart," he concluded in response to Buckley's prompting. See Maher, *Kerouac*, p. 469 for an account of this sad episode. Kerouac died a year later.

5. Kerouac, *On the Road* (New York: Signet, 1985). Since I will be working closely with this book here, page numbers will be indicated in parentheses.

6. For background on Dylan's trip to Colorado, see Clinton Heylin, *Bob Dylan behind the Shades: A Biography* (New York: Simon & Schuster, 1991), pp. 40–42. It is in Central City that Kerouac acknowledges the forces of cultural commercialization ("the arty types" [p. 35]) that would later destroy his own career. As Tim Major recalls the beauty of the old frontier town ("Think how it was a hundred — what the hell, only eighty, sixty years ago"), Sal bitterly comments on the tourists, "Yeah, but *they're* here" (p. 44). This is also where he names his friends as "rising from the underground, the sordid hipsters of America, a new beat generation that I was slowly joining" (p. 46). A central city indeed.

7. Dylan would return to the motif of the auto journey in the 1986 song "Brownsville Girl," which was cowritten with Sam Shepard and unfolds in a Kerouackian space. There is, for example, a visit to a "wrecking yard" owned by "Henry Porter," and his bitter, disaffected wife, Ruby, that resembles the visit to Bull Lee in *On the Road*. And, again, the journey functions as a kind of narrative unit that makes possible play with entries and exits from fiction. In "Brownsville Girl" what is at issue is the relationship between fictional illusion and the world outside of art. A brief account of the motif of the "open road" in popular culture may be found in Greil Marcus's "The Myth of the Open Road," in his *Bob Dylan* (New York: Perseus, 2010), pp. 133–47.

8. Dylan's own account of this journey may be found in *Chronicles: Volume One*, pp. 256–58. His deep knowledge of *On the Road* may be inferred from his recitation (or reading) of an extended key passage from the novel in Martin Scorsese's 2005 documentary about him, *No Direction Home*. Wilentz quotes Ginsberg quoting Dylan to the effect that he knew Kerouac's *Mexico City Blues* as early as 1959. "It blew my mind," Dylan is supposed to have said. Here is Wilentz: "It was the first poetry he'd read that spoke his own American language, Dylan said — or so Ginsberg said he said" (*Bob Dylan in America*, p. 59). Wilentz's skepticism is useful since it reminds us that Dylan's influences move far beyond the canon of American poetry.

9. See *Inferno*, Canto I, vv.13–18: "Ma poi ch'i' fu al piè d'un colle giunto, / là dove terminava quella valle / che m'avea di paura il cor compunto, / guardai in alto, e vidi le sue spalle /

vestite già de' raggi del pianeta / che mena dritto altrui per ogne calle." I have used the Robert Durling/Ronald Martinez edition and translation (Oxford: Oxford University Press, 1991). The literary scenarios I evoke here are central to Dante's work, and Kerouac would have known them, as a reader of Dante. As Gerald Nicosia shows throughout *Memory Babe: A Critical Biography of Jack Kerouac* (New York: Grove Press, 1983), Kerouac's reading was extremely broad. However, most accounts of Kerouac's work pay little attention to the intertextual aspects of his work, beyond the usual suspects (Whitman, Twain, Thomas Wolfe, et al.). Indeed, given how much of Kerouac's career was dominated by his struggles with form, it would be irresponsible not to look carefully at his use of different generic registers and literary tradition.

10. My mention of the French meaning of Des Moines is not idle. Kerouac was from a Quebecois family, thought of himself as "Ti-Jean" (Petit Jean), was bilingual in French, and was very widely read in French literature. It would be impossible for him not to have noticed the literal meaning of Des Moines as the location of Sal's brief but powerful askesis and conversionary self-alienation. Kerouac's journals suggest that this moment of alienation (located firmly in Des Moines) was one of the first things he wrote of *On the Road*, in early 1950, in the form of the fragment titled "Gone on the Road: Chapter One: An Awkward Man": "It all began when I came awake and a terrible, certainly most terribly beautiful thing was TAKING PLACE only for a few moments but enough to make the change in my life that led to the events I implore God to help arrange in my mind so I may bring them to light." See *Windblown World: The Journals of Jack Kerouac, 1947–1954*, ed. Douglas Brinkley (New York: Viking, 2004), p. 363. He goes on to describe this conversionary moment in some detail, with the wish, "and may the Angels of the Eternal Dream bear witness." On Kerouac's identity as a Francophone writer, see Hassan Melehy, *Kerouac: Language, Poetics, & Territory* (New York: Bloomsbury, 2016).

11. I rely for my understanding of the end of the *Paradiso*, again, on the Robert Durling/Ronald Martinez translation and edition (Oxford: Oxford University Press, 2011). Some circumstantial background: Paul Maher Jr. notes that Kerouac began working seriously on *On the Road* in the summer of 1950, following the commercial and critical failure of his first novel, *The Town and the City*, and his return from Mexico. This was a period during which he was most intensively in dialogue with Allen Ginsberg, who was at that time involved in a systematic study of Dante and Cezanne (presumably in preparation for the infernal vision that would become "Howl," a few years later). See Maher, *Kerouac*, p. 217.

12. My thanks to Elise Zell for the etymology of Dean's last name.

13. Obviously, one could present other versions of Laura as possible inspirations for Sal's beloved, perhaps not least the Gene Tierney character in the 1944 Otto Preminger film of that name. However, they all go back to Petrarch.

14. My reading and citation of Petrarch rely on Robert Durling's translation and edition, *Petrarch's Lyric Poems* (Cambridge, MA: Harvard University Press, 1976). The

historical question of how Kerouac, and later Dylan, read Petrarch, and through which editions and translations, is, of course, open. Many inexpensive editions of selections of Petrarch's poetry in English circulated in the 1950s and 1960s. And, of course, translating Petrarch was a classic exercise for English poets in the sixteenth and seventeenth centuries. One can certainly speculate that Ginsberg, a friend to both Kerouac and Dylan and a tireless ambassador for poetry, might have had a hand. Thus, Ginsberg in a letter to Kerouac from May 18, 1948: "School is over and I have been reading Dante, which I have found very inspiring. I finished the *Divine Comedy* during the term, and am reading books including the *Vita Nuova*. . . . I think I am going to write a sonnet sequence. I want to read Petrarch and Shakespeare, Spencer [*sic*] and Sidney, etc. and learn about sonnets from beginning to end, and write a series on love, perfectly, newly conceived. I conceived the whole idea all at once seeing the first word in a title embedded in a page of the *Vita Nuova*." See *Jack Kerouac and Allen Ginsberg: The Letters*, eds. Bill Morgan and David Stanford (New York: Viking, 2010), p. 36. A complete bilingual version of Petrarch's *Canzoniere*, trans. Anna Maria Armi, had been published in 1946 by Pantheon, in New York, under the title *Sonnets and Songs*. In his notebooks from late 1949 and early 1950 Kerouac writes of his interest in Dante's use of numbers and includes Petrarch among those on his lists of books to read or "Sublimities to Learn." The journals during this period alternate between comments about his reading and thoughts about the soon-to-be written *On the Road*. See *Windblown World*, pp. 233–60. Whether the onomastically sensitive Kerouac saw a pun on the "beat generation" in Dante's beloved, Beatrice, we will probably never know.

15. On the complex interplay of momentary intensity and narrative direction in the Petrarchan sonnet sequence see Roland Greene, *Post Petrarchism* (Princeton: Princeton University Press, 1991), ch. 1. On the role of fragmentation in Petrarchan poetics as a response to Dante's poetics see Robert Durling's magisterial introduction to *Petrarch's Lyric Poems*.

16. We need only think of the titles of Kerouac's many post–*On the Road* projects — *Visions of Gerard*, *Visions of Cody*, and so on, as well as Dylan's "Visions of Johanna" — to evoke this tradition. It is thus not coincidental that Dylan's one earlier use of Kerouac had come in some phrases taken from *On the Road* and inserted into what is his perhaps his most "visionary" song, "Desolation Row," of 1965. Wilentz mentions these borrowings on pp. 50–51 of *Bob Dylan in America*.

17, To read the album biographically and literally, in other words, makes no more sense than to read *On the Road* as if Sal Paradise were "only" Jack Kerouac and Dean Moriarty were Neal Cassady.

18, *Petrarch's Lyric Poems*, p. 50. What is at issue here is less some literal citation of Petrarch by Dylan than the general tradition of Petrarchist poetry and the history of the love sonnet that comes out of Petrarch: Wyatt, Sidney, Shakespeare, up to at least Baudelaire. The Petrarch quote is chosen more or less at random since the trope of the lady's presence scattered in nature (as air, as flower, etc.) is stock in Petrarchist poetry. On landscape, the female body, and Petrarchan desire see Greene, *Post Petrarchism*, ch. 5.

19. The interview was with Chris MacGregor. Quoted in the Bob Dylan "Who's Who," available through the *Expecting Rain* website (www.expectingrain.com), from an interview published in *New Musical Express* on April 22, 1978. The fact that Petrarch was obsessed with Plutarch makes the mistake especially lovely. It should be noted that "Tangled Up in Blue" is one of the songs in his playlist that Dylan has since performed most frequently and altered most dramatically in performance. In 1984 it was rerecorded on the *Real Live* album. The reference to Petrarch gets replaced by the Bible during his "Christian period" in the late 1970s, and many other revisions appear over time. It is illuminating that one of the most frequent has been to change the line as follows: "Written by Charles Baudelaire in the nineteenth century." The substitution of Baudelaire, perhaps the greatest writer of sonnets in modern poetry, for Petrarch, suggests that, wherever we are, we are in sonnet-land here. The identification with Dante is made by Aidan Day in *Jokerman: Reading the Lyrics of Bob Dylan* (Oxford: Blackwell, 1988), p. 62. For a general account of the relationship between Petrarchan poetry and modern popular song, see María Rosa Menocal, *Shards of Love* (Durham, NC: Duke University Press, 1993). Menocal ends, however, with a close reading of Eric Clapton's "Layla," and skirts the edges of Dylan's work.

20. I note that the version of the lyric in *Lyrics* does not structure "Tangled Up in Blue" as a sonnet sequence. It buries rhymes internally, no doubt for reasons of space. On the changing relationship between line and verse form in Dylan see Charles O. Hartman, "Dylan's Bridges," *New Literary History* 46.4 (2015), pp. 738–42.

21. The jump from a triad based on the tonic to one based a step below on the flatted seventh is occasionally used to create drama in popular song, as, for example, by The Rolling Stones; see the opening riff to "(I Can't Get No) Satisfaction," among many other examples. However, these are passing chords, and it is rare indeed to set the exposition of an entire story over such a pattern. In a discussion of one of Dylan's later songs, "I Believe in You," the musicologist Wilfrid Mellers calls this "the shock chord." See his "God, Mode and Meaning in Some Recent Songs of Bob Dylan," in *The Dylan Companion*, eds. Elizabeth Thomson and David Gutman (New York: Da Capo, 2000), p. 256.

22. *Petrarch's Lyric Poems*, p. 270. I note in passing that the "breeze before which my life flees" just alluded to names Laura through the pun on breeze ("l'aura"). Laura is present even when absent, named even when turned into air.

23. Heylin (*Bob Dylan behind the Shades*, p. 242) quotes acquaintances of Dylan who assert that "You're Gonna Make Me Lonesome When You Go" was written for Ellen Bernstein, a Columbia Records employee with whom he was spending time. However, here, again, poetic echo trumps biography as the motif of the lady's hair links this song to at least two other tracks on the record.

24. Greil Marcus is one of the few writers about the album to note its coherence, the

fact that it is basically a group of fragments of the same story. See his brief review "An Album of Wounds," *Bob Dylan*, pp. 63–65.

25. For a discussion of the narrative structure of the song see Aidan Day's reading in *Jokerman: Reading the Lyrics of Bob Dylan* (London: Blackwell, 1988), pp. 51–66. Day goes on to work through a number of alternative versions of the lyrics that have been used in subsequent performances, testing out their implications. See as well Carrie Brownstein's brief account of the song in her article "Blood on the Tracks (1975)," in *The Cambridge Companion to Bob Dylan*, ed. Kevin J. H. Dettmar (Cambridge: Cambridge University Press, 2009), pp. 157–58, and Michael Gray's critique of "poststructuralist" readers of Dylan in chs. 8–9 of *Song and Dance Man III* (New York: Continuum, 2000).

26. For an account of Raeben's influence, with quotations of Dylan's comments on it, see Heylin, *Bob Dylan behind the Shades*, pp. 240–42.

27. The theme of difference in perspective is one that Dylan explored as early as his third album, with "you were right from your side / but I was right from mine," of "One Too Many Mornings" (1964). Here, however, that ethical statement becomes an ideological and formal principle. For a good discussion of "One Too Many Mornings," see Christopher Ricks, *Dylan's Visions of Sin* (New York: HarperCollins, 2003), pp. 430–33. Ricks also has interesting things to say about Dylan's use of form, though not with reference to the songs I study here, in the opening chapter of the same book. It is worth noting that the line "[she] froze up inside" may evoke "Visions of Johanna," one of Dylan's most powerful "visionary" songs, exemplary of the kind of poetics he is here rejecting. It was originally titled "Seems Like a Freeze-Out." Thanks to Diana Thow for pointing out this echo to me.

28. This appropriation of the lyric voice is then repeated (along with a transformation of the "bird that flew" image) three songs later in "You're a Big Girl Now": "Bird on the horizon, sittin' on a fence / He's singin' a song for me at his own expense / And I'm just like that bird, oh, singin' just for you" (p. 484). For a more thematic, less structural approach to the question of "conversion" in Dylan see the wide-ranging and insightful discussion in Rob Wilson's *Be Always Converting, Be Always Converted: An American Poetics* (Cambridge, MA: Harvard University Press, 2009), ch. 6. See also Chapter 5 of this book.

29. "No one else could sing that tune" is the last line from "Up to Me," a song recorded but left off of the album and released later on a compilation. It concludes with the most explicit of all of these scenes of performance: "If we never meet again / Baby remember me / How my lone guitar played sweet for you / That old time melody / And the harmonica around my neck / I blew it for ya free / No one else could play that tune / You knew it was up to me" (p. 349).

30. We might recall Theodor Adorno's description of lyric form. "Its universality is ... not the universality of simply communicating what others are unable to communicate," writes Adorno. Rather, form elevates the poem to the level of universality "by making manifest something not distorted, not grasped, not yet subsumed." For Adorno the modern

lyric becomes the site at which language breaks free from the reification imposed on it by mass society and cliché, precisely through acknowledgment of its own aesthetic difficulty and difference, "something in which what is possible transcends its own impossibility." *Blood on the Tracks* seems to project something like the special kind of mimesis Adorno evokes. See Theodor W. Adorno, "On Lyric Poetry and Society," in *Notes to Literature*, trans. Shierry Weber Nicholson (New York: Columbia University Press, 1991), vol. 1, pp. 38, 50.

31. For example see — or, perhaps better, avoid — Paul McCartney's "The Lovely Linda," from 1970, and John Lennon's "Oh, Yoko," from 1971.

32. See Durling, *Petrarch's Lyric Poems*, p. 264.

33. The lyrics of "If You See Her, Say Hello" fit perfectly over the melody of "Tangled Up in Blue," the song with which, as I noted earlier, it is most closely related thematically. Metrically, they are the same song. Moreover, the middle section of each verse of "Idiot Wind" ("They say I shot a man named Gray / And took his wife to Italy") is replayed in "Lily, Rosemary and the Jack of Hearts" ("The curtain had been lifted / And the gamblin' wheel shut down"). "Buckets of Rain" replays "You're a Big Girl Now." Furthermore, the lyrical motifs that unify the album are matched by recurring musical motifs or gestures. Thus, measure eleven of "Simple Twist of Fate" features a powerfully strummed chord progression, leading to the climax of the verse, of I-V-IV. The same figure appears in measure eight, at the climax, of each verse of "You're a Big Girl Now," and, implicitly, figured by the melody, in measures twelve and thirteen of "If You See Her, Say Hello." When expanded to two beats per chord it forms the entire chordal pattern of "Shelter from the Storm."

34. Pete Hamill, liner notes to *Blood on the Tracks*. It is worth noting that this is the only time, since his first album, that Dylan had included a laudatory or interpretive essay by another hand as part of the package. Clearly, a professional relaunch was felt to be needed.

35. On the cultural importance of romance, see Fredric Jameson's seminal discussion in *The Political Unconscious: Narrative as a Socially Symbolic Act* (Ithaca, NY: Cornell University Press, 1981), ch. 2. I cite Andreas Huyssen's discussion of the same cultural moment as the moment of *Desire* (without, however, reference to Dylan) in "The Search for Tradition: Avant-Garde and Postmodernism in the 1970s," ch. 9 of his *After the Great Divide: Modernism, Mass Culture, Postmodernism* (Bloomington: Indiana University Press, 1986), p. 173.

36. This is the claim of Andrew Kirelle in "'Desire': Bob Dylan's Sloppiest Masterpiece Turns 40," *Daily Beast*, online.

37. For a demonstration of the "New York mozambique" see www.youtube.com/watch? v=M1gG5I8j4Mo. For the maxixe: www.youtube.com/watch? v=_o2ZkEforyg. Thanks to Rob Kaufman for linking this song to these Latin traditions.

38. On Dylan's use of the bridge as a structural element that both breaks up formal patterns and effects transformations, see Charles O. Hartman, "Dylan's Bridges," *New Literary History* 46.4 (2015), pp. 737–57.

39. Here is Adorno: "The rebellion against semblance, art's dissatisfaction with itself,

has been an intermittent element of its claim to truth from time immemorial.... Art, whatever its material, has always desired dissonance, a desire suppressed by the affirmative power of society with which aesthetic semblance has been bound up. Dissonance is effectively expression; the consonant and harmonious want to soften and eliminate it." Theodor Adorno, *Aesthetic Theory*, trans. Robert Hullot-Kentor (Minneapolis: University of Minnesota Press, 1997), p. 105.

40. It may not be by accident that this is virtually the only song on *Desire* on which violin and harmonica seem to be in actual dialogue, exchanging riffs leading into the first verse, about four seconds in. The two musical "voices" that suggest the difference between exoticism (violin) and blues-inflected skepticism (harmonica) speak to each other, as if setting up the structural juxtaposition of story and commentary.

41. Joseph Conrad, *Victory*, ed. Tony Tanner (New York: Knopf, 1998), pp. 384–85. The links between the actual plot of the novel and the story in the song are tenuous, though it is worth noting that, like the song, the novel is presented through multiple narrators.

42. Wilfrid Mellers has noted Dylan's increasing interest in a "divided self" (foreshadowing some of the work on his Christian-influenced albums at the end of the decade) on 1977's *Street Legal*. See "God, Mode and Meaning in Some Recent Songs of Bob Dylan," p. 253. His claim that this emphasis is of a piece with Dylan's very earliest work, from which the development is "both natural and inevitable," seems less obvious to me, however.

43. See "Songs of Redemption," Ginsberg's commentary on the album, included as an insert, dated "10 November 1975."

44. *Petrarch's Lyric Poems*, p. 36. This is the end of the first sonnet, where Petrarch acknowledges that he has too long been "the talk of the crowd."

CHAPTER FIVE: TURN, TURN AGAIN

1. I cite Elijah Cook Jr., as Harry Jones, in Howard Hawks's 1946 film version of *The Big Sleep*, speaking to Bob Steele, as Canino. "Naw, you just got good sense," answers Canino, before he kills him.

2. Saint Augustine, *Confessions*, trans. Whitney J. Oats, in *Basic Writings of Saint Augustine* (New York: Random House, 1948), vol. 1, p. 126.

3. The classic discussion of the psychodynamics of conversion is in William James's *The Varieties of Religious Experience*. I have consulted the Library of America edition of that text, ed. Bruce Kuklick (New York, 1987). Also important for conceptualizing the structure of conversion (and placing Christian conversion in historical context) is A. D. Nock, *Conversion: The Old and the New in Religion from Alexander the Great to Augustine of Hippo* (Oxford: Clarendon Press, 1933). An extended philosophical and philological meditation on the same problems may be found in Kenneth Burke's *The Rhetoric of Religion: Studies in Logology* (Boston: Beacon Press, 1961). See esp. ch. 1, "On Words and the Word." For a lyrical discussion of Dylan's achievement that stresses his interest in change and "conversion"

see Rob Wilson, *Be Always Converting, Be Always Converted: An American Poetics* (Cambridge, MA: Harvard University Press, 2009), pp. 185–98.

4. The intertwining of different forms of rejection, turning, and reversal suggested here might be seen as well in the critical accounts of Dylan's work during this period, which range from antagonism from reviewers and fans that he had changed direction (chronicled in Clinton Heylin's *Trouble in Mind: Bob Dylan's Gospel Years — What Really Happened* [New York: Overamstel, 2017]) to claims that this work is simply of a piece with Dylan's earlier work (by, for example, Michael Gray, in *Song and Dance Man III* [London: Continuum, 2000], 210). My argument, as will be seen, is that rhetoric of the work, by turns hostile, passive, and determined, offers a reflection on the impact, on both the individual and the larger community, of crises of the late Carter and early Reagan years.

5. See Michael Gray's fine discussion of this song in *Song and Dance Man III*, 428ff. He notes the strangeness of this moral moment but reads it slightly differently from the way I do. In his Nobel Prize speech, Dylan evoked Erich Maria Remarque's World War I novel *All Quiet on the Western Front* as an important text. His vision here, which acknowledges that both the violent and the peaceful are prey to the same mortality, is a Remarquian moment. It pushes beyond an attempt to read the song as a flat allegory about "good guys" versus "bad guys." It indicates that even in the time when Dylan's work appeared to be excessively "moralistic" ("You either got faith or you got unbelief there ain't no neutral ground" [p. 570] as he said several years earlier in "Precious Angel") easy positionings that allow for self-righteous finger pointing are not always opened up by the songs. As I'm suggesting here, that may in part have to do with the difficulties of representing personal crisis, political upheaval, and cosmic disarray through the same form.

6. See Memphis Slim's introduction to the live version of the tune on his album *All Kinds of Blues.*

7. On the place of *metanoia* in rhetorical theory, see Heinrich Lausberg's classic guide *Elemente der literarischen Rhetorik* (Munich: Max Hueber Verlag, 1949). I have consulted the Italian version, *Elementi di retorica* (Bologna: Il Mulino, 1969), #384, 207. For a nuanced discussion of the relationship between gestures of conversion/turning and the lyric tradition, see David Marno, *Death Be Not Proud: The Art of Holy Attention* (Chicago: University of Chicago Press, 2016), esp. ch. 5. On *metanoia*, see p. 159.

8 The references to "R. J." and "Ray" are citations of Bill Saluga's ridiculous "Raymond J. Johnson, Jr." comedy skit, which may be found at www.youtube.com/watch?v=qoYsfbq3vMc. Here, in characteristically expansive fashion, Dylan yokes together comedy, autobiography, and social satire for a deadly serious purpose. Thanks to Charles O. Hartman for pointing me toward this reference.

9. Saint Augustine, *Confessions*, p.120.

10. "Gonna Change My Way of Thinking" is built on what seems to be the first half of Eric Clapton's famous guitar riff to Cream's "Sunshine of Your Love" (1967).

11 Most commentators on Dylan's turn to Christianity (and, I suppose, implicitly, his appropriation of AAVE expressions, though this is not noted) focus on the biographical dimension, his broken marriage and his involvement with several African American women. See, for some background on this, Sean Wilentz, *Bob Dylan in America* (New York: Vintage, 2011), 180ff. Clinton Heylin's *Trouble in Mind: Bob Dylan's Gospel Years—What Really Happened*, is a book-length compilation of reviews and interview snippets about this period in Dylan's life. Michael Gray, in *Song and Dance Man III*, ch. 7, argues that Dylan's divorce was the overriding force behind his conversion. He speaks of "Dylan's voyage from Sara to Jesus" (p. 220) and claims, without irony, that "the quest for salvation might be called the central theme of Bob Dylan's entire output" (p. 208).

12. Cited from www.azlyrics.com/lyrics/johnlennon/< god.html.

13. As Christopher Ricks points out, the opening of the lyric quotes the Otto Harbach/Jerome Kern song, "Smoke Gets in Your Eyes": "They asked me how I knew, that my love was true." Dylan complicates the situation by moving it to the present tense and pursuing its implications. See Ricks, *Dylan's Visions of Sin* (New York: HarperCollins, 2003), p. 351.

14. Dylan's fondness for the fourth played over a major chord is a veritable tic that appears multiple times in his songs, from the opening guitar/organ riff on 1966's "I Want You," and the powerfully strummed introduction to "Desolation Row" (1965) to the first measures of "Tangled Up in Blue" (1975). Here it makes the melody itself, marked out on electric keyboard over a jangling guitar.

15. See the discussion of the modal structure of some of these tunes (as well as, more extensively, the songs on *Street Legal*) by Wilfrid Mellers in "God, Mode and Meaning in Some Recent Songs of Bob Dylan," *The Dylan Companion,* ed. Elizabeth Thomson and David Gutman (New York: Da Capo Press, 2000), pp. 247–60.

16. We can note in passing Dylan's memory, recounted in Martin Scorsese's film *No Direction Home*, of finding a copy of the Monroe recording in the basement of his parents' newly purchased home back in Hibbing, Minnesota.

17. In his discussion of the song, Ricks notes the transitive/intransitive tension within "sustain." He cites scriptural uses of the verb and calls Dylan's use "an imaginative exception." This is fine as far as it goes. However, I think it is important to notice the musical sense of "sustain." See Ricks, *Dylan's Visions of Sin*, p. 349.

18. William Blake, "Auguries of Innocence" in *The Poetry and Prose of William Blake,* ed. David V. Erdman (New York: Doubleday, 1970), pp. 481–87.

19. See Gray's extended discussion in *Song and Dance Man III*, ch. 12. He stresses Dylan's deep debt to Blake, right up to his appropriation in this song of Blake's seven-foot poetic line. However, his judgment of the song is quite harsh. Wilentz, by contrast, calls it "a beautifully wrought composition" (*Bob Dylan in America*, p. 180). My reading argues that the rhetorical excesses of the song, which Gray sees as its weakness, reflect and perform the spiritual and psychological confusions the lyric recounts.

20. I cite the Revised Standard Version, taken from the *New Oxford Annotated Bible*, eds. Herbert G. May and Bruce M. Metzger (New York: Oxford University Press, 1973).

21. William Shakespeare, *Hamlet*, V.ii, 215–18. Cited from the Arden Shakespeare, ed. Harold Jenkins (London: Methuen, 1982).

22. Thus, Genesis 5:15: "And the Lord put a mark on Cain, lest any who came upon him should kill him." Two verses earlier Cain declares, "My punishment is more than I can bear," a line echoed by Dylan in 1997's "Not Dark Yet," "Sometimes my burden is more than I can bear" (p. 800).

23. See Day's reading of this lyric in his book, *Jokerman: Reading the Lyrics of Bob Dylan* (Oxford: Blackwell, 1988), ch. 7.

24. *The Collected Poems of W. B. Yeats*, ed. Richard J. Finneran (New York: Macmillan, 1989), p. 187.

25. See Gray, *Song and Dance Man III*, pp. 481ff.

26. I cite the Richmond Lattimore translation of the *Odyssey* (New York: Harper, 1967), p. 27. In his Nobel speech Dylan mentions the *Odyssey* as one of his favorite books.

27. For extended discussions of where the St. James Hotel might be, see Wilentz, *Bob Dylan in America*, p. 202, and Gray, *Song and Dance Man III*, ch. 15. Gray's account of why "St. James Infirmary" is being used is especially insightful. Wilentz appreciatively calls the song "a leap in Dylan's American art" (p. 183). Greil Marcus's thoughtful account of the place of the song in Dylan's work calls it "the last word." He notes that part of the function of art is to reveal lives that are not ours, and that this is what happens in "Blind Willie McTell." None of these critics, however, notices this song as epic. See Marcus's discussion "Dylan as Historian," in his *Bob Dylan: Writings, 1968–2010* (New York: PublicAffairs Books, 2010), pp. 155–61.

CHAPTER SIX: "A WISP OF STARTLED AIR"

1. I recovered the lyrics of "Jim Jones" from Eyolf Østrem's now-defunct website dylan-chords.com.

2. Theodor W. Adorno, "On Beethoven's Late Style," in *Essays on Music*, trans. Susan H. Gillespie, ed. Richard Leppert (Berkeley: University of California Press, 2002), p. 566. For an exposition and gloss on Adorno, see Edward W. Said, *On Late Style: Music and Literature against the Grain* (New York: Pantheon Books, 2006). For a broad critique and qualification of Adorno's fragment, as well as of Said's gloss, see the essays in *Late Style and its Discontents: Essays in Art, Literature, and Music*, eds. Gordon McMullan and Sam Smiles (Oxford: Oxford University Press, 2016), esp. section V. For a good overview of the question of the "late," coming out of Adorno's famous fragmentary essay, see Joe Paul Kroll, "Sorry They're Late," *Times Literary Supplement*, January 2, 2018.

3. The technique of setting a short-lined rhyming couplet at the center of the stanza, as a kind of anchor or transitional step between larger clusters of lines, seems to be useful

to Dylan in these songs. It can be seen in a number of places. See the discussion of "When the Deal Goes Down" later in this chapter.

4. F. Scott Fitzgerald, *The Great Gatsby* (New York: Scribner, 2004), p. 110. The Fitzgerald citation has been noted as well by several other commentators. See, for example, Eric Lott, "Love and Theft," in *The Cambridge Companion to Bob Dylan,* ed. Kevin J. H. Dettmar (Cambridge: Cambridge University Press, 2009), p. 168, and Sean Wilentz, *Bob Dylan in America* (New York: Vintage, 2011), p. 274. None of these writers explores the irony of the citation, or the broader context in Fitzgerald.

5. Without wanting to oversell "Ballad of a Thin Man," I simply point out its special status in Dylan's oeuvre. It is one of only a very small number of Dylan recordings from the 1960s written in a minor key. And it is one of a handful of songs from that era that actually features Dylan's piano playing. Perhaps more interesting, it is the first time ever that he writes a song with a bridge between the verses. On the importance of this moment, and on Dylan's bridges more generally, see Charles O. Hartman's essay "Dylan's Bridges," *New Literary History* 46.4 (2015), pp. 737–57.

6. On the citations in "Tryin' to Get to Heaven," see Michael Gray, *Song and Dance Man III* (London: Continuum, 2000), ch. 19.

7. In an interview with Mikal Gilmore from the time of the release of *Love and Theft*, Dylan describes himself as a man among the ruins, feeling like he is walking about in Pompeii. See "Bob Dylan, at 60, Unearths New Revelations," *Rolling Stone*, November 22, 2001.

8. For insightful commentary on this recording and song, from which I have learned much, see Janet Gezari and Charles O. Hartman, "Dylan's Covers," *Southwest Review* 95.1–2 (2010), pp. 152–66.

9. See *Robert Johnson: The New Transcriptions*, ed. Pete Billman (New York: Hal Leonard, 1999), pp. 96–98, as well as Peter Guralnick, *Searching for Robert Johnson* (New York: Dutton, 1989). Here, again, see Gezari and Hartman, "Dylan's Covers," for background and analysis.

10. Henry Timrod, *The Collected Poems of Henry Timrod: A Variorum Edition*, eds. Edd Winfield Parks and Aileen Wells Parks (Athens: University of Georgia Press, 2007), p. 45. Paul H. Hayne suggests in his sketch of the poet's life from his edition of Timrod, *The Poems of Henry Timrod* (New York: Hale and Sons, 1873), that the "Rhapsody" dates from 1848 or thereabouts. See pp. 24–26. The Timrod echoes have been noted, mostly in passing, by a number of writers on Dylan. See, for example, Richard F. Thomas, *Why Bob Dylan Matters* (New York: Dey Street Press, 2017), pp. 246–47. Robert Reginio notes Timrod's appearances in Dylan's late songs and links them to Dylan's supposed recognition that "American popular music is the story of white America's 'love' of black culture, a culture shaped by manifold acts of thievery." See his essay "'Nettie Moore': Minstrelsy and the Cultural Economy of Race in Bob Dylan's Late Albums," in *Highway 61 Revisited: Bob Dylan's Road from Minnesota to the World*, eds. Colleen Josephine Sheehy and Thomas Swiss (Minneapolis: University of Minnesota Press, 2009), pp. 213–24.

11. I note in passing that Dylan's first line recalls two classic tunes, one by Cole Porter and another by the doo-wop group the Five Satins (from 1956), both titled "In the Still of the Night." My emphasis on the generic implications of the Timrod citation supplements the reading by Gezari and Hartman, which focuses on Dylan's rejection of Timrod's nostalgia. See "Dylan's Covers," p. 160.

12. The bulk of the song was composed by Roy Turk and Fred E. Ahlert. Consulted on lyricsfreak.com, in February 2018.

13. For background on the recording and composition of "Where the Blue of the Night Meets the Gold of the Day," see Gary Giddins, *Bing Crosby: A Pocketful of Dreams: The Early Years 1903–40* (New York: Little, Brown, 2001), pp. 259–61. On Crosby's interest in minstrelsy and blackface, see pp. 83–87. On Dylan's "borrowings," generally during this period, see "Critic's Notebook: Plagiarism in Dylan, or a Cultural Collage?" by Jon Pareles, *New York Times*, July 12, 2003. On the Timrod borrowings, see Motoko Rich, "Who's This Guy Dylan Who's Borrowing Lines from Henry Timrod?" *New York Times*, September 14, 2006. Robert Polito's essay "Bob Dylan's Memory Palace" also unpacks some of Dylan's references in these songs, placing them in the context of early modern practices of citation through the work of Jonathan Spence on Matteo Ricci. As he notes, citation of commonplaces and of other poets is a consistent feature of poetic history. He notes the intensification of Dylan's citational practice in these late songs. His essay appears in Sheehy and Swiss, *Highway 61 Revisited*, pp. 140–53.

14. T. S. Eliot, *The Waste Land and Other Poems* (New York: Harcourt Brace Jovanovich, 1962), p. 46.

15. *Ibid.*, p. 8.

16. On the complex processes of "deixis" or pointing/indication in Dylan's work, see Charles O. Hartman, "Dylan's Deixis," forthcoming in *Polyvocal Dylan*, eds. Joshua Toth and Nduka Otiono (London: Palgrave Macmillan).

17. For the Haggard lyric, see azlyrics.com.

18. The Ovid connection was first discovered by Cliff Fell, a poet from New Zealand, who suggested that Dylan had been reading Peter Green's Penguin translation of Ovid. These details are reported by Richard F. Thomas in *Why Bob Dylan Matters*, p. 243. Thomas lists several more parallels between Ovid's text and Dylan's lyrics discovered by Fell. Curiously, Thomas's commentary links the exile poems not to Dylan's tragic characters or the bleak landscape Dylan paints but to the songwriter: "In the inner exile he created for his own protection, and from which he sends us his songs, Bob Dylan discovered and invoked Ovidian exile poetry, the poetry coming at the end of the career of Ovid" (p. 245). As should be clear by now, my interest is in the songs, rather than the presumed psychology of the writer. I have consulted the reedition of the Green translation, *Ovid: The Poems of Exile* (Berkeley: University of California Press, 2005).

19. In an insightful treatment of these songs that reached me as I was completing my

own work, Heinrich Detering points out that the reference to the "steel rails hum" parallels the language of Goebel Reeves's "Hobo's Lullaby," which was recorded by Woody Guthrie in 1944 and later, in 1972, by his son Arlo. See Detering's fine monograph *Die Stimmen aus dem Limbus: Bob Dylans späte Song Poetry* (Munich: Siemens Stiftung, 2012), p. 38.

20. The song was Léo Daniderff's "Je cherche après Titine," nicely distorted into a mixture of different languages and nonsense phrases by Chaplin.

CONCLUSION: FRANKNESS

1. For the Pinsky references, see, again, *Democracy, Culture and the Voice of Poetry* (Princeton: Princeton University Press, 2002), pp. 46–47. On the material permutations of voice, see Steven Connor, "The Strains of the Voice," available at www.stevenconnor. com, as well as the material on sobs in Connor's book *Beyond Words: Sobs, Hums, Stutters and Other Vocalizations* (London: Reaktion Books, 2014), ch. 4. For a systematic study of vocal production, see Kate Heidemann, "A System for Describing Vocal Timbre in Popular Song," *Music Theory Online* 22.1 (2016), pp. 1–17.

2. For an impressive study of Dylan's vocal timbre across a broad swath of time, see Steven Rings's essay "A Foreign Sound to Your Ear: Bob Dylan Performs 'It's Alright, Ma (I'm Only Bleeding),' 1964–2009," *Music Theory Online* 19.4 (2013), pp. 1–39. On the institutional settings of Dylan's changing vocal style, see Daniel Karlin, *The Figure of the Singer* (Oxford: Oxford University Press, 2013), ch. 9. Karlin's entire argument offers insights into how the idea of the "singer" intertwines with poetic composition and collecting over the past two hundred years.

3. Lyrics retrieved from www.azlyrics.com.

4. Such tricks are not unheard of elsewhere. It is not unusual for tenors to distort the pronunciation of the lyric to Puccini's aria "Nessun dorma," as they jerk their voices up to hit the high B at the climax of the song. My thanks to Kate van Orden for pointing me toward this Dylanesque moment in the classical canon.

Bibliography/Discography

Adorno, Theodor W. 1983. *Prisms.* Trans. Samuel and Shierry Weber. Cambridge, MA: MIT Press.

———. 1997. *Aesthetic Theory.* Trans. Robert Hullot-Kentor. Minneapolis: University of Minnesota Press.

———. 2002. *Essays on Music.* Ed. Richard Leppert. Trans. Susan H. Gillespie. Berkeley: University of California Press.

Adorno, Theodor W., and Max Horkheimer. 1972. *Dialectic of Enlightenment.* Trans. John Cumming. New York: Seabury Press.

Alighieri, Dante. 1991. *Inferno.* Trans. Robert Durling and Ronald Martinez. Oxford: Oxford University Press.

Attali, Jacques. 1985. *Noise: The Political Economy of Music.* Trans. Brian Massumi. Minneapolis: University of Minnesota Press.

Augustine, Saint. 1948. *Basic Writings of Saint Augustine.* Trans. Whitney J. Oats. New York: Random House. 2 volumes.

Benjamin, Walter. 1999a. *The Arcades Project.* Ed. Rolf Tiedemann. Trans. Howard Eiland and Kevin McLaughlin. Cambridge, MA: Harvard University Press.

———. 1999b. "Some Remarks on Folk Art." In *Walter Benjamin: Selected Writings*, vol. 2, pp. 278–82. Ed. Michael Jennings. Cambridge, MA: Belknap Press.

Blake, William. 1970. *The Poetry and Prose of William Blake.* Ed. David V. Erdman. New York: Doubleday.

Bourdieu, Pierre. 1993. *The Field of Cultural Production.* Ed. Randal Johnson. New York: Columbia University Press.

Brecht, Bertolt. 1992. *Brecht on Theater: The Development of an Aesthetic.* Ed. and Trans. John Willett. New York: Hill & Wang.

Burke, Kenneth. 1961. *The Rhetoric of Religion: Studies in Logology.* Boston: Beacon Press.

Byrne, David. 2013. *How Music Works.* Edinburgh: Canongate Books.

Cantwell, Robert. 1996. *When We Were Good: The Folk Revival.* Cambridge, MA: Harvard University Press.

Connor, Steven. 2004. "The Strains of the Voice." Online at www.stevenconnor.com.

———. 2009. "Writing the White Voice." Online at www.stevenconnor.com.

———. 2014. *Beyond Words: Sobs, Hums, Stutters and Other Vocalizations*. London: Reaktion Books.

Conrad, Joseph. 1998. *Victory*. Ed. Tony Tanner. New York: Knopf.

Cran, Rona. 2014. *Collage in Twentieth-Century Art, Literature, and Culture: Joseph Cornell, William Burroughs, Frank O'Hara, and Bob Dylan*. Burlington, VT: Ashgate.

Culler, Jonathan. 2015. *Theory of the Lyric*. Cambridge, MA: Harvard University Press.

Day, Aidan. 1988. *Jokerman: Reading the Lyrics of Bob Dylan*. London: Blackwell.

Detering, Heinrich. 2012. *Die Stimmen aus dem Limbus: Bob Dylans späte Song Poetry*. Munich: Siemens Stiftung.

Dettmar, Kevin J. H. 2009. *The Cambridge Companion to Bob Dylan*. Cambridge: Cambridge University Press.

Doyle, Peter. 2005. *Echo and Reverb: Fabricating Space in Popular Music Recording, 1900–1960*. Middletown, CT: Wesleyan University Press.

Dylan, Bob. 2004a. *Chronicles: Volume One*. New York: Simon & Schuster.

———. 2004b. *The Lyrics: 1962–2001*. New York: Simon & Schuster.

———. 2014. *The Lyrics: Since 1962*. Ed. Christopher Ricks, Lisa Nemrow, and Julie Nemrow. New York: Simon & Schuster.

Eliot, T. S. 1962. *The Waste Land and Other Poems*. New York: Harcourt Brace Jovanovich.

———. 1964. *Selected Essays of T. S. Eliot*. New York: Harcourt Brace Jovanovich.

Gary, Romain. 1983. "The Life and Death of Emil Ajar." Trans. Barbara Wright. In *King Solomon*. New York: Harper & Row.

Gezari, Janet, and Charles O. Hartman. 2010. "Dylan's Covers." *Southwest Review* 95. 1–2, pp. 152–66.

Giddins, Gary. 2001. *Bing Crosby: A Pocketful of Dreams: The Early Years 1903–40*. New York: Little, Brown.

Gilmore, Mikal. 2001. "Bob Dylan, at 60, Unearths New Revelations." *Rolling Stone*, November 22, 2001.

Ginsberg, Allen. 1988. *Collected Poems: 1947–1980*. New York: Harper & Row.

Gitlin, Todd. 1987. *The Sixties: Years of Hope, Days of Rage*. New York: Bantam Books.

Gray, Michael. 2000. *Song and Dance Man III: The Art of Bob Dylan*. London: Continuum.

Greene, Roland. 1991. *Post Petrarchism*. Princeton: Princeton University Press.

Guralnick, Peter. 1989. *Searching for Robert Johnson*. New York: Dutton.

Guthrie, Woody. 1983. *Bound for Glory*. New York: Penguin.

Gutman, David, and Elizabeth Thomson. 1990. *The Dylan Companion*. London: Macmillan.

Hajdu, David. 2001. *Positively 4th Street: The Lives and Times of Joan Baez, Bob Dylan, Mimi Baez Fariña and Richard Fariña*. New York: Farrar, Straus and Giroux.

Hartman, Charles O. 1991. *Jazz Text: Voice and Improvisation in Poetry, Jazz, and Song.* Princeton: Princeton University Press.

_____. 2015a. "Dylan's Bridges." *New Literary History* 46.4, pp. 737–57.

_____. 2015b. *Verse: An Introduction to Prosody.* Oxford: Blackwell.

_____. 2017. "Dylan's Deixis." Forthcoming in *Polyvocal Dylan.* Eds. Joshua Toth and Nduka Otiono. London: Palgrave Macmillan.

Hass, Robert. 2017. *A Little Book on Form: An Exploration into the Formal Imagination of Poetry.* New York: HarperCollins.

Heidemann, Kate. 2016. "A System for Describing Vocal Timbre in Popular Song." *Music Theory Online: A Journal of the Society for Music Theory* 22.1, pp. 1–17.

Heylin, Clinton. 1991. *Bob Dylan behind the Shades: A Biography.* New York: Simon & Schuster.

_____. 2017. *Trouble in Mind: Bob Dylan's Gospel Years — What Really Happened.* New York: Overamstel Publishers.

Hollander, John. 1975. *Vision and Resonance: Two Senses of Poetic Form.* New York: Oxford University Press.

_____. 1981. *The Figure of Echo: A Mode of Allusion in Milton and After.* Berkeley: University of California Press.

Homer. 1967. *The Odyssey.* Trans. Richmond Lattimore. New York: Harper.

Hughes, John. 2013. *Invisible Now: Bob Dylan in the 1960s.* Burlington, VT: Ashgate.

Huyssen, Andreas. 1986. *After the Great Divide: Modernism, Mass Culture, Postmodernism.* Bloomington: Indiana University Press.

Jackson, Virginia, and Yopie Prins, eds. 2014. *The Lyric Theory Reader: A Critical Anthology.* Baltimore: Johns Hopkins University Press.

James, William. 1987. *Writings 1902–1910.* Ed. Bruce Kuklick. New York: Library of America.

Jameson, Fredric. 1981. *The Political Unconscious: Narrative as a Socially Symbolic Act.* Ithaca, NY: Cornell University Press, 1981.

_____. 1999. *Brecht and Method.* London: Verso.

_____. 2007. *The Modernist Papers.* London: Verso.

_____. 2012. *A Singular Modernity.* London: Verso.

Johnson, Robert. 1999. *Robert Johnson: The New Transcriptions.* Ed. Pete Billman. New York: Hal Leonard.

Karlin, Daniel. 2013. *The Figure of the Singer.* Oxford: Oxford University Press.

Kaufman, Robert. 2005. "Lyric's Constellation, Poetry's Radical Privilege." *Modernist Culture* 1.2, pp. 209–34.

_____. 2008. "Lyric Commodity Critique, Benjamin, Adorno, Marx, Baudelaire, Baudelaire, Baudelaire." *PMLA* 123.1, pp. 207–15.

Kerouac, Jack. 1976. *The Dharma Bums.* New York: Penguin.

_____. 1985. *On the Road.* New York: Signet.

———. 2004. *Windblown World: The Journals of Jack Kerouac, 1947–1954*. Ed. Douglas Brinkley. New York: Viking.

Kerouac, Jack, and Allen Ginsberg. 2010. *Jack Kerouac and Allen Ginsberg: The Letters*. Eds. Bill Morgan and David Stanford. New York: Viking.

Lausberg, Heinrich. 1969. *Elementi di retorica*. Bologna: Il Mulino.

Lott, Eric. 1993. *Love and Theft: Blackface, Minstrelsy and the American Working Class*. New York: Oxford University Press.

Maher, Paul, Jr. 2004. *Kerouac: The Definitive Biography*. New York: Taylor.

Marcus, Greil. 2005. *Like a Rolling Stone: Bob Dylan at the Crossroads*. New York: Perseus.

———. 2010. *Bob Dylan: Writings 1968–2010*. New York: Perseus.

———. 2011. *The Old, Weird America: The World of Bob Dylan's Basement Tapes*. New York: Picador.

Marno, David. 2016. *Death Be Not Proud: The Art of Holy Attention*. Chicago: University of Chicago Press.

Marqusee, Mike. 2005. *Wicked Messenger: Bob Dylan and the 1960s*. New York: Seven Stories Press.

May, Herbert G., and Bruce M. Metzger, eds. 1973. *The Oxford Annotated Bible*. Oxford: Oxford University Press.

Melehy, Hassan. 2016. *Kerouac: Language, Poetics, & Territory*. New York: Bloomsbury.

Mellers, Wilfrid. 1985. *A Darker Shade of Pale: A Backdrop to Bob Dylan*. New York: Oxford University Press.

———. 1987. *Music in a New Found Land: Themes and Developments in the History of American Music*. New York: Oxford University Press.

Menocal, María Rosa. 1993. *Shards of Love: Exile and the Origins of the Lyric*. Durham, NC: Duke University Press.

Nicosia, Gerald. 1983. *Memory Babe: A Critical Biography of Jack Kerouac*. New York: Grove Press.

Nock, A. D. 1933. *Conversion: The Old and the New in Religion from Alexander the Great to Augustine of Hippo*. Oxford: Clarendon Press.

Østrem, Eyolf. www.dylanchords.

Ovid. 2005. *Ovid: The Poems of Exile*. Trans. Peter Green. Berkeley: University of California Press.

Pareles, Jon. 2003. "Critic's Notebook: Plagiarism in Dylan, or a Cultural Collage?" *New York Times*, July 12, 2003.

Pennebaker, D. A. 1967. *Don't Look Back*. Video.

Petrarch, Francis. 1976. *Petrarch's Lyric Poems*. Trans. Robert Durling. Cambridge, MA: Harvard University Press.

Pinsky, Robert. 2002. *Democracy, Culture and the Voice of Poetry*. Princeton: Princeton University Press.

Rich, Motoko. 2006. "Who's This Guy Dylan Who's Borrowing Lines from Henry Timrod?" *New York Times*, September 14, 2006.

Ricks, Christopher. 1984. *The Force of Poetry*. Oxford: Clarendon Press.

_____. 1999. *The Oxford Book of English Verse*. Oxford: Oxford University Press.

_____. 2003. *Dylan's Visions of Sin*. New York: HarperCollins.

Rimbaud, Arthur. 1957. *Illuminations*. Trans. Louise Varèse. New York: New Directions.

_____. 1961. *A Season in Hell and the Drunken Boat*. Trans. Louise Varèse. New York: New Directions.

_____. 2005. *Complete Works, Selected Letters*. Trans. Wallace Fowlie and Seth Whidden. Chicago: University of Chicago Press.

Rings, Steven. 2013. "A Foreign Sound to Your Ear: Bob Dylan Performs 'It's Alright, Ma (I'm Only Bleeding),' 1964–2009." *Music Theory Online* 19.4, pp. 1–39.

_____. 2015. "Analyzing the Popular Singing Voice: Sense and Surplus." *Journal of the American Musicological Society* 68.3, pp. 663–72.

Said, Edward W. 2006. *On Late Style: Music and Literature against the Grain*. New York: Pantheon Books.

Sandburg, Carl. 1990. *The American Songbag*. New York: Harcourt Brace Jovanovich.

Scorsese, Martin. 2005. *No Direction Home*. Video.

Shakespeare, William. 1982. *Hamlet*. Ed. Harold Jenkins. London: Methuen.

Sheehy, Colleen J., and Thomas Swiss, eds. 2009. *Highway 61 Revisited: Bob Dylan's Journey from Minnesota to the World*. Minneapolis: University of Minnesota Press.

Sidney, Philip. 1989. *The Major Works*. Ed. Katherine Duncan-Jones. Oxford: Oxford World's Classics.

Silverman, Jerry, ed. 1975. *The Folk Song Encyclopedia*. 2 volumes. New York: Hal Leonard.

Smith, Harry. 1997. *Anthology of American Folk Music*. 3 discs. Washington, DC: Smithsonian Folkways Recordings.

Smith, Patti. 2010. *Just Kids*. New York: Ecco.

Sterne, Jonathan, ed. 2012. *The Sound Studies Reader*. London: Routledge.

Swiss, Thomas, Jean Sloop, and Andrew Herman, eds. 1998. *Mapping the Beat: Popular Music and Contemporary Theory*. London: Blackwell.

Szendy, Peter. 2008. *Listen: A History of Our Ears*. Trans. Charlotte Mandell. New York: Fordham University Press.

Thomas, Richard F. 2017. *Why Bob Dylan Matters*. New York: Dey Street Press.

Thomson, Elizabeth, and David Gutman, eds. 2000. *The Dylan Companion*. New York: Da Capo Press.

Timrod, Henry. 1873. *The Poems of Henry Timrod*. Ed. Paul H. Hayne. New York: Hale and Sons.

_____. 2007. *The Collected Poems of Henry Timrod: A Variorum Edition*. Ed. Edd Winfield Parks and Aileen Wells Parks. Athens: University of Georgia Press.

Tomlinson, Gary. 1999. *Metaphysical Song: An Essay on Opera*. Princeton: Princeton University Press.

Van Ronk, Dave, with Elijah Wald. 2006. *The Mayor of MacDougal Street: A Memoir*. New York: Da Capo Press.

Whitesell, Lloyd. 2008.. *The Music of Joni Mitchell*. Oxford: Oxford University Press.

Whitman, Walt. 1992. *Leaves of Grass*. Ed. Justin Kaplan. New York: Library of America.

Wilentz, Sean. 2011. *Bob Dylan in America*. New York: Vintage.

Wilson, Rob. 2009. *Be Always Converting, Be Always Converted: An American Poetics*. Cambridge, MA: Harvard University Press.

Wolff, Daniel J. 2017. *Grown-Up Anger: The Connected Mysteries of Bob Dylan, Woody Guthrie, and the Calumet Massacre of 1913*. New York: HarperCollins.

Yeats, William Butler. 1989. *The Collected Poems of W. B. Yeats*. Ed. Richard J. Finneran. New York: Macmillan.

DISCOGRAPHY: ALBUMS BY BOB DYLAN USED IN THIS BOOK

Bob Dylan, Columbia, CK94239 (1962)

The Freewheelin' Bob Dylan, Columbia, CK92396 (1963)

The Times They Are a-Changin', Columbia CK94240 (1964)

Another Side of Bob Dylan, Columbia CK92402 (1964)

Bringing It All Back Home, Columbia, CK92401 (1965)

Highway 61 Revisited, Columbia, CH90324 (1965)

Blonde on Blonde, Columbia, CK92400 (1966)

John Wesley Harding, Columbia, CK92395 (1967)

Nashville Skyline, Columbia, CH90319 (1969)

New Morning, Columbia, KC30290 (1970)

Self Portrait, Columbia 30290 (1970)

Pat Garrett and Billy the Kid, Columbia, CK32460 (1973)

Planet Waves, Asylum, 7E 1003 (1974)

Before the Flood, Sony, B01SF8GIG (1974)

Blood on the Tracks, Columbia, CK33235 (1975)

Desire, Columbia, CK92303 (1976)

Hard Rain, Columbia, B0012GMUP4 (1976)

Street Legal, Columbia, CH90338 (1977)

Slow Train Coming, Columbia, CK92397 (1979)

Saved, Columbia, CK36553 (1980)

Shot of Love, Columbia, CK37496 (1981)

Infidels, Columbia, CK38819 (1983)

Biograph, Columbia, C3K 65298 (1985)

Oh Mercy, Columbia 45281 (1989)

Under the Red Sky, Columbia, CK46794 (1990)

The Bootleg Series, vols. 1–3, Rare and Unreleased, Columbia C3K 47382 (1991)

Folksinger's Choice: Live Radio Performance, March 11, 1962, Left Field Media, LFMCD501 (1992)

Good as I Been to You, Columbia, CK53200 (1992)

World Gone Wrong, Columbia, CK57590 (1993)

Bob Dylan's Greatest Hits, vol. 3, Columbia, CK66782 (1994)

Time Out of Mind, Columbia, CK68556 (1997)

Love and Theft, Columbia, CK 89575 (2001)

Modern Times, Columbia 82876876062 (2006)

The Bootleg Series, vol. 8, Tell Tale Signs, Columbia 88697357952 (2008)

Together through Life, Columbia, 88697438933 (2009)

The Bootleg Series, vol. 9, The Witmark Demos: 1962–1964, Columbia 88697761792 (2010)

Tempest, Columbia, 88725457602 (2012)

The Minneapolis Hotel Tape, & The Gaslight Café, BDA, BDACD103 (2012)

The Bootleg Series, vol. 10, Another Self Portrait, Columbia, 88883734872 (2013)

The Bootleg Series, vol. 11, The Basement Tapes Complete, Sony Legacy 88875016131 4 (2014)

The Bootleg Series, vol. 12, The Best of the Cutting Edge, Columbia, 88875224422 (2015)

Shadows in the Night, Columbia, 88875057962 (2015)

Fallen Angels, Columbia, 88985308022 (2016)

List of Songs Cited

"Absolutely Sweet Marie" (copyright © 1966 by Dwarf Music; renewed 1994 by Dwarf Music)

"Ain't Talkin'" (copyright © 2006 by Special Rider Music)

"All Along the Watchtower" (copyright © 1968 by Dwarf Music; renewed 1996 by Dwarf Music)

"All I Really Want to Do" (copyright © 1964 by Warner Bros. Inc.; renewed 1992 by Special Rider Music)

"All the Tired Horses" (copyright ©1970 by Big Sky Music; renewed 1998 by Big Sky Music)

"As I Went Out One Morning" (copyright ©1968 by Dwarf Music; renewed 1996 by Dwarf Music)

"Ballad of a Thin Man" (copyright ©1965 by Warner Bros. Inc.; renewed 1993 by Special Rider Music)

"The Ballad of Frankie Lee and Judas Priest" (copyright ©1968 by Dwarf Music; renewed 1996 by Dwarf Music)

"Beyond Here Lies Nothin'" (copyright © 2009 by Special Rider Music and Ice Nine Publishing)

"Beyond the Horizon" (copyright © 2006 by Special Rider Music)

"Black Diamond Bay" (copyright © 1975 by Ram's Horn Music; renewed 2003 by Ram's Horn Music)

"Blind Willie McTell" (copyright © 1983 by Special Rider Music)

"Blowin' in the Wind" (copyright © 1962 by Warner Bros. Inc.; renewed 1990 by Special Rider Music)

"Brownsville Girl" (copyright © 1986 by Special Rider Music)

"Buckets of Rain" (copyright ©1974 by Ram's Horn Music; renewed 2002 by Ram's Horn Music)

"Changing of the Guards" (copyright © 1978 by Special Rider Music)

"Chimes of Freedom" (copyright © 1964 by Warner Bros. Inc.; renewed 1992 by Special Rider Music)

"Cold Irons Bound" (copyright © 1997 by Special Rider Music)

"Desolation Row" (copyright © 1965 by Warner Bros. Inc.; renewed 1993 by Special Rider Music)

"Dignity" (copyright © 1991 by Special Rider Music)

"Don't Think Twice, It's Alright" (copyright © 1963 by Warner Bros. Inc.; renewed 1991 by Special Rider Music)

"Down the Highway" (copyright © 1963, 1967 by Warner Bros. Inc.; renewed 1991, 1995 by Special Rider Music)

"Every Grain of Sand" (copyright © 1981 by Special Rider Music)

"Floater (Too Much to Ask)" (copyright © 2001 by Special Rider Music)

"Girl from the North Country" (copyright © 1963 by Warner Bros. Inc.; renewed 1991 by Special Rider Music)

"Gonna Change My Way of Thinking" (copyright © 1979 by Special Rider Music)

"Gotta Serve Somebody" (copyright © 1979 by Special Rider Music)

"The Groom's Still Waiting at the Altar" (copyright © 1981 by Special Rider Music)

"A Hard Rain's a-Gonna Fall" (copyright © 1963 by Warner Bros. Inc.; renewed 1991 by Special Rider Music)

"Honey, Just Allow Me One More Chance" (copyright © 1963, 1966 by Warner Bros. Inc.; renewed 1991, 1994 by Special Rider Music)

"Hurricane" (copyright © 1975 by Ram's Horn Music; renewed 2003 by Ram's Horn Music)

"I Believe in You" (copyright © 1979 by Special Rider Music)

"I Dreamed I Saw St. Augustine" (copyright © 1968 by Dwarf Music; renewed 1996 by Dwarf Music)

"I Shall Be Free" (copyright © 1963, 1967 by Warner Bros. Inc.; renewed 1991, 1995 by Special Rider Music)

"I Shall Be Free No. 10" (copyright © 1971 by Special Rider Music; renewed 1999 by Special Rider Music)

"I Want You" (copyright © 1966 by Dwarf Music; renewed 1994 by Dwarf Music)

"Idiot Wind" (copyright © 1974 by Ram's Horn Music; renewed 2002 by Ram's Horn Music)

"If You See Her, Say Hello" (copyright © 1974 by Ram's Horn Music; renewed 2002 by Ram's Horn Music)

"Isis" (copyright © 1975 by Ram's Horn Music; renewed 2003 by Ram's Horn Music)

"It Ain't Me, Babe" (copyright © 1964 by Warner Bros. Inc.; renewed 1992 by Special Rider Music)

"It Takes a Lot to Laugh, It Takes a Train to Cry" (copyright © 1965 by Warner Bros. Inc.; renewed 1993 by Special Rider Music)

"It's Alright, Ma (I'm Only Bleeding)" (copyright © 1965 by Warner Bros. Inc.; renewed 1993 by Special Rider Music)

"Joey" (copyright © 1975 by Ram's Horn Music; renewed 2003 by Ram's Horn Music)

"Jokerman" (copyright © 1983 by Special Rider Music)

"Just Like a Woman" (copyright © 1966 by Dwarf Music; renewed 1994 by Dwarf Music)

"Just Like Tom Thumb's Blues" (copyright © 1965 by Warner Bros. Inc.; renewed 1993 by Special Rider Music)

"Legionnaires' Disease" (copyright © 1981 by Special Rider Music)

"License to Kill" (copyright © 1983 by Special Rider Music)

"Like a Rolling Stone" (copyright © 1965 by Warner Bros. Inc.; renewed 1993 by Special Rider Music)

"Lily, Rosemary and the Jack of Hearts" (copyright © 1975 by Ram's Horn Music; renewed 2002 by Ram's Horn Music)

"The Lonesome Death of Hattie Carroll" (copyright © 1964, 1966 by Warner Bros. Inc.; renewed 1992, 1994 by Special Rider Music)

"Love Sick" (copyright © 1997 by Special Rider Music)

"Masters of War" (copyright © 1963 by Warner Bros. Inc.; renewed 1991 by Special Rider Music)

"Meet Me in the Morning" (copyright © 1974 by Ram's Horn Music; renewed 2002 by Ram's Horn Music)

"Mississippi" (copyright © 1996 by Special Rider Music)

"Moonlight" (copyright © 2001 by Special Rider Music)

"Mozambique" (copyright © 1975 by Ram's Horn Music; renewed 2003 by Ram's Horn Music)

"Mr. Tambourine Man" (copyright © 1964, 1965 by Warner Bros. Inc.; renewed 1992, 1993 by Special Rider Music)

"My Back Pages" (copyright © 1964 by Warner Bros. Inc.; renewed 1992 by Special Rider Music)

"Nettie Moore" (copyright © 2006 by Special Rider Music)

"New Morning" (copyright © 1970 by Big Sky Music; renewed 1998 by Big Sky Music)

"New Pony" (copyright © 1978 by Special Rider Music)

"No Time to Think" (copyright © 1978 by Special Rider Music)

"Not Dark Yet" (copyright © 1997 by Special Rider Music)

"Obviously 5 Believers" (copyright © 1966 by Dwarf Music; renewed 1994 by Dwarf Music)

"Oh, Sister" (copyright © 1975 by Ram's Horn Music; renewed 2003 by Ram's Horn Music)

"One More Cup of Coffee (Valley Below)" (copyright © 1975, 1976 by Ram's Horn Music; renewed 2003, 2004 by Ram's Horn Music)

"One More Weekend" (copyright © 1970 by Big Sky Music; renewed 1998 by Big Sky Music)

"One Too Many Mornings" (copyright © 1964, 1966 by Warner Bros. Inc.; renewed 1992, 1994 by Special Rider Music)

"Only a Pawn in Their Game" (copyright © 1963, 1964 by Warner Bros. Inc.; renewed 1991, 1992 by Special Rider Music)

"Percy's Song" (copyright © 1964, 1966 by Warner Bros.; renewed 1992, 1994 by Special Rider Music)

"Po' Boy" (copyright © 2001 by Special Rider Music)

"Queen Jane Approximately" (copyright © 1965 by Warner Bros. Inc.; renewed 1993 by Special Rider Music)

"Quit Your Lowdown Ways" (copyright © 1963, 1964 by Warner Bros. Inc.; renewed 1991, 1992 by Special Rider Music)

"Restless Farewell" (copyright © 1964, 1966 by Warner Bros. Inc.; renewed 1992, 1994 by Special Rider Music)

"Romance in Durango" (copyright © 1975 by Ram's Horn Music; renewed 2003 by Ram's Horn Music)

"Sad-Eyed Lady of the Lowlands" (copyright © 1966 by Dwarf Music; renewed 1994 by Dwarf Music)

"Señor (Tales of Yankee Power)" (copyright © 1978 by Special Rider Music)

"She Belongs to Me" (copyright © 1965 by Warner Bros. Inc.; renewed 1993 by Special Rider Music)

"Shelter from the Storm" (copyright © 1974 by Ram's Horn Music; renewed 2002 by Ram's Horn Music)

"Sign on the Window" (copyright © 1970 by Big Sky Music; renewed 1998 by Big Sky Music)

"Slow Train" (copyright © 1979 by Special Rider Music)

"Song to Woody" (copyright © 1962, 1965 by Duchess Music Corporation; renewed 1990, 1993 by MCA)

"Spanish Harlem Incident" (copyright © 1964 by Warner Bros. Inc.; renewed 1992 by Special Rider Music)

"Spirit on the Water" (copyright © 2006 by Special Rider Music)

"Standing in the Doorway" (copyright © 1997 by Special Rider Music)

"Stuck Inside of Mobile with the Memphis Blues Again" (copyright © 1966 by Dwarf Music; renewed 1994 by Dwarf Music)

"Subterranean Homesick Blues" (copyright © 1965 by Warner Bros. Inc.; renewed 1993 by Special Rider Music)

"Sugar Baby" (copyright © 2001 by Special Rider Music)

"Summer Days" (copyright © 2001 by Special Rider Music)

"Sweetheart Like You" (copyright © 1983 by Special Rider Music)

"Talkin' New York" (copyright © 1962, 1965 by Duchess Music; renewed 1990, 1993 by MCA)

"Tangled Up in Blue" (copyright © 1974 by Ram's Horn Music; renewed 2002 by Ram's Horn Music)

"Things Have Changed" (copyright © 1999 by Special Rider Music)

"Time Passes Slowly" (copyright © 1970 by Big Sky Music; renewed 1998 by Big Sky Music)

"The Times They Are a-Changin'" (copyright © 1963, 1964 by Warner Bros. Inc.; renewed 1991, 1992 by Special Rider Music)

"To Ramona" (copyright © 1964 by Warner Bros. Inc.; renewed 1992 by Special Rider Music)

"Tombstone Blues" (copyright © 1965 by Warner Bros. Inc.; renewed 1993 by Special Rider Music)

"Too Much of Nothing" (copyright © 1967, 1970 by Dwarf Music; renewed 1995, 1998 by Dwarf Music)

"Tryin' to Get to Heaven" (copyright © 1997 by Special Rider Music)

"Union Sundown" (copyright © 1983 by Special Rider Music)

"Visions of Johanna" (copyright © 1966 by Dwarf Music; renewed 1994 by Dwarf Music)

"Went to See the Gypsy" (copyright © 1970 by Big Sky Music; renewed 1998 by Big Sky Music)

"When the Deal Goes Down" (copyright © 2006 by Special Rider Music)

"When the Ship Comes In" (copyright © 1963, 1964 by Warner Bros. Inc.; renewed 1991, 1992 by Special Rider Music)

"Where Are You Tonight? (Journey through Dark Heat)" (copyright © 1978 by Special Rider Music)

"With God on Our Side" (copyright © 1964 by Warner Bros. Inc.; renewed 1991 by Special Rider Music)

"Workingman's Blues #2" (copyright © 2006 by Special Rider Music)

"You're Gonna Make Me Lonesome When You Go" (copyright © 1974 by Ram's Horn Music; renewed 2002 by Ram's Horn Music)

Index

ACCOMPANIMENT, FUNCTION OF, 20–21.
Adorno, Theodor, 38, 148, 194–95.
Alden, Harold, 193.
Alliteration, 65, 67, 68, 92, 93, 194, 227, 244 n.19.
Altamont Festival, 144.
American history, 33, 38, 39, 75, 188–89.
Armstrong, Louis, 189, 215, 231.
Arnold, Eddy, 179.
Art, as dialogic, 14.
Asch, Moses, 29.
Ashbery, John, 86.
Assonance, 61, 77.
Asylum Records, 143.
Audience expectation, 120, 122.
Augustine, Saint, *Confessions*, 161, 162, 164, 166, 175, 179.
Authenticity, 17, 27, 28, 30, 31–32, 34–35, 64, 67, 75–76, 148, 152.
Authority, artistic, 20, 22, 26–27, 37–38, 39, 75, 81, 84–85, 86, 93, 106, 161, 167, 181, 187, 190, 207, 218.
Authority, unmasking of, 75.
Automobile culture, 45, 49, 59.

BACKUS, JIM, 69.
Baez, Joan, 46, 60.
Bakhtin, Mikhail M., 14, 35.
Band, The, 24, 83, 114, 117, 119.
Baudelaire, Charles, 88, 102, 239 n.12; "To a Woman Passing By," 90.
Beat Generation, 85, 98, 150, 154.
Beatles, The, 15, 20, 83, 200; *Let it Be*, 101.
Beethoven, Ludwig van, 112, 194–95.

Belafonte, Harry, 68, 103.
Berlin, Irving, "How Deep Is the Ocean," 64.
Berry, Chuck, 112, 226, 239 n.14; "Johnny B. Goode," 182; "Roll Over Beethoven," 112.
Billy the Kid, 18.
Blake, William, 86, 88, 176, 247 n.7, 260 n.19; "Auguries of Innocence," 175–76.
Blue of the Night, 215.
Blues, 11, 49–50, 112, 131, 132, 148, 165, 167–68, 189–90, 193, 195, 201, 203–204, 211, 215, 218–19, 220; Chicago-style, 83, 209; culture, 84; structure, 99–100; "talking blues," 51–52, 57, 58, 71, 78, 80.
"Blue Velvet," 108.
Boccaccio, Giovanni, 57.
Borges, Jorge Luis, "Kafka and his Precursors," 54.
"Bound for Glory," 49.
Brecht, Bertolt, 22, 38–39, 68, 71–73, 80.
Broonzy, Big Bill, 59.
Browne, Jackson, 158.
Burroughs, William S., *Naked Lunch*, 124.
Byrds, The, 77.
Byrne, David, 11.

CANON CREATION, 29–30, 56.
Capitalism, 17, 112, 186, 210, 239 n.12.
Carné, Marcel, *Children of Paradise*, 157.
Carroll, Hattie, 115.
Carter, Jimmy, 160, 190.
Carter, Rubin, 149, 150, 152.
Carthy, Martin, 40.
Cash, Johnny, 41.
Cento, 207.

Chandler, Raymond, 18; *The Long Goodbye,* 19.

Chaplin, Charles, 210, 222.

Child, Francis James, 68.

City Lights Books, 85.

Clayton, Paul, 32–33, 35; "Who's Gonna Buy You Ribbons When I'm Gone?," 60–61.

Clinton era, 206.

Cohen, Leonard, 17, 182, 229.

Columbia Records, 25, 30, 143.

"Come All Ye Bold Tarriers," 76.

Commodification, 32, 66, 78.

Communitarianism, 78, 80.

Como, Perry, 229.

Conrad, Joseph, *Victory,* 150, 151.

Consumerism, 13, 28, 31, 66, 75, 78, 80, 88.

Cooper, James Fenimore, 98.

Crosby, Bing, 211, 213–16, 223, 226, 230; "Where the Blue of the Night Meets the Gold of the Day," 211, 213–15, 216.

DADA, 87.

Daniel, Arnaut, 207.

Dante Alighieri, 19, 85, 132, 162, 179, 188, 207; *Divine Comedy,* 126, 127, 128, 129–30.

Day, Aidan, 183.

Day, Doris, 229.

Dean, James, 69.

Deleuze, Gilles, 28.

"Delia," 60.

Demeny, Paul, 96–97.

Denver, John, 144.

Disco music, 144.

Divine Comedy (Dante), 129–30, 162.

Donne, John, 133.

"Don't Let Your Deal Go Down," 211.

Don't Look Back (Pennebaker), 228.

"Driftin' Too Far from the Shore," 171.

Dunbar, Sly, 182.

Dutchman, 33.

Dylan, Bob: adoption of rock-based sound, 85, 86; American standards, recordings of, 231–32; "archaic voice," 36–37, 52, 69, 89, 172, 177, 179, 221; Christian songs, 162–63, 168, 181, 186, 188; *Chronicles: Volume One,* 23, 25, 32, 36, 46, 71, 119, 209; compositional technique, 84, 93, 100, 103, 105, 203; conversion to Christianity, 159–60; density of songs, 15–16, 19; as disruptor, 10–11, 32; "Greenwich Village" voice, 37, 221;

"hobo voice," 35–36, 64; late style, 195–96, 204, 206, 207–10, 218; as maker/poet, 93; marriage, 126, 131, 141; melody, approach to, 66, 89, 153, 226; Minnesota origin, 25, 36, 54–55, 125–26; multivoiced nature of lyrics, 35, 221; "Okie" voice, 59, 70, 221; performance style, 73; *Renaldo and Clara,* 157; retirement from performing, 83; *Tarantula,* 97; as troubadour, 139–40; use of sonnet structure, 132–35, 136; using Black English locutions, 168, 172; the "ventriloquist," 218; "vision music," 85, 89–91, 92–96, 102, 105–106, 108–14, 117, 130, 137, 140–41, 154, 188, 228; vocal style, 34–35, 66, 105, 170, 228–31; as "voice of a generation," 10, 29, 119–20, 138, 140, 142.

Dylan, Bob, albums: *Another Side of Bob Dylan,* 45, 78–80, 89, 90, 113; *The Basement Tapes,* 24, 83, 114, 117, 240 n.19; *Before the Flood,* 117, 223; *Blonde on Blonde,* 83, 98, 103, 105, 106, 114, 115, 117, 122, 123, 163, 201, 232; *Blood on the Tracks,* 117, 119, 121–22, 124, 125–26, 130–32, 136, 140, 142–44, 145, 150, 151, 152, 153, 154, 157, 159, 162, 183, 194, 196, 218, 257 n.30; *Bob Dylan,* 25, 51; *Bringing It All Back Home,* 83, 94, 98, 99; *Desire,* 117, 119, 121, 123, 125, 144–45, 148, 150, 152, 153, 154, 157, 159, 162, 163, 179, 186, 194, 258 n.40; *Fallen Angels,* 231; *The Freewheelin' Bob Dylan,* 25, 49, 56, 59, 61, 68; *Good as I Been to You,* 152, 193, 210; *The Great White Wonder,* 83; *Hard Rain,* 233; *Highway 61 Revisited,* 83, 98, 106, 114, 182, 218, 251 n.28; *John Wesley Harding,* 83, 114, 117, 119, 123, 240 n.19; *Live at Budokan,* 157; *Love and Theft,* 193, 196, 200, 203, 204, 207–208, 262 n.7; *Modern Times,* 193, 210–11, 218, 222–23, 230; *Nashville Skyline,* 119, 123, 229, 240 n.19; *New Morning,* 119, 123; *Planet Waves,* 119, 123; *Saved,* 157; *Self Portrait,* 17, 117, 119, 123, 179; *Shadows in the Night,* 231; *Shot of Love,* 157; *Slow Train Coming,* 157, 159, 164, 169; *Street Legal,* 119, 157, 158, 162, 163, 186, 211, 258 n.42, 260 n.14; *Tell Tale Signs,* 203; *Tempest,* 231; *Time Out of Mind,* 193, 194, 195, 196, 197, 198, 199, 200, 207, 208; *The Times They Are a-Changin',* 45, 59, 75, 76; *Together through Life,* 193, 198; *Triplicate,* 231; *World Gone Wrong,* 152, 193, 230.

Dylan, Bob, songs: "Absolutely Sweet Marie," 106, 122; "Ain't Talkin'," 222; "All Along the Watchtower," 115–17, 149, 150, 183; "All I Really Want to Do," 80; "All the Tired Horses," 123; "As I Went Out One Morning"; "Ballad of a Thin Man," 21, 98, 103, 206–207, 262 n.5; "The Ballad of Frankie Lee and Judas Priest," 115; "Beyond Here Lies Nothin'," 198; "Beyond the Horizon," 211; "Black Diamond Bay," 150–52, 153; "Blind Willie McTell," 187–91, 227, 261 n.27; "Blowin' in the Wind," 45, 59, 62–67, 69, 70, 71, 74, 76–77, 92, 227, 244 n.16; "Boots of Spanish Leather," 123, 147; "Brownsville Girl," 196–97, 252 n.7; "Buckets of Rain," 126, 131, 139, 257 n.33; "Changing of the Guards," 159, 168, 211; "Chimes of Freedom," 90–95, 96, 102, 105, 106, 107, 109, 110, 111, 113–14, 197, 248 n.15; "Cold Irons Bound," 196, 200; "Country Pie," 123; "Day of the Locusts," 124; "Dear Landlord," 115; "Desolation Row," 106, 111–12, 113–14, 216–17, 219, 254 n.16, 260 n.14; "Dignity," 18–20; "Don't Think Twice, It's Alright," 35, 59, 60–61, 63, 65, 73, 79, 142, 233; "Down the Highway," 49–50; "Duquesne Whistle," 230; "Every Grain of Sand," 174–80, 181, 227; "Floater (Too Much to Ask)," 208, 209; "Girl from the North Country," 39–40, 42–43, 60, 62, 66, 95, 145, 150, 243 n.18; "Gonna Change My Way of Thinking," 163, 259 n.10; "Gotta Serve Somebody," 157, 164–67, 168, 169, 171, 172, 173, 174, 177, 181, 185; "A Hard Rain's a-Gonna Fall," 36, 59, 62, 68–71, 75, 76, 93, 94, 183, 227, 230; "Hazel," 123; "Highlands," 204; "Highway 61 Revisited," 112; "Honey, Just Allow Me One More Chance," 56, 61, 220; "Hurricane," 149, 150, 164; "I Believe in You," 168, 169–74, 181, 182, 190, 255 n.21; "Idiot Wind," 131, 141, 142, 233, 257 n.33; "I Dreamed I Saw St. Augustine," 114, 161; "If Not for You," 123; "If You *See* Her, Say Hello," 135, 138, 142–43, 147, 157–58, 257 n.33; "I'll Be Your Baby Tonight," 123, 142; "I Shall Be Free," 57–58; "I Shall Be Free No. 10," 78, 80, 244 n.16; "Isis," 152–53; "It Ain't Me, Babe," 80; "It's Alright, Ma (I'm Only Bleeding)," 17, 98, 165, 264 n.2; "It

Takes a Lot to Laugh, It Takes a Train to Cry," 220; "I Want You," 260 n.14; "Jim Jones," 193–94, 195; "Joey," 149–50; "John Wesley Harding," 150; "Jokerman," 182–86, 187, 189, 190; "Just Like a Woman," 98, 100, 102–104, 105, 250 n.28; "Knocking on Heaven's Door," 21; "Lay, Lady, Lay," 21, 123, 229; "Legionnaires' Disease," 159; "Leopard-Skin Pillbox Hat," 204; "The Levee's Gonna Break," 223; "License to Kill," 186, 187; "Like a Rolling Stone," 21, 29, 83, 98, 100–102, 103, 104, 105, 142, 177, 251 n.28; "Lily, Rosemary and the Jack of Hearts," 124, 125, 136, 140, 183, 257 n.33; "The Lonesome Death of Hattie Carroll," 72–75, 112, 115, 117, 245 n.25; "Love Minus Zero/No Limit," 123; "Love Sick," 195, 196; "Masters of War," 62, 76, 98, 164; "Meet Me in the Morning," 125, 131; "Mississippi," 196, 197, 200, 201–204, 205, 206, 208, 214, 226; "Moonlight," 208; "Mozambique," 145–46, 149; "Mr. Tambourine Man," 94, 96, 104–105, 106, 107, 114, 176, 197; "My Back Pages," 89–90, 91, 96, 99, 102, 104; "Nettie Moore," 218; "New Morning," 123; "New Pony," 158; "Not Dark Yet," 196, 198, 261 n.22; "Nothing Was Delivered," 114; "No Time to Think," 159, 168; "Oh, Sister," 146, 150, 152; "On a Night like This," 123; "One More Cup of Coffee (Valley Below)," 145, 149, 152, 153; "One More Weekend," 123, 242 n.13; "One Too Many Mornings," 256 n.27; "Only a Pawn in Their Game," 75; "Peggy Day," 229; "Percy's Song"; "Pledging My Time," 105; "Po' Boy," 208; "Queen Jane Approximately," 98, 164, 251 n.28; "Quit Your Lowdown Ways," 36, 168; "Restless Farewell," 231; "Romance in Durango," 147–48, 149, 150, 152; "Sad-Eyed Lady of the Lowlands," 105, 199, 250 n.28; "Sara," 152; "Señor (Tales of Yankee Power)," 158; "She Belongs to Me," 99–100, 105, 106, 123, 250 n.24; "Shelter from the Storm," 126, 131, 196, 197, 257 n.33; "Simple Twist of Fate," 131; "Slow Train," 159–60, 163, 168; "Something There Is about You," 124; "Song to Woody," 51, 54, 56, 69; "Spanish Harlem Incident," 123; "Spirit on the Water," 210; "Standing in the Doorway," 197–98, 199,

202; "Stuck Inside of Mobile with the Memphis Blues Again," 105, 113, 201, 206, 226; "Subterranean Homesick Blues," 218; "Sugar Baby," 196; "Summer Days," 204–206, 207, 208; "Sweetheart Like You," 187; "Talkin' New York," 39, 51–54, 58; "Tangled Up in Blue," 125–26, 131–35, 136–39, 140, 141, 142, 145, 147, 151, 155, 174, 177–78, 223, 227, 255 n.19, 255 n.20, 257 n.33, 260 n.14; "Tell Me that It Isn't True," 123; "The Groom's Still Waiting at the Altar," 163, 188; "The Man in Me," 123; "Things Have Changed," 198, 228; "This Wheel's on Fire," 114; "Thunder on the Mountain," 204; "Till I Fell in Love With You," 198–200; "Time Passes Slowly," 123; "The Times They Are a-Changin'," 45, 59, 62, 71, 75, 76, 91, 111, 193–94; "To Be Alone with You," 123; "Tombstone Blues," 112, 208; "Tonight I'll Be Staying Here with You," 123, 229; "Too Much of Nothing," 242 n.13; "To Ramona," 78–80; "Tryin' to Get to Heaven," 196, 198, 200, 207, 210; "Union Sundown," 219; "Visions of Johanna," 106–10, 111, 113, 114, 116, 122, 218, 227, 232–33, 254n16, 256 n.27; "Wedding Song," 123; "Went to See the Gypsy," 117, 124; "When He Returns," 159; "When the Deal Goes Down," 211–14, 222, 227; "When the Ship Comes In," 71; "Where Are You Tonight? (Journey through Dark Heat)," 159; "The Wicked Messenger," 115; "Winterlude," 123; "With God on Our Side," 36, 37, 39, 59–60, 75; "Workingman's Blues #2," 196, 218–22; "You Angel You," 123; "You're a Big Girl Now," 131, 256 n.28; "You're Gonna Make Me Lonesome When You Go," 88, 124, 131, 136, 255 n.23.
Dylan, Sara, 121.

EISENSTEIN, SERGEI, 16.
Eliot, T. S.:"Love Song of J. Alfred Prufrock," 19, 217; "The Hollow Men," 19; "Tradition and the Individual Talent," 26, 54.
Ellington, Duke, 16.
Elliot, Ramblin' Jack, 46.
Energy crisis, 160.
Epic narrative, 188–89.
Epiphany (Joycean), 90.
Evers, Medgar, 75.

Exile, poet as, 29.
Ezekiel, Book of, 19.

FAULKNER, WILLIAM, 98.
Ferlinghetti, Lawrence, 85.
Fields, W. C., 86.
Financial Times, 19.
Fitzgerald, F. Scott, 205, 207.
Folk music culture, 27–32, 77–78, 80–81, 239n14, 244 n.11.
Folk song, American standards as, 231.
Folk song style, 26–27, 62, 250 n.28.
Folkways Records, 29, 30.
Foster, Stephen, 193.
French Impressionists, 16.

GALLO, JOEY, 149–50.
Gary, Romain, 120.
Generation of 1927, 122.
Gershwin, George, 193.
Ginsberg, Allen, 85–86, 154, 253 n.11, 254 n.14; "Howl," 85, 121.
Gray, Michael, 176, 185, 207.
Great American Songbook, 193.
Great Gatsby, The (Fitzgerald), 92, 205–207, 210, 218.
Greeley, Horace, 121.
Greenwich Village, 27, 28, 30.
Guattari, Félix, 28.
Guinizelli, Guido, 207.
Guthrie, Arlo, 264 n.19.
Guthrie, Woody, 18, 22, 25, 26–27, 32, 36, 39, 41, 45, 46, 47, 48, 49, 51, 59, 72, 79, 84, 87, 101, 117, 122, 148, 205, 216, 226, 244 n.11, 264 n.19; Bound for Glory, 47, 81; "Hard Travelin'," 56–57, 61; "I Ain't Got No Home," 34; "1913 Massacre," 54–55, 56; "Pastures of Plenty," 44; "Pretty Boy Floyd," 39, 53, 54, 150; "Talking Dust Bowl Blues," 36, 51, 52; "The Sinking of the Reuben James," 34; "This Land Is Your Land," 244 n.19; "Union Maid," 53; "We Shall Be Free," 57, 80.

HAGGARD, MERLE, "WORKIN' MAN BLUES," 218–19.
Hamill, Pete, 143.
Hammond Jr., John, 46.
Happening, 87.
Harmonica, symbolic associations, 148–49.

Hartman, Charles O., 104.
"Help Me Rhonda" (Beach Boys), 108.
Hemingway, Ernest, 121.
Hendrix, Jimi, 115.
"Hokum" song, 220.
Holiday, Billie, 30.
Holiday Inn, 215.
Holmes, Odetta. *See* Odetta
Homer, 188, 189.
"Honey Babe Let the Deal Go Down," 211.
Hopkins, John "Lightnin'," 50.
Houston, Cisco, 55.
Hunter, Robert, 230.
Huyssen, Andreas, 144.

"I DREAMED I SAW JOE HILL," 114.
Iranian Revolution, 160.
"I Think We're Alone Now" (Tommy James and the Shondells), 168.
Izambard, Georges, 96.

JAGGER, MICK, 35.
James, William, 162.
Jameson, Fredric, 88, 144.
Jazz standards, harmonic traits of, 182.
Jobim, Antônio Carlos, "How Insensitive," 158.
John of the Cross, Saint, 179.
Johnson, Lonnie, 218.
Johnson, Robert, 211, 213, 215, 223; "Hot Tamales," 220.
Johnson, Samuel, 187.
Joyce, James, 30, 56, 98; "The Dead," 212.

KAFKA, FRANZ, 54.
Keats, John, 185.
Kerouac, Jack, 18, 47–49, 87, 121–22, 125, 127, 138, 140, 144, 150, 162, 252 n.3, 252 n.4, 252 n.6, 253 n.9, 253 n.10, 253 n.11, 254 n.14; *The Dharma Bums,* 48; *On the Road,* 47–48, 49, 122, 124, 126–31, 150, 152, 154, 254 n.14, 254 n.17.
King, Carole, 158.
Kingston Trio, The, 30–32, 59, 103, 179.
Knopfler, Mark, 182.

"LA BAMBA," 101.
Labor movement, 28.
Lanois, Daniel, 199.

Late style, of artistic production, 194–95.
Leadbelly (Huddie Ledbetter), 29, 56; "Irene Goodnight," 31.
Leigh, Caroline, 231.
Lennon, John, 10, 141; "God," 168–69.
Levy, Jacques, 144, 150, 151.
"Lily of the West," 60.
Lomax, Alan, 29.
Lomax, John, 29.
London, Jack, 18, 152.
"Lord Randall," 68–70.
Lott, Eric, 207–208.
"Louie, Louie" (The Kingsmen), 101.
Lyric poetry, 12, 14.

MALE IDENTITY, 158.
Mallarmé, Stéphane, 68.
Martí, José, "Guantanamera," 34.
Marvell, Andrew, 19.
McCartney, Paul, 35, 141; "When I'm Sixty-Four," 38.
McClure, Michael, 85.
McTell, Blind Willie, 187–88, 189, 190.
Meaning, songs as bearers of, 9.
Menocal, María Rosa, 29.
Metanoia, 164.
Middle East oil crisis, 160.
Miller, Henry, *The Time of the Assassins,* 87.
Mississippi Sheiks, The, 211, 213, 215.
Mitchell, Joni, 17, 229.
Modernism, 16–17, 19, 22, 26, 28, 51, 56, 68, 72, 85–88, 90–92, 96, 98, 148, 217, 223, 232, 239 n.14.
Modern Times (Chaplin), 210, 222.
Monroe, Bill, 171.
Moore, Henry, 16.
Morrison, Jim, 87.
Morrison, Toni, 10.
Mozambique, 146.
"My Last Fair Deal Gone Down," 211.

NABOKOV, VLADIMIR, 16.
Narrative, and balladlike forms, 58.
Neruda, Pablo, 10.
Newbern, Hambone Willie, "Rollin' and Tumblin'," 211.
New Lost City Ramblers, The, 25, 46.
Newport Folk Festival, 45, 83, 85.
Nobel Prize in Literature, 9, 10.

"No More Auction Block for Me," 62, 64, 65, 69.
Nyro, Laura, 17.

ODETTA, 62.
Odyssey, 188, 189.
Oh! Calcutta!, 144.
Ono, Yoko, 169.
Orbison, Roy, 158.
Ovid, Tristia (Book of Sorrows), 220.
Owens, Buck, "Truck Driving Man," 145.

PARIS COMMUNE, 28.
Parker, Charlie, 16.
Pasternak, Boris, 10.
Paul, Saint, 19, 20.
Pennebaker, D. A., 228.
Pennies from Heaven, 215.
Persona, of the singer, 18, 20–22, 32, 34–36, 38,
    46, 49–51, 57–62, 71, 74, 78–79, 97, 105, 110,
    113, 135, 137, 142, 154, 165, 168, 175, 205–206.
Perspectival poetics, 136–37, 144.
Peter, Paul and Mary, 45, 59, 63, 66, 242 n.13.
Petrarch, 121, 128, 131, 132, 139, 143; Canzoniere,
    129–30, 136, 142, 207.
Picasso, Pablo, 16.
Pilgrimage, 122, 127, 128, 177, 189.
Pinsky, Robert, 12, 13, 227, 228.
"Pirate Jenny" (Brecht and Weill), 71, 72, 75.
Pitt, William, 187.
Poetics, defined, 13.
Politics of songs, 12.
Pollock, Jackson, 16; "Number 1, 1948," 80.
Poole, Charlie, 211, 213.
Popular song, classic structure of, 203.
Porter, Cole, 193; "Begin the Beguine," 47.
Pound, Ezra, 15, 217.
Powell, William, 206.
Presley, Elvis, 215, 229.
Protestant hymns, 175.
Protest music, 27–28, 61–63, 67, 75, 76, 77,
    84, 89, 90–91, 93, 98, 104, 110, 112, 149, 217,
    239 n.14.
Proust, Marcel, 92.

RAEBEN, NORMAN, 137.
Rainey, Ma, 112.
Rambler cliché. See Wanderer persona.
Ray, Nicholas, 69.
Ray (Dylan friend), 32–33, 35.

Reagan/Thatcher years, 182, 186–87, 190, 196.
Rebel without a Cause, 69.
Reddy, Helen, 169.
Redemption and reconciliation, 92–94, 115,
    117, 123, 200, 209.
"Red Sails in the Sunset," 211.
Religious conversion, 161, 163–64.
Rhetorical density, 146–48, 177–80, 227.
Rhyme, 52, 61, 65–66, 68, 77, 103, 111, 146, 171,
    172–73, 174, 183, 194, 214, 219, 227, 232, 255
    n.20.
Rich, Charlie, 86.
Richards, Johnny, 231.
Rimbaud, Arthur, 16, 18, 22, 86–91, 96–97, 99,
    104, 106, 109, 111, 116–17, 131–32, 144, 145,
    188, 205, 246 n.7; "After the Flood," 117;
    "Alchemy of the Word," 87, 89; "Bridges,"
    116; Illuminations, 116; A Season in Hell,
    88, 89, 90, 131; "The Drunken Boat," 88,
    91–92, 95.
Rivera, Scarlet, 148.
Robbins, Marty, "El Paso," 17, 148, 150.
Robeson, Paul, 62.
Robinson, Smokey, 86.
Rock and roll music, 83, 86, 96, 158, 182, 188,
    217, 239 n.14.
Rodgers, Jimmie, 46, 200; "Blue Yodel #10,"
    80.
Rossetti, Dante, 133.
Rotolo, Suze, 50, 71.

SACHS, NELLY, 10.
Salinger, J. D., 120.
San Francisco press conference, 85, 86, 117.
"Scarborough Fair," 40–42.
"Scarlet Ribbons," 103.
Seeger, Mike, 25–26, 30, 31, 32, 33, 34, 46, 78.
Seeger, Pete, 25, 31, 36; "Guantanamera," 34;
    "If I Had a Hammer," 75, 93; "Turn, Turn,
    Turn," 34.
Self, invention and reinvention of, 32, 34, 39,
    41, 46, 57–59, 61, 66, 84, 86, 97–98. See also
    Visionary poetics.
Shakespeare, Robbie, 182.
Shakespeare, William, 17, 133, 176; Romeo and
    Juliet, 164.
Shepard, Sam, 196.
Shore, Dinah, "Buttons and Bows," 103.
Sidney, Philip, 133.

"Silver Dagger," 60.

Simon, Paul, 11; *Graceland,* 101–102.

Simon and Garfunkel, 40, 41, 77, 242 n.18.

Sinatra, Frank, 30, 158, 193, 231–32.

Slim, Memphis, 165, 226; "Mother Earth" ("Consolation Blues"), 164.

Smith, Harry, *Anthology of American Folk Music,* 30.

Smith, Patti, 87.

Sonnet: articulated musically, 133–35; Baudelairean, 88; and perspective, 136; Petrarchan, 132–33, 136, 137.

Spenser, Edmund, 133.

Spoelstra, Mark, 33.

Springsteen, Bruce, 144.

"St. James Infirmary," 189–90.

"Statesboro Blues" (McTell), 188.

Stendhal, 19.

Stravinsky, Igor, 16.

Style, defined, 13–14.

Symbolism, 132.

TAYLOR, JAMES, 158.

Terry, Sonny, 55, 57.

"This World Is Not My Home," 34.

Threepenny Opera (Brecht and Weill), 71.

Timrod, Henry, 213, 215, 223; "Ethnogenesis," 212; "Rhapsody of a Southern Winter Night," 212–13.

Tin Pan Alley, 47, 182, 231.

Tolstoy, Leo, 98.

"Tom Dooley," 30.

Tommy James and the Shondells, 168.

Twain, Mark, 40.

"Twist and Shout," 101.

UNIONS, 27, 45, 53, 72, 75, 79.

Unmasker persona, 57–58, 59, 78, 81, 84, 97–98, 101, 102, 105, 115, 161, 164–65.

VALLEE, RUDY, 215.

Van Heusen, Jimmy, 193.

Van Ronk, Dave, 46, 60, 68, 87.

Veloso, Caetano, 11.

Verlaine, Paul, 88.

Verne, Jules, *Twenty Thousand Leagues under the Sea,* 217.

Vietnam War, 45, 131, 141, 144.

Virgil, *Eclogue* I, 213.

Vision, multiplicity of, 97, 99, 104.

Visionary poetics, 85–89, 91–92, 104–105, 114, 117, 130. *See also* Rimbaud, Arthur

"Voice": and collective space, 38–43; and persona, 35–38.

WANDERER PERSONA, 46–47, 49, 50, 57–58, 59, 60, 75, 81, 83, 85, 105, 110, 122, 205, 218.

Watergate, 121, 144.

Waters, Muddy, 22.

Weavers, The, 31.

Weber, Max, 17.

Welles, Orson, 16.

"Which Side Are You On, Boys," 217.

White, Josh, 29.

Whitman, Walt, 19, 38, 247 n.7.

"Wild Thing" (The Troggs), 101.

"Wildwood Flower," 34.

Williams, Hank, "Jambalaya," 15.

Women's movement, 158.

Woodstock, New York, 83.

Woodstock Festival, 119, 144.

Woolf, Virginia, 16, 92; "The Moment," 90.

Wyatt, Thomas, 133.

YEATS, WILLIAM BUTLER, "The Second Coming," 184.

"You and Me against the World" (Reddy), 169.

Young, Lester, 120.

"Young at Heart" (Leigh and Richards), 231–32, 233.

ZIMMERMAN, ROBERT. *See* Dylan, Bob

Zydeco, 15.

Zone Books series design by Bruce Mau
Typesetting by Meighan Gale
Printed and bound by Maple Press